p39 — overwriting

SHAKESPEARE STUDIES

EDITORIAL BOARD

Harry Berger Jr.
  The University of California, Santa Cruz

David M. Bevington
  The University of Chicago

Catherine Belsey
  University of Wales College of Cardiff

Michael Bristol
  McGill University

S. P. Cerasano
  Colgate University

Barry Gaines
  The University of New Mexico

Jean E. Howard
  Columbia University

Lena Cowen Orlin
  University of Maryland, Baltimore County

John Pitcher
  St. John's College, Oxford

Maureen Quilligan
  Duke University

Alan Sinfield
  The University of Sussex

Peter Stallybrass
  The University of Pennsylvania

SHAKESPEARE STUDIES VOLUME XXVII

EDITED BY
LEEDS BARROLL

BOOK-REVIEW EDITOR
Susan Zimmerman

Madison • Teaneck
Fairleigh Dickinson University Press
London: Associated University Presses

© 1999 by Associated University Presses, Inc.

All rights reserved. Authorization to photocopy items for internal or personal use, or the internal or personal use of specific clients, is granted by the copyright owner, provided that a base fee of $10.00, plus eight cents per page, per copy is paid directly to the Copyright Clearance Center, 222 Rosewood Drive, Danvers, Massachusetts 01923 [0-8386-3835-X/99 $10.00 + 8¢ pp, pc.]

Associated University Presses
440 Forsgate Drive
Cranbury, NJ 08512

Associated University Presses
16 Barter Street
London WC1A 2AH, England

Associated University Presses
P.O. Box 338, Port Credit
Mississauga, Ontario
Canada L5G 4L8

The paper used in this publication meets the requirements
of the American National Standard for Permanence of Paper
for Printed Library Materials Z39.48-1984.

International Standard Book Number 0-8386-3835-X (vol. xxvii)
International Standard Serial Number 0582-9399

All editorial correspondence concerning *Shakespeare Studies* should be addressed to the Editorial Office, *Shakespeare Studies*, Fine Arts 447, University of Maryland (Baltimore County), Baltimore, Maryland 21250. Manuscripts submitted without appropriate postage will not be returned. Orders and subscriptions should be directed to Associated University Presses, 440 Forsgate Drive, Cranbury, New Jersey 08512.

Shakespeare Studies disclaims responsibility for statements, either of fact or opinion, made by contributors.

PRINTED IN THE UNITED STATES OF AMERICA

Contents

Foreword	9
Contributors	11

Forum: Harry Berger, Jr.'s *Making Trifles of Terrors: Redistributing Complicities in Shakespeare*

Introduction LENA COWEN ORLIN	19
What "womanhood denies" the Power of "tongues to tell" LYNN ENTERLINE	25
Complicity and the Genesis of Shakespearean Dramatic Discourse ANGUS FLETCHER	37
Imaginary Anti-Theatricality: Harry Berger's Drama of Passive Aggression LOIS POTTER	42
Recovering the Terror of Trifles MARSHALL GROSSMAN	51
Reading Harry Berger STANLEY CAVELL	65

Review Articles

Hen-pecked Husbands and Light-Tailed Wives: The Courts in Early Modern England S. P. CERASANO	77
History and Literary History CONSTANCE JORDAN	94

Contents

Articles

Mingling Vice and "Worthiness" in *King John*
ROBERT WEIMANN 109

The Language of Treason in *Richard II*
DERMOT CAVANAGH 134

Women's Letters and Letter Writing in England 1540–1603: An Introduction to the Issues of Authorship and Construction
JAMES DAYBELL 161

Beauty's Poisonous Properties
TANYA POLLARD 187

Reviews

David J. Baker, *Between Nations: Shakespeare, Spenser, Marvell, and the Question of Britain*

Christopher Highley, *Shakespeare, Spenser, and the Crisis in Ireland*
DYMPNA C. CALLAGHAN 213

Michael D. Bristol, *Big Time Shakespeare*
SCOTT CUTLER SHERSHOW 219

Viviana Comensoli, *"Household Business": Domestic Plays of Early Modern England*
MARION WYNNE-DAVIES 223

John D. Cox and David Scott Kastan, eds., *A New History of Early English Drama*
PHYLLIS RACKIN 225

Mario DiGangi, *The Homoerotics of Early Modern Drama*
DENISE ALBANESE 230

Elizabeth Fowler and Roland Greene, eds., *The Project of Prose in Early Modern Europe and the New World*
BRUCE AVERY 233

Richard Halpern, *Shakespeare Among the Moderns*
KIERNAN RYAN 236

Jonathan Hart, ed., *Reading the Renaissance: Culture, Poetics, and Drama*
ELIZABETH FOWLER 241

Contents

David Hillman and Carla Mazzio, eds., *The Body in Parts: Fantasies of Corporeality in Early Modern Europe*
GRAHAM HAMMILL 248

Jean E. Howard and Phyllis Rackin, *Engendering a Nation: A Feminist Account of Shakespeare's English Histories*
SUSAN FRYE 253

Coppélia Kahn, *Roman Shakespeare: Warriors, Wounds, Women*
LYNN ENTERLINE 257

Jacques Lezra, *Unspeakable Subjects: The Genealogy of the Event in Early Modern Europe*
JONATHAN CREWE 260

Claire McEachern and Debora Shuger, eds. *Religion and Culture in Renaissance England*
ELIZABETH HANSON 266

Michael Neill, *Issues of Death: Mortality and Identity in English Renaissance Tragedy*
EMILY C. BARTELS 273

R. Malcolm Smuts, ed. *The Stuart Court and Europe: Essays in Politics and Political Culture*
PAULINE CROFT 276

Helen Wilcox, ed., *Women and Literature in Britain 1500–1700*
SUSANNE WOODS 279

W. B. Worthen, *Shakespeare and the Authority of Performance*
CARY M. MAZER 282

Index 289

Foreword

SHAKESPEARE STUDIES is very pleased to offer in Volume XXVII its fifth Forum, which examines the seminal contributions of Harry Berger, Jr. to contemporary studies in Shakespeare. Organized by Lena Cowen Orlin, who is also a contributor, the Forum takes Peter Erickson's 1998 edition of Berger's essays, *Making Trifles of Terrors: Redistributing Complicities in Shakespeare*, as a focal point for commentary on the wide-ranging import of Berger's scholarship. Other contributors to the Forum include Stanley Cavell, Lynn Enterline, Angus Fletcher, Marshall Grossman, and Lois Potter.

Volume XXVII also continues a recent innovation by featuring two review articles which comment at length on important historical and theoretical issues in early modern studies. S. P. Cerasano examines four books on legal history (by Giese, Gowing, Kaplan, and Kermode/Walker) in a larger survey of the status of scholarship—and the many unexplored areas—in this complex field. Constance Jordan interrogates the vexed relationships between literary history, cultural studies, and social studies by contrasting the methodologies and accomplishments of two recent studies (by Cressy and Manley) of early modern life.

Plans for Volume XXVIII include yet another innovation (to take the place of the Forum in this edition). Peter Stallybrass will organize a collection of brief essays on "Material Cultures" which will combine the work of scholars in a variety of fields to offer a wide-ranging view of new developments in this exciting area of study.

Leeds Barroll

Contributors

DENISE ALBANESE is Associate Professor of English and Cultural Studies at George Mason University. She is author of *New Science, New World*, and is at work on a study connecting the "unnatural practices" of sodomy, occultism, and natural philosophy.

BRUCE AVERY is Assistant Professor of English at San Francisco State and author of the essay "Gelded Continents" in the anthology *Playing the Globe*, a collection on Shakespeare and geography.

EMILY C. BARTELS is Associate Professor of English at Rutgers University (New Brunswick). She is author of *Spectacles of Strangeness: Imperialism, Alienation, and Marlowe*, and editor of *Critical Essays on Christopher Marlowe*, and is currently working on a book, *Before Slavery: English Stories of Africa*.

DYMPNA CALLAGHAN teaches English at Syracuse University. Her latest book is *Shakespeare Without Women*.

DERMOT CAVANAGH is a Lecturer in English at the University of Northumbria at Newcastle upon Tyne. He is currently completing a book on "disorderly" language in the Tudor history play.

STANLEY CAVELL, having retired last year as Professor of Philosophy at Harvard in order to get more writing done, is getting more writing done.

S. P. CERASANO, Professor of English at Colgate University, is co-editor of *Renaissance Drama by Women*. She is currently writing a biography of Edward Alleyn and editing *Globe Plays* for Penguin Books.

JONATHAN CREWE teaches Renaissance literature at Dartmouth. He is the author of numerous books and articles, and is currently editing Shakespeare as well as completing a book on early modern residues in contemporary global culture.

PAULINE CROFT is Senior Lecturer in History at Royal Holloway, University of London. She has published extensively on the political and cultural history of late Elizabethan and Jacobean England.

JAMES DAYBELL is a final year doctoral student in the History Department at Reading University. He is currently engaged in a thesis on "Women's letters and letter writing in England, 1560–1603." He is also the editor of a forthcoming volume of essays on women's letter writing in England 1450–1700.

Contributors

LYNN ENTERLINE is Associate Professor of English at Vanderbilt University and is author of *The Tears of Narcissus: Melancholia and Masculinity in Early Modern Writing*, and *The Rhetoric of the Body from Ovid to Shakespeare* (forthcoming).

ANGUS FLETCHER is Distinguished Professor of English and Comparative Literature at CUNY. On the editorial board of the *Shakespeare International Yearbook*, he is the author, most recently, of *Colors of the Mind: Conjectures on Thinking in Literature*.

ELIZABETH FOWLER is Assistant Professor of English at Yale University. Her work on medieval and early modern representations of the person—from legal person to economic person to fictional character—is forthcoming as *The Human Figure in Words*.

SUSAN FRYE is Associate Professor of English at the University of Wyoming. The author of *Elizabeth I: The Competition for Representation* and co-editor with Karen Robertson of *Maids and Mistresses, Cousins and Queens: Women's Alliances in Early Modern England*, she is completing a book on the relation between the domestic and literary production of early modern women.

MARSHALL GROSSMAN is Professor of English at the University of Maryland, College Park. His most recent book is *The Story of All Things: Writing the Self in Renaissance English Narrative Poetry*.

GRAHAM HAMMILL is Assistant Professor of English at the University of Notre Dame. He is currently completing a book on Caravaggio, Marlowe, and Bacon entitled *Sexuality and Form*.

ELIZABETH HANSON is Associate Professor of English at Queen's University (Canada) and the author of *Discovering the Subject in Renaissance England*. She is currently working on a study of economic knowledge and Renaissance drama.

CONSTANCE JORDAN is Professor of English at Claremont Graduate University. She is currently at work on a study of early modern ideas of property.

CARY M. MAZER is Associate Professor of English and Chair of the Theatre Arts Program at the University of Pennsylvania. In addition to writing about Shakespearean performance history, he has directed plays and has worked as a dramaturg and theater critic.

LENA COWEN ORLIN is Research Professor of English at the University of Maryland Baltimore County and Executive Director of the Shakespeare Association of America. Her current project has the working title, *Locating Privacy in Early Modern England*.

TANYA POLLARD is a doctoral candidate in Comparative Literature at Yale University. Her thesis "Dangerous Remedies: Poison and Representation in the Renaissance," examines links between dissimulation and the vulnerability of the body in early modern English plays and medical writings.

LOIS POTTER is Professor of English at the University of Delaware. She is currently completing a book on *Othello* for the Shakespeare in Performance series of the University of Manchester Press.

Contributors

PHYLLIS RACKIN is Professor of English in General Honors at the University of Pennsylvania. Her most recent books are *Stages of History: Shakespeare's English Chronicles* and, with Jean E. Howard, *Engendering a Nation: A Feminist Account of Shakespeare's English Histories*. She is working now on a revisionist study of Shakespeare's representations of women.

KIERNAN RYAN is Professor of English Language and Literature at Royal Holloway, University of London, and a Fellow of New Hall, University of Cambridge. His latest book is a critical reader, *Shakespeare: The Last Plays*. He is currently working on a study of Shakespearean comedy and romance.

SCOTT CUTLER SHERSHOW is Associate Professor of English at Miami University in Oxford, Ohio. He is the author of *Puppets and 'Popular' Culture* and of articles on Renaissance drama and the theory of cultural studies.

ROBERT WEIMANN is Professor of Drama and Performance Theory at the University of California, Irvine. He is currently completing a book-length study of "author's pen" and "actor's voice" in Shakespeare's theatre.

SUSANNE WOODS is Professor of English at Franklin and Marshall College and the author of *Lanyer: A Renaissance Woman Poet* (1999).

MARION WYNNE-DAVIES is Senior Lecturer in English Literature at the University of Dundee. Her publications include, with S. P. Cerasano, *Gloriana's Face: Women, Public and Private, in the English Renaissance* (1992), and *Renaissance Drama by Women: Texts and Contexts* (1996).

SHAKESPEARE STUDIES

FORUM: HARRY BERGER, JR.'S *MAKING TRIFLES OF TERRORS: REDISTRIBUTING COMPLICITIES IN SHAKESPEARE*

Introduction

Lena Cowen Orlin

TALKING WITH THE AUTHORS who here respond to Harry Berger, Jr.'s *Making Trifles of Terrors: Redistributing Complicities in Shakespeare*,[1] I came to regard this project of response as a sort of intellectual stress test. Berger, of course, set the pace. If the catchwords of the volume—complicities, communities, discourses, representation—reverberate through the following essays, so, too, does the word *smart*. But it is not just, as Marshall Grossman writes, that "most of us are not as smart as Harry." There is also the fact that Berger works so hard, reading widely and deeply, working through and selectively incorporating elements from the theories and methodologies of recent decades, thinking in the most exacting and unsentimental manner, writing with discipline for clarity as well as wit. Stanley Cavell pauses over a challenge Berger has put, remarking, "now *there* is an issue worth engaging" (emphasis added). Lynn Enterline begins that "this is about as difficult an essay to write as any I can remember." Angus Fletcher notes Berger's view that we are "not very smart if we fail to read Shakespeare, actively, ingeniously, dialogically"; Lois Potter, that Berger "insist[s] on the right to be as intelligent about Shakespeare as he has often been about, for instance, Spenser." If each registers in some degree a sense of being put to the test, it is a test that allows for more than one set of answers, as the five contributors productively demonstrate.

This forum, the fifth in a series organized by *Shakespeare Studies*, is the first to treat of a single volume of contemporary scholarship. Other issues of the journal have dealt with textual editing, with the field of women's studies, with the disputed authorship of *A Funeral Elegy*, and with race and the study of Shakespeare. *Making Trifles of Terrors*, the subject of this year's forum, is a collection of Shakespearean essays by one of the preeminent scholar/teachers in the field.

The volume has a long biography. One piece in the collection, on *King Lear*, was first published in 1979; another on *Macbeth* in 1980; a third on *The Merchant of Venice* in 1981; a fourth and fifth on *Much Ado about Nothing* and (again) *Macbeth* in 1982; and so on, through 1984, 1985, 1987, 1989, and six more essays, these principally concerning the *Henriad*. There are, further, three previously unpublished pieces, including a study of *Measure for Measure* and the namesake chapter bearing a variation on the collection's title and featuring its epigraph: "Hence it is that we make trifles of terrors, ensconcing ourselves into seeming knowledge, when we should submit ourselves to an unknown fear." (The quotation is from *All's Well That Ends Well*; I might have identified the character to whom these lines are given were it not that Berger's theory of complicities, which, in one strand, suggests that meanings are shared out among the community of a play's characters, renders the speech prefix unnecessary here.) Also new for this volume is the preface, which makes something rich and strange even of the conventional business of "acknowledging." In his description of the influence on him of Stanley Cavell, Berger gives us a short course on how he reads: with respect and with resistance, evidently with equal intensity. This level of engagement with the ideas of others is how the critical project advances, the preface suggests by showing, whether the "others" are undergraduate students or distinguished philosophers. The process is rejoined by Cavell in the last of the forum's responses.

Making Trifles of Terrors is not, as might be expected for a collection with a twenty-year life span, a miscellany. It is a coherent, sustained work of scholarship that lays out a critical practice and illustrates its range and consequence. The reader is attendant, in the active French sense of the word, at the evolution of that practice and the refinement of its arguments. Marshall Grossman talks about one of the ways in which Berger allows himself to be seen in—that is, revealed by—his work; this is another. In particular, we witness Berger responding to the critical stimuli of the 1970s and 1980s, to feminism, new historicism, cultural materialism and to Foucault, Derrida, Benveniste, Greimas, and Lacan. The editor of the volume, Peter Erickson, observes that "Much of the excitement and vitality of Berger's current work comes from its dramatization of the struggle between two powerful desires: the need to open himself to the challenge of new methodological influences and the need to incorporate them into his previous system."

Introduction 21

As befits the moment in his introduction, Erickson writes of a contained system: Berger's intellectual history as it shapes Berger's critical product. The forum respondents break out of this box, showing that what Berger has done makes new ways of doing. For example: while, among his own autobiographical remarks, Berger writes of having undertaken to "assimilate" some of the challenges of feminist criticism, Lynn Enterline demonstrates that, in fact, his work goes further to suggest "new avenues for feminist critique." Berger's crucial intervention into the feminist dialogue, she says, is to introduce a Lacanian hypothesis: that characters are "the effect rather than the cause of their language." With this, Berger is able to extricate his analyses from the "epigenetic or developmental paradigm" of the psychoanalytic readings of Shakespeare that have prevailed elsewhere. As Enterline explains, Berger negotiates a space for both psychoanalytic and historicist work by "insist[ing] on a return to the question of the subject's production in and by various social texts." Shakespearean tests, she continues, "do more than repeat or rehearse the objectification and subjection of women. Rather, they ask us to witness this process as it happens; most important, they dramatize its effects on the characters to whom it happens." Enterline concludes that Berger's model makes it possible for us to see that Shakespeare "invites us . . . to ask how Hermione, Lucrece, and Isabella feel about the exceedingly narrow confines of the language-games that, by dint of their position in culture, are available to them to play." Like Berger, Enterline closes with *Measure with Measure*, and specifically with the end of one set of language-games in Isabella's silence.

Similarly, although Berger acknowledges skating toward the "vertiginous vortex of Lacanian conundrums" (demurring, however, that he has erected self-protective mechanisms against "being sucked down into those depths and lost forever"), Marshall Grossman outlines a "direction toward which a further collaboration between Shakespeare and Lacan might lead." On the one hand, there is Lacan's "the unconscious is structured like a language"; on the other, Berger's "reading of linguistic complicities" which, "distributed among Shakespeare's characters, collectively structure the symbolic of these plays." Taking as his text the Prince always already known as King, Hal/Henry V, Grossman sets out to "nudge" Berger toward the notion of "the psychoanalytical transference as a model . . . which explains what it is the Shakespearean text does in and to its readers and how it does it." Specifically, the model may suggest "how it comes about that these texts enable us—perhaps, force us—to do something ethical with words." Transference, Grossman continues, is "the way we think through what we cannot think about, by attaching the emotional import of one set of relations to another set of relations and subtly supplementing their grammar with the impertinencies of rhetoric. Thus, reading Shakespeare, "we redistribute his language not only within the community of the plays, but between them and our own ... and in this way, we and [Prince] Harry meet and are changed by having met."

Grossman briefly engages Berger's reputation for "anti-theatrical polemic"; so does Lois Potter. For Grossman, "a reading includes a performance and a performance at least evokes a reading," the two productive of a "creative tension" in which each is, in a word, complicitous. And so, he says, he remains "agnostic," suspecting that Berger's reputed anti-theatricalism is "rooted very much in a particular critical context." Potter goes further by terming Berger's anti-theatricalism "imaginary": he is "not so much attacking the theater as setting himself on the side of complexity." She recognizes that Berger "hears" Shakespeare's characters with unusually keen ears; Angus Fletcher uses the same auditory locution for Berger's sensitive register for language. Neither Grossman nor Potter is persuaded that Berger's readings are insusceptible of performance, and Potter gives a number of instances in which the theatre has proved itself capable of Bergerian subtleties, contradictions, ambivalences, and discontinuities.

These are what Enterline calls Berger's "language-game[s] of dark corners and disowned desires," what Fletcher identifies as the volume's overarching theme of "complicitous bad faith." Of the five forum authors, Potter is the most concerned to address in its own terms Berger's theory of "redistributed complicities," and specifically, the complicity between victim and villain. As Potter summarizes, the "good" characters tend to "[seek] occasion[s] to suffer wrong so that there can be no doubt that [they are] in the right." What Potter calls "the Berger approach" does insinuate itself into his reader's textual strategies—it has happened to me, when I was teaching so unlikely a play as *Henry VIII*—and the effect that is generated can seem severely cynical or, as Potter also calls it, pessimistic. "One looks in vain," she says of *Making Trifles of Terrors*, "for any example of goodness that is not in some way vitiated." Potter is not the only respondent to pause over what Peter Erickson characterizes as "the curious contrast between the quirky attractiveness of Berger's manner and the bleakness of his message." It may be the same sense of contradiction that leads Fletcher to emphasize the "pedagogical burden" Berger accepts, and Stanley Cavell to describe "what strikes [him], attractively, as a pedagogical conscience." Potter is finally resolved that the bleakness, like Berger's anti-theatricality, is imaginary. What it comes down to is that Berger does not succumb to that confusion of dramatic characters and "real" people on which theater depends in order to elicit its emotional response. "If we have to sacrifice the emotional response," Potter says (not without some regret), there are compensations in the form of "enhanced" understandings. She concludes that the concept of complicity is best understood as "the extent to which characters themselves have a vested interest in keeping their play going," that, for example, Macduff is more loyal to the tragedy of *Macbeth* than to the family whose deaths he allows. "It has nothing to do with life," Potter observes, "and everything to do with the pleasure we take in art."

For Angus Fletcher, *Making Trifles of Terrors* illuminates the intellectual pleasures peculiar to dramatic art. He emphasizes Berger's argument that the distribution of complicities, particularly that distribution by which "the self-reflexive undoings of character . . . are to be found throughout the texture of whole plays," is "a consequence of the nature of dramatic discourse." When Fletcher takes up the issue of the differences between the Shakespearean play in performance and that play as read, he is especially concerned with the philosophical issue of the differing temporal frameworks of each, an issue Grossman engages, too. On stage, Fletcher notes, the play "unfolds linearly." On the page, however, "we are led to crisscross back and forth over the many ambiguous verbal interactions expressing that linear action—until we get a fix on the many walls (internal as much as external) that close down a character's power of expression." In the end, "the Shakespearean text is replete with its self-cancellations." On stage, the actors must effect their own "intellective deletions," because they cannot possibly put in play all those meanings that are made available to them. On the page, these meanings compel interpretation: "such an involuted, cross-referencing, complicitous Text requires the tenacious close reading" that Berger deploys. "If we don't accept that these plays are successfully overwritten," argues Fletcher, "we shall be denying their manifest nature." Berger's New Critical strategies, Fletcher suggests, are required of the interpreter of a Shakespearean play, as they are not required of the reader of a legal document, even of a poem. But the theory of complicities produces a "more social, political, communal reading of the dramatic ironies" than are customarily thrown up by the practice of close reading.

Making Trifles of Terrors prompts Stanley Cavell, too, to reflect on both critical practice and the nature of drama. For the former, he writes of "the violence of the practice of criticism," and particularly of "the complex surface of [Berger's] evocative, conversational prose harboring motives of deadly seriousness about literature." For the latter, he leads the reader on an excursion through Henry James, Emerson, and Wittgenstein that builds a network of associations among the fear of breath, the fear of death, the fear of speech, and the fear of letting speech come to an end—the last a fear that "the genre of drama lives upon." This is a meditation that powerfully and poetically resists recounting here. Indeed, it has been my aim throughout not to summarize the responses that follow but to point some of the ways in which they reflect on each other, as well as on *Making Trifles of Terrors*. One recurring motif is—and here, I borrow a term from Fletcher—the "exfoliation" of meanings. Thus, I omit much, and for no one more than for Cavell, who, in a moving tribute to Berger's "weave of insights," writes: "I have never seen so steadily before . . . why I have so often found myself recurring, in uncovering intersections of philosophy and literature, to the genre of drama."

Perhaps it is inevitable that a forum such as this will have the air of tribute. If so, then I hope it is a tribute of the sort that the author of *Making Trifles of Terrors* would value: unsentimental, "endlessly pushing the inquiry further," in Erickson's words. Grossman insists that Berger is inimitable, but Grossman also gives sufficient indication of why the editor of this journal would choose to devote this sort of attention to a single volume of interpretation: it is "Harry's courage in the transference—his willingness to, as it were, be seen by Shakespeare and to let us see Shakespeare seeing Harry—that generates those inimitable readings . . . and leaves so much working through for the rest of us."

Notes

1. Harry Berger, Jr., *Making Trifles of Terrors: Redistributing Complicities in Shakespeare*, ed. Peter Erickson (Stanford: Stanford University Press, 1997).

What "womanhood denies" the Power of "tongues to tell"

Lynn Enterline

Perhaps it is best to begin by acknowledging a stubborn fact: this is about as difficult an essay to write as any I can remember. In *Making Trifles of Terrors*, Harry Berger unfolds the many unlovely, self-interested desires and motives that lurk in the "dark corners" of various Shakespearean speakers' utterances. What most interests me about these unacknowledged motives is that they so often seem simultaneously obscure and compelling to the speakers themselves. Shining a kind of bright readerly light on such dark corners, Berger traces subtle modulations of self-defense and self-blame in a series of ethically ambiguous interactions in Shakespeare's plays. He turns the light on, not to judge Shakespeare's speakers, but because he wants to think about how they may judge themselves. Unacknowledged motives, particularly a speaker's suspicion about his or her own complicity in actions or desires she is working hard to lay at someone else's door, emerge from these speeches precisely because Berger cannily recasts the idea of self-representation rhetorically. That is, he understands such pronouncements as Lear's "I am more sinned against than sinning" less as self-representation than as an exercise in self-persuasion. Such a book—concerned as it is with vicissitudes of address and self-knowledge, with the shaping pressures and obliquities of one's own language—carries peculiar perils for anyone trying to write about it. The warning sign, *caveat scriptor*, has therefore loomed large over my reflections as I thought about how to respond.

Chief among the things I learned from Berger's way of looking at what I would call the rhetorical conditions of Shakespearean subjectivity is that a sentiment like the one with which I opened this essay—"this is difficult" or "this writing is hard for me to do"—may set out to praise its object, that is, "this is a rich and complex book and therefore it is hard to write about." But it also draws, however briefly, on what Berger identifies as "the victim's discourse." That is, acknowledging my difficulty with writing this essay also registers a complaint: "this book is asking me to work very hard." Nor does Berger's way of reading stop there; it also tells me that such a statement does not entirely evade the effects of my effort to persuade myself of something else my words do not openly proclaim. If I present myself to myself (and to the world) as someone who is working diligently on a difficult essay about a complex book, then I am also laboring to persuade myself that I am a smart person. Since I've learned this much from Berger's book, I can think of no better way to account for my motives in writing this paragraph than to quote his own account of why he listened to Peter Erickson and put together the essays that make up *Making Trifles of Terrors*: "He made me do it" (xxii).

If you are struck as much as I am by the shuttle between "self-inculpation and self-exculpation" in the preceding account of just a few opening words, or by the suspicious displacement of agency from one party (me) to another party (him), then you have become involved in the language-game of dark corners and disowned desires that Berger signals in his subtitle, "Redistributing Complicities." As *Making Trifles of Terrors* continually reminds us, however, everyone must assume some place as the place from which to speak—and then do the best she can with the cultural baggage that comes along. The place I claim here as the one from which to speak to others about the complex questions of address raised in Berger's book is (not surprisingly) that of a literary critic whose habits, training, experience, and desires mean that she approaches such ethico-rhetorical issues as a feminist. Having gotten that much said, what I propose to do here is outline what seem to me some of the most compelling contributions Berger's book makes to feminist criticism of Shakespeare. What I want to suggest is that Berger's account of Shakespearean subjectivity draws on such criticism in order to further it, and thus constitutes a kind of invitation to new avenues for feminist critique. (Already I tread on the dangerous Lacanian ground of the future anterior—recasting what the book has been for what I declare it is in the process of becoming—but we can return to that later.) First things first: what Berger calls the "positional discourse of gender" is axiomatic in this thinking about Shakespearean drama. He views it as one among several culturally inflected positions that circumscribe the various "ethical discourses" speakers employ. But Berger approaches the discourse of gender, and the question of positionality, somewhat obliquely, through analyses that concentrate primarily on the question of what it means, in Shakespeare's plays, to represent oneself to oneself or to others. It may take a little time, but I would like to demonstrate why such obliquity is both necessary and important.

Berger is quite clear that he conceives of Shakespeare's characters as the effect rather than the cause of their language. He turned to Lacanian theory, he tells us, because he wanted to "extricate" his account of subjectivity and gender from the "disabling" shadow of "biological destiny" that lies heavily over the "epigenetic or developmental paradigm" advanced in many psychoanalytic accounts of Shakespeare's plays in the last twenty years (215). For feminist readers, I believe, such an extrication is crucial. If we give sufficient weight to the recursive projections of the mirror stage and the force of the future anterior in Lacan's writing or attend to the "other Freud" that Lacan finds in Freud's texts—his push in the direction of semiotics in *Interpretation of Dreams*; his refusal to adjudicate between event and fantasy at the "origin" of psychic life; his theory of retrospective action; his discovery that present transferences and countertransferences shape the "truth" of the subject's history in the analytic session—something important happens. What the thesis of "the speaking-subject" means for psychoanalytic theory (Freud's included) is that it quickly exceeds the contours of its own plot, its own chronological narratives of stages and development. Recall, in this regard, the way Slavoj Žižek describes the difference the hypothesis of the Symbolic makes to the question of the subject's history and the subject-in-history. We do not "discover" the meaning of symptoms or excavate them "from the hidden depth" of a subject's past, but construct them "retroactively." If analysis "produces the truth," then that "truth" is "the signifying frame which gives the symptoms their symbolic place and meaning." What this means is that, "as soon as we enter the symbolic order, the past is always present in the form of historical tradition and the meaning of those traces is not given; it changes continually with the transformation of the signifier's network."[1] Substitute "Shakespearean text" for "symbolic order" in the preceding account, and I think you begin to entertain the kind of reading Berger calls for.

Feminist theorists in other fields have, of course, made similar claims about the work of retrospection, because they want to argue that the trope of the maternal body is precisely that, a trope—that if we are to extricate our concepts of motherhood from its apparent imprisonment in the bedrock of biological destiny, we must pay close attention to the recursive effects of the Symbolic order on what is too easily posited as pre-linguistic (whether this positing is done by an author, a patient, an analyst, or a literary critic).[2] Here, Berger recalls Lisa Lowe's objection, in an essay on *Coriolanus*, that psychoanalytic studies treating mother-son relations as the "genetic cause," rather than a persuasive cultural fantasy, "obscures the extent to which social, cultural, and political circumstances influence family structure." The break that Lacan's theory of the Symbolic order produces—the break with an "epigenetic" or developmental plot—has not yet found much of a place in readings of gender in Shakespeare, although I think this is changing. Berger's mode of psychoanalytic reading, accordingly, advocates a shift "from causal to effectual and structural frameworks" (216). I tried to advocate a similar shift by writing a book that analyzed early modern tropes of the maternal body, including Shakespeare's, according to the proposition that accounts of origin such as mother-son bonds (whether in a literary or a theoretical text) are retroactive, recursive cultural fantasies shaped by the symbolic order the mother is claimed to precede.[3]

Berger puts forward his Lacanian hypothesis—that characters are the effect rather than the cause of their language—in order to move beyond the epigenetic mode of feminist psychoanalytic work in Shakespeare. At the same time, however, such an approach opens up a variety of ways to explore the possible intersections between psychoanalytic and historical accounts of early modern subjectivity. The position that recursive, culturally inflected fantasies shape how and what bodies, genders, and desires mean proposes a kind of symptomology of the speaking subject in culture. It makes room for both psychoanalytic and historical feminists because it insists on a return to the question of the subject's production in and by various social texts. How specific a critic wants to get about the texts against which to read these symptoms and fantasies will, I suspect, be a decision at once personal (a question of taste) and institutional (a question of graduate training).

Berger's distinctive way of investigating language's action on Shakespearean subjectivity moves freely between Lacan, Austin, and Wittgenstein. *Making Trifles of Terrors* focuses on the "language-games" or "ready made community practices" various Shakespearean speakers draw upon to represent themselves because Berger is interested in "socially constructed patterns not only of behavior but also of self-representation" (325). The idea of language-games allows him to modify—or perhaps particularize—Lacan's notion of the Symbolic order in a way that seems crucial for feminism:

> the men and women who represent themselves to themselves and each other as players of roles are (whether or not they are aware of it) simultaneously being represented as the roles, the characters, the dramatic personae, written and performed by—by whom, or rather, by what? By the motives, desires, the fears, inscribed in language. Not, however, language *tout court,* not even in what Lacan calls the "symbolic" *tout court,* but in the "discourse networks" of specific "social texts" (324).

Such a shift from symbolic to social text signals one way historical and psychoanalytic critiques of the early modern subject might meet (and perhaps move beyond one of our field's least productive antinomies). Certainly it signaled to me a way of opening what he calls "the positional discourses" central to psychoanalysis—those of gender, sexuality, and generation—to the larger social field: the interplay of various positions of authority (or lack of it) in "social texts," the "discourse networks" within which, or alongside which, the positional transactions of the family take their place. As he puts it, "in Shakespeare's text, the family is embedded in, and indeed identical with, a political order" oriented around "father power" (232).

Berger's argument about the language of Shakespearean subjectivity goes something like this: Shakespeare's speakers draw on, and are given recognizable shape by, a series of "ethical discourses" within which they represent themselves to each other and, more important, to themselves. His taxonomy of these ethical discourses—the victim's, the villain's, the revenger's, the sinner's, the hero's, the donor's—is arresting enough. Each has its own peculiar, and at times hilariously familiar, "rationale or scenario," "its own 'argument' (in one of the older meanings of the term)" (231). These discourses are stories Shakespeare's characters either tell themselves or work hard to get told by others. (Heroes like Coriolanus or Othello, for instance, are peculiarly vulnerable: drawing on the hero's discourse means that you have to work hard to get other people to praise you without acknowledging to yourself or to others that is what you are doing.) Berger carefully names these ethical discourses according to their "stereotypical character," a naming that reflects his larger concern with "culturally constructed and constrained patterns of motivation" and thus with the various, often conflicting "social texts" within which Shakespeare wrote (229 and 324).

Berger's way of illuminating self-representation as self-persuasion, moreover, plunges into the middle of scenes of address—be it to another or to oneself. In these scenes of address, one or more of these ethical discourses surfaces, but—and, for me, this is a crucial move—the content of what gets said, what the speaker's words mean, quickly runs onto the shoals of other less explicit meanings (the general effect of polysemy heightened by Shakespeare's incessant punning) or of what those words *do* (the general effect of performatives but made particularly evident in a theater historically intertwined with religious ritual).[4] My brief summary of how Berger's generally Austinian interest in perlocutionary and illocutionary force modulates into issues of hidden motives and self-persuasion will, I hope, be sufficient for the present purpose of this essay—that of suggesting that his analysis of unacknowledged complicities is poised between a rhetorical and a psychoanalytic critique of speaking subjectivity. In "rhetorical," I include the social, and would simply remind readers of Berger's own apt summary of rhetoric elsewhere as a field of action that is at once "tropological and transactional."[5] Another way of thinking about this complex intersection is to observe that Berger's insistence on the scene of address requires us to consider, in some detail, the effects both of persuasion and of the Other on the way Shakespeare's characters think about themselves.

Since even the most committed Lacanian thinker may feel her mind go blank when reading that enigmatic word, "the Other," I'd like to compare the rhetorical scene I take Berger to be describing to what Žižek describes as the Other's place in subjectivity. As I have said, Berger shifts the emphasis away from self-representation—from a static model of the self's knowledge (or ignorance) about itself and the representations that reflect such personal history—to a dynamic, temporally disjunctive, ongoing process of address that includes persuading oneself as much as persuading others. Analyzing various "auditors in the speaker" (307)—most notably, in this regard, Prince Harry and Duke Vincentio—Berger proposes finely nuanced accounts of feeling and ambiguated motives without personifying these characters as selves whose history precedes the play in which they take part. Through the idea of various ethical discourses available to speakers and acting on them, Berger reads the scene of address and linguistic action (with all its unanticipated effects) in light of the constraints of socially determined discourses.

In other words, if Shakespeare and Berger ask us to eavesdrop on the "auditor in the speaker" and attend to the unacknowledged motives that hide in the "dark corners of" his or her discourse—Cordelia's "To your professed bosomes / I commit him" or Vincentio's "let our pleasures be executed" (305 and 421)—they are asking us to listen to the pressure exerted by the Other inside. By this, I mean that the movement of self-persuasion is not a closed circle. Žižek describes a similar movement, calling it "symbolic identification." Our identification as speaking subjects, he writes, is "with the very place from where we are being observed, from where we look at ourselves so that we appear to ourselves to be likeable, worthy of love." This description accords well enough with Berger's description of the saint's or the hero's discourses, but his scheme includes those of sinner, villain, and revenger as well. In fact, Berger asks us to pay particular attention to subjects talking to themselves or to others from the place where they see themselves as unlikable and unworthy of love—a "reversal into its opposite" of truly Freudian provenance. My point here is the *dislocation* Berger charts in these moments of self-persuasion, a dislocation that aligns these analyses with a number of psychoanalytic theorists.[6] As Žižek describes this displacement, "the crucial break that psychoanalysis must accomplish is to induce [the subject] to realize how he is himself this other for whom he is acting a role—how his being-for-the-other is his being-for himself, because he is himself already symbolically identified with the gaze for which he is playing his role" (104–5).

Because a speaker's idea of what counts as "worthy" or "unworthy" will carry with it all the culturally inflected baggage of gender, sexuality, and generation that defines that speaker's social position, this dislocating identification quickly ushers us onto the domain of feminist critique. What makes this work important for contemporary feminists is that Berger's theory of various ethical discourses—with all the determinations of gender difference that attend them—insists on the fact that the Other within the speaker is the place where we can begin to unravel its social inscription. That is, if the ethical discourses are "primarily ethico-psychological," nonetheless, "they are always situated in specific situational scenarios" (231). His model proposes a kind of socially textured version of Benveniste's site of enunciation—such shifters as I/you/s/he/it bear the mark of the institutional structures within which these positions are deployed—and thus requires readers to consider the position of authority, or lack of it, from which a speaker speaks (as sinner, saint, donor, and so on). For Berger, Shakespeare's characters face the "positional exigencies" of a patriarchally organized family structure, a structure that sets the parameters within which speakers deploy various ethical discourse to play their "self-justifying language-games" (232). Vexed relations of sexuality, gender, and generation, therefore, place considerable pressure on the way these discourses are spoken or received. Thus, the same discourse—the victim's discourse—sounds very different when it falls from Lear's lips than when it falls from Cordelia's.

I would like to conclude by illustrating this abstract summary with one of the more compelling examples in Berger's book: Isabella's attempt to persuade Angelo to spare her brother in *Measure for Measure*. Berger notes that it is Isabella's "discourse of virtue that seduces Angelo, the 'sense' of sensuality appealing to him from the 'sense' of her rational, occasionally casuistic, persuasions.... He is stirred by *a duplicity of speech that produces her sexuality as an unintended effect* of her Christian rhetoric" (406, emphasis mine). Thus, it is no accident that the nun who first talks with Isabella understands retiring from the world of men quite specifically—as having no conversation with them.

> *Isabella.* Who is't that calls?
> *Francisca.* It is a man's voice. Gentle Isabella,
>   Turn you the key, and know his business from him;
>   You may, I may not; you are yet unsworn.
>   When you have vow'd, you must not speak with men
>   But in the presence of a prioress;
>   Then if you speak, you must not show your face,
>   Or if you show your face, you must not speak
>   (I.4.8–13)

Given what happens when Angelo hears Isabella speak, we may come to reflect that the nun was not wrong.

As I read Berger's account of Isabella's discursive predicament, I could not help but remember the many other Shakespearean women caught by the unintended effects of their own discourse, whose meanings go astray as soon as they fall on a man's ears. One thinks of Lucrece's infelicitous words of prayer to Tarquin (when she calls herself a "troubled ocean" that tries to "soften" Tarquin's "stone" "with continual motion" [589–93]); Lavinia's unintended reference to the very sexual act she tries to fend off ("one thing more / That womanhood denies my tongue to tell. / O, keep me from their worse than killing lust / Tumble me into some loathsome pit" [2.3.173–76]); or the unhappy effects of Hermione's "potent tongue" when her words fall on Leontes' jealous ears. My point is not that this bind of unintended meaning applies only to women in Shakespeare. Berger's book demonstrates in considerable detail how this problem—the surprises lying in wait in language's dark corners—shapes the self-representations of either gender. But the misfiring Berger so cannily describes turns, in the case of all four women, specifically to sex (and only sex) as the domain that determines how they will be heard. In these predicaments, we see Shakespeare define the exceedingly important, and culturally inflected, position of a woman's chastity in early modern England precisely—and discursively—by writing dialogues in which a woman, speaking to her male interlocutor to try to persuade him of one thing, unhappily discovers that he has heard something else. And that "something else," in the chaste woman's case, is the sexual meaning she is at pains to prevent. This is positionality with a vengeance, a telling index of the cultural pressure that places exceedingly narrow boundary markers around the field of what a woman can possibly say. This does not mean that Shakespeare's women are excluded from language (the erroneous objection that was sometimes raised against French feminism when it reached American shores) or that they are utterly imprisoned by it. Rather, it means that Shakespeare's women, like all his subjects, create limited forms of agency out of their own linguistic vulnerability;[7] and that when they take up their position in discourse, they find, like all his speaking subjects, that the form of their discursive subjection betrays the particular imprint of their culture's binary machine of difference. Taken together, what the cases of Isabella, Lucrece, Lavinia, and Hermione suggest to me is that their speech is marked by the imprint or trace of what counts as "chaste" in the early modern period. And that, in Shakespeare's texts, chastity is pushed beyond the cultural *desideratum* that a woman remain silent to designate an impossible, paradoxical place no one ever occupies—a vanishing point that lies outside the errancies of discourse and therefore seems to solicit its own violation merely by being talked about. Another way to put this observation might be that female chastity is a figure—the figure for a dream about a place outside linguistic errancy which is therefore at risk the moment a woman opens her mouth.

The repeated misfiring of a woman's speech in Shakespeare's texts means to me that under the particular material circumstances that defined early modern discourses about gender difference, the positional exigencies defining a woman's vulnerability and agency in language were, by contrast to those defining a man's, especially limiting. What Berger's focus on character as effect rather than cause of a speaker's own discourse allowed me to think, in a different way, is that these texts do more than repeat or rehearse the objectification and subjection of women. Rather, they ask us to witness this process as it happens; most important, they *dramatize its effects on the characters to whom it happens*. It thus seems to me that these texts offer particularly eloquent moments of what Althusser would call "internal distance" from the very ideology from which they also derive.[8]

As feminist work has demonstrated, the narrator in *The Rape of Lucrece* holds Collatine's *words* responsible for the violence done her; both *Titus Andronicus* as a whole and Lavinia herself blame a specific discourse for her rape; the opening scene of the *Winter's Tale* charts the cataclysmic effects of Hermione's rhetoric. Like Angelo's sexualized reading of Isabella's Christian discourse, each of these texts insists that language inaugurates the deeply gendered forms of violence that ensue—and that we think long and hard about that inauguration. But most important to the way I read *Making Trifles of Terrors* is the fact that each of these Shakespearean texts also ensures that the object of such linguistic violence is also its subject. In other words, they ask us to worry a lot about what these women think and feel about their socio-linguistic positioning and about what limited forms of agency might be available to them—how they might, in short, speak to what "womanhood denies" their "tongue[s] to tell." Probably one of the more resonant moments of resistance in this regard is Hermione's protest in Leontes' courtroom. She speaks of her position and begins a ringing testimony of her various emotions by reminding her audience and herself how she will be heard:

> Since what I am to say must be but that
> Which contradicts my accusation, and
> The testimony on my part no other
> But what comes from myself, it shall scarce boot me
> To say "Not guilty." Mine integrity
> Being counted falsehood, shall (as I express it)
> Be so received
>
> (3.2.26–28).

Lucrece, too, speaks at length about the impossibility of speaking in her case. Produced out of the contradiction of having "more woe than words," Lucrece emerges as a character precisely by way of her meditations on the pain of being forced to speak about an event that lies beyond the power of words to say. (I note in passing that such representations of womanhood as the predicament of speaking about an unspeakable event point to an important place where contemporary psychoanalytic work on trauma might enrich historical analyses of gender and rape.) Even Lavinia, the Shakespearean woman whose agency in language seems reduced to nothing, nonetheless manages to point out the text of her subjection (the *Metamorphoses*) and to write the three words that turn the play's action into revenge. As readers often note, moreover, the play spends a lot of time showing how the men who claim to want to know what Lavinia is thinking and feeling all too quickly turn her into a sign for their own grief. If Marcus's swift turn from "O that I knew thy heart" to the desire to rail at the "beast" who violated her "to ease *my* mind" (2.4.34–35) isn't enough to make us notice this shift, Titus says he wants to take Lavinia with him to gaze into a pool that, in this Ovidian play, sounds suspiciously like that of Narcissus (3.1.123–29). My point here is that *Titus* makes this narcissistic turn evident, asks us to watch it happen, and therefore reinforces *our* desire to know the very feelings *they* seem to forget.

It seems to me that the question the men in *Titus Andronicus* keep raising and evading—what is Lavinia thinking and feeling about her corporeal-linguistic violation?—does more than surface in the texts I mention here. It becomes the foundational question they pose about their female characters. Shakespeare invites us, by way of his characters' own rhetoric, to ask how Hermione, Lucrece, and Isabella feel about the exceedingly narrow confines of the language-games that, by dint of their position in culture, are available to them to play. If we read these female characters as the retroactive effect of the misfiring imposed on them by their own language and by the (socially specific) Other that inhabits that language, then they take their shape and texture—their distinctive personality—around a troubling, and deeply cultural, contradiction. Lacan, of course, describes this contradiction as the predicament peculiar to women—that of having to become subjects of the very discourse that makes them the privileged objects of desire and fear. I want to conclude my response to the feminist aspects of *Making Trifles of Terrors* with Berger's account of the saint's discourse in Isabella's and Angelo's dialogue, then, for this reason: his way of approaching the question of character in Shakespeare tells me that Isabella's much noted silence at the end of *Measure for Measure* speaks volumes.

Notes

1. *The Sublime Object of Ideology* (London: Verso, 1989): 56. All future citations in the text are to this edition.

2. See Jacqueline Rose, *Sexuality in the Field of Vision* (London: Verso, 1986): 79; Judith Butler, *Gender Trouble: Feminism and the Subversion of Identity* (London: Routledge, 1990): 80–81; Cynthia Chase, "Transference as Trope and Persuasion," in Shlomith Rimmon-Kenan, ed., *Discourse in Psychoanalysis and Literature* (London: Methuen, 1987): 223.

3. For further discussion, see *The Tears of Narcissus: Melancholia and Masculinity in Early Modern Writing* (Stanford: Stanford University Press, 1995): 18–38.

4. Here, I refer readers to Berger's discussion of the work of Stephen Greenblatt and Steven Mullaney on pp. 329–34.

5. "Narrative as Rhetoric in *The Faerie Queene*," *English Literary Renaissance* (1991): 3–48.

6. In this regard, see also Samuel Weber's chapter on Lacan's "staging" of the subject, in *Return to Freud: Jacques Lacan's Dislocation of Psychoanalysis*, trans. Michael Levine (New York: Cambridge University Press, 1991).

7. Here, I too quickly summarize Berger's account of what his approach means for questions of agency. Interested readers should see his discussions on pp. 223–28 and 322–28 especially.

8. "Ideology and Ideological State Apparatuses," in *Lenin and Philosophy*, trans. Ben Brewster (New York: Monthly Review Press, 1971): 133, 152–56.

Complicity and the Genesis of Shakespearean Dramatic Discourse

Angus Fletcher

As always, there is the distinction between substance and form. My own theoretical interests lead me to ponder the shaping of Harry Berger's commentaries into what is clearly an essayistic form. On the role of commentary in the criticism of Shakespeare, I shall indeed have something to say. Initially, however, I am struck by a persistent theme in these essays, and by its uncanny pertinence to broader problems of understanding American attitudes in the present period. This is the theme of complicitous bad faith, which inevitably becomes Berger's chief concern, as soon as he develops his affinity with the Shakespearean commentaries of Stanley Cavell. Berger has been thinking about the hidden complicities of Shakespearean characters for years, but the use of Cavell's acknowledgment-thesis gives a yet sharper edge to the proceedings. Throughout the plays discussed here, Berger finds different aspects of a behavior Cavell relates to acknowledgment—if I do not know something, Cavell says, that implies a blank spot of ignorance; there's something missing in the body of my knowledge. But if I fail or refuse to acknowledge something, the point is that almost the opposite situation pertains: "A 'failure to acknowledge' is the presence of something, a confusion, an indifference, a callousness, an exhaustion, a coldness." Cavell most powerfully aligns this second failure, this acknowledgment-gap, when (like Berger) he shows that, in *Lear* and elsewhere, characters refuse or fail to reveal themselves to others, and in that masking gesture fail to "acknowledge others." We are looking at the tremendously complex system of ethical reciprocations which add up to the workings of a community, and as soon as we include an emotional inwardness and deeper self in our account, we almost perforce enter the field of complicity. This term has achieved a sort of neutrality, so that it falls short of conspiratorial involvement in wrongdoing, although one is surprised to learn that "complicit" as meaning criminal involvement is a very late (twentieth-century) usage.

The remarkable thing, then, is that Berger can show such atmospheres and activities of personal, social, and political complicity in the plays. He can show that Rumor is far more than a convenient personification for a history play, the Duke in *Measure for Measure* something rather more devious and controlling than even his detractors had thought, that the "discourse of honor" is more sharply shot through with dishonoring doubleness than we can imagine Hotspur laboring against. Many of the self-reflexive undoings of character we associate most extremely, let us say, with an Iago or a Claudius are to be found throughout the texture of whole plays. And that, Berger argues, is a consequence of the nature of dramatic discourse. On this idea, he is flexible; it helps to take his view ("*Discourse* is the sort of modest, recessive term people use to define and discuss other things without bothering to define and discuss *it*. As a result it has become an all-purpose instrument denoting anything from the narrow confines of a speech event to the amplitude of social and political practices"). Berger gives a catalogue of typical recent usages, from Benveniste, Greimas, Foucault, and others. I read this book's usage as implying that a discourse (for example, "the villain's discourse," or "the sinner's discourse") is a discernible elaboration of a set of language-games which gives the fashion in which a dramatic character speaks and bespeaks his "characteristic" approach to life. As Berger argues in many ways, and in great depth for different persons in the plays, each discourse carries with it its own rationale or scenario, or, in the older sense, its "argument" (231).

This emphasis on discourse involves a problematic notion of Shakespearean drama in general, which it is Berger's purpose to develop in the light of his apparent distaste for performance-centered criticism, and against which he counterposes a strongly text-centered criticism. Performance and theatrical business here are held to project the "circumstances" of the action, whereas the characters' articulated discourse, embedded in a "community" of relevant speech, projects the much deeper level of what Berger calls the "conditions" in which and through which the character expresses a form of life. If "circumstances" of actions are, at bottom, mostly an affair of theatrical stage business, then unquestionably they get us to thinking about the surface of the drama, about what works on stage as the play unfolds linearly as a piece of theatrical practice. Audiences pay to see this done well. But if, on a more obscure plane, the action is motivated around deep-lying psychic and social "conditions," then we are led to crisscross back and forth over the many ambiguous, verbal interactions expressing that linear action—until we get a fix on the many walls (internal as much as external) that close down a character's powers of expression. "Freedom of expression" comes to seem less likely, if not impossible. Yet expression continues, so that finally the Shakespearean text is replete with its self-cancellations, all the while reaching for greater rhetorical force and direct drive. The combination is irresistibly textual, in Berger's rich understanding of that term.

Nothing could be more obvious, and yet no less problematic than this paradoxical mixture. Berger's own reaction to it, as both scholar and teacher, is to accept the pedagogical burden it imposes. His view is that we are foolish and not very smart if we fail to *read* Shakespeare, actively, ingeniously, dialogically. If we do not accept that these plays are successfully overwritten, we shall be denying their manifest nature.

Theatrical, as well as literary, history shows how Shakespeare strains the bounds of what is possible for the stage, all the while liberating the "imaginary auditor," Berger's ideal reader. Vertiginous virtuosity is what this reader expects, whether early comic euphuism or late romantic compactions, or the deeply troubled expressive manners of plays like *Troilus and Cressida* or *All's Well*. One supposes that, for such language to translate from page to stage, there must be a sort of intellective deletion—the actors cannot possibly use all the meanings of the text, and if they tried to, their performances would instantly bog down in a self-reflexive morass. Berger deserves the highest praise for raising the question of the textual overplus, especially since he gives an account, via the idea of complicity, of its genesis. Thus, he shows how Rumor as personification, versus Rumor as dramatic participant, are at odds with each other, the result of which is that Rumor's discourse complexifies the play at large. In *Measure*, the Duke is shown to be involved in the "Vienna problem," a discursive network from which the Duke cannot extract an honestly independent standpoint, whereas, in fact, he "enjoys" the complicitous disguises his own mind accepts as a form of self-blinding vision. In a world of such complicities the Shakespearean text betrays the normally private complications one tries to control and repress from public view, with the general dramatic consequence that no single speech is ever written so as to affirm an unconditional sense of self. The actions (and their scripts) rush forward, but the texts, available to synchronous reading, to "flipping back and forth," virtually force the active reader into a mode of retrospective and prospective interrogation. Actors take a pragmatic view of cutting the textual superflux, as they have also traditionally cut or changed the scripts they are handed; from Berger's viewpoint, however, it seems significant that Hamlet is by far the most talkative of Shakespeare's personae, followed by Falstaff, Richard III, and (!) Iago (although, if we throw in *Merry Wives*, Falstaff wins by a couple of hundred lines). What is curious is that the imaginary auditor seems to go in an opposite, antitheatrical direction, always increasing his or her sense of lexical density and semantic amplitude. One even wonders whether Hamlet is not to be seen as the one who reads, the *überleser* of tragedy. He is certainly, unlike other Shakespearean heroes, an academic of sorts. In principle, Berger will call Hamlet an interpreter, the hero of the kind of text emerging throughout the canon.

The oldest and strongest model for interpretation is, of course, biblical, so that we might finally want to compare Berger's "text" with a scriptural equivalent, and further to analyze the parallel question of textual canonicity in both cases. But it can be more simply observed that interpretive commentary elicits a special kind of response, which might be called "another commentary." This is not to say that such readings are condemned to life in a self-reflexive jail of competing commentaries—here, there are many pages of the most astute ethical analysis, of psychoanalytic insight, of insight into broader theatrical layouts in the plays discussed. On a deeper level, however, the effect of Berger's work is to call for further responses in the same vein, that is, further text-centered discoursings. These essays are, as it were, vastly extended analytic footnotes for a folio Shakespeare the size of Central Park; they take the textual moment and expand it to unusual size, so that we thereby begin to perceive the microstructure usually hidden by our map. Whether Berger's method is closer to allegory than it seems is a question of theory which may not need posing; if it were, we could ask how complicitous expression shares in the obsessive self-entanglement allegory always reveals.

Another question always returns for me, in the context of such matters of method: the idea suggested by Wittgenstein when he asked if Shakespeare were not, after all, "the inventor of language." The texts may exfoliate in all directions, as Berger shows, and we may wonder what, besides a play-filling network of complicitous speeches, can be said to produce the richness of the Shakespearean text. The hermeneutics of suspicion in whatever guise tends to imagine a prolixity of mind—the duplicity resulting from complicity, expressions, and meanings which, in John Donne's words, "about, and about must go"—and if the Text is that level of utterance at which Shakespeare expresses such convolutions of possible meaning, then, with Berger, we will see the Text as Shakespeare's inmost resource. Certainly such an involuted, cross-referencing, complicitous Text requires the tenacious close reading Berger gives it. I may imagine, of course, a more random purpose to the "prolixity" than is presented here. I may also imagine that Shakespeare's Text looks like a deep level of complicitous discoursing, whereas, in fact, its depth comes from the poet indeed being a sort of "inventor of language." Then the poet would be like some crazed carpenter building a barn with decorations as delicate as Grinling Gibbons. Berger himself proposes at one point that we think of the playwright as inventing dramatic scripts on the expressive model of the brilliantly inturning Sonnets. Perhaps as good a cue to the way Berger reads his Shakespeare is to say that he *hears* it, as when he supposes, "If I listen to the Duke's words with his ears" (394), in the sense that Berger wants to take Lionel Abel's metatheater (and all similar sophistications of self-reflexivity) quite a few steps further along the road toward the complete commentary on all the possible countermoves within the rhetoric of the plays. In this, Berger, as he has often noted about his own criticism, continues in the New Critical line of delving for ironies (for what irony can exist, especially in a play, without the revelation of a complicity?), but the beauty of the new complicity theory is that it allows for a much more social, political, communal reading of the dramatic ironies.

One wants to say, in conclusion, that rarely have the Shakespearean texts been so genially followed into their depths as they are here. I find it tantalizing that among those plays yielding so effectively to this deep reading, none is more apposite than *Measure for Measure*, to which the book devotes its final, very long essay. *Measure* is the perfect proof text for Berger's interpretive aim, and his account (simply to make a critical, if not interpretive remark about it) is absolutely splendid, a classic interpretive text in its own right. I am happy at this outcome, if not completely surprised; for, among Shakespeare's plays, *Measure* most closely approaches the textual mystery Kafka invented and reinvented, the mystery called "judgment." My job here is merely to respond to Berger: I must say that the interpretive mode truly finds its mark in this final chapter; nor do I think the allusion to Watergate misplaced.

Imaginary Anti-Theatricality: Harry Berger's Drama of Passive Aggression

Lois Potter

In *Imaginary Audition* (1989), Harry Berger (in an imaginary dialogue with the imaginary Gary Taylor and Richard Levin) responded to a kind of criticism that is often called theater-orientated. This criticism usually (a) claims that the response of an "innocent" spectator is the most valid guide to a play, and therefore (b) disallows some readings (such as the one Berger wanted to offer) on the grounds that they cannot be performed and therefore cannot be intended. The pendulum swing between those who think that criticism is too complex and those who think that it isn't complex enough has been going on long enough to be called a perpetual motion. In suggesting that Shakespeare's plays are both theatrical and anti-theatrical (and that the second quality enriches the first), Berger was not so much attacking the theater as setting himself on the side of complexity as opposed to what he sees as reductive criticism.

Making Trifles of Terrors, selected and edited by Peter Erickson, is a collection of fourteen of Berger's Shakespearean essays; many of these predate *Imaginary Audition*; three are published for the first time in this volume. Nearly half are on what used to be called the Second Tetralogy and will probably be subsumed in a forthcoming book, to be called *Harrying*. Two are on the Lear and Gloucester families in *King Lear*. There are also two essays on *Macbeth* and one each on *Much Ado*, *Merchant of Venice*, and *Measure for Measure*. While Erickson (or Berger) might perhaps have gone further in reducing repetition between essays, I can see why they did not. For one thing, not many people read this kind of book from cover to cover; for another, Berger's argument is complex, constantly developing, and benefits from reiteration.

As Erickson says in his perceptive introduction, Berger's approach is "moral" and "political." But it is moral in a special sense.

That is, it is concerned with characters' perceptions of good and evil, but whereas moral criticism usually involves seeing the characters in the same terms that they themselves use, Berger's essays complicate the study of morality in two major ways: first, by a concept of performance that has only the speaker's self for audience, and second, by insisting on the complicity between villains and victims. There is a victims' discourse, as there is a villains' discourse, and in theatrical terms one is as powerful as the other; thus, both types of characters are participants in a competition, although perhaps they are not fully aware that they are competing. It is important to realize that Berger is eager—if not, I think, always able—to avoid inviting us to take part in what he calls "the voyeuristic power of divine judgment" (279).

Berger's two essays on the comedies, which come first in the book, show how easily manipulation of the victim's role—suffering and forgiveness—comes to women. Portia's words to Bassanio about the ring she gives him, the loss of which will "be my vantage to exclaim on you," become one of the key phrases of the book, a character's unconscious admission that she (like many other characters) is seeking occasion to suffer wrong so that there can be no doubt that she is in the right. *Much Ado* ends with Hero recognizing the advantage she gains by forgiving Claudio, and thus proving that comedy is "an experience that ends in the nick of time" (24). Obviously, these essays are influenced by feminist writing. In some ways, they are a welcome relief from the usual insistence that (fictitious) women can do no wrong, since Berger starts from exactly that position and shows how deadly it is. However, anyone who thinks that this study of manipulative victimization sounds misogynistic need only turn to the essays on the tragedies and histories, which occupy most of the rest of this volume, to find numerous men who carry the art much further.

All do offend, he says—all. One might think *Lear* already a cruel play, but Berger's reading makes it even more cruel. Gloucester's true feelings toward his children are inadvertently revealed when he says, not that he loves Edmund as much as Edgar, but that Edgar is "no dearer" to him than Edmund (57). Lear himself says that he is kind to "Poor Tom" because he identifies the beggar with himself; Gloucester does not say, but Berger infers, that Gloucester takes enormous risks to help Lear because he identifies Lear with himself. Of course, if good actions are always going to have mixed motives, it would seem to follow that evil characters are less than purely evil. But Berger, although he hints that both Edmund's villainous bravado and Edgar's apparent self-abasement may cover very similar feelings toward a father who has rejected them, does not pursue the possibility of arousing sympathy for a vulnerable Edmund. What interests him is the extent to which villains are enabled—perhaps even compelled—by the willing complicity of the "good" characters, who use them rather as More's Utopians use the brutish Zapoletes, to enable them to go on being good. Macbeth is not an evil principle whose expulsion restores goodness to the universe; his society chooses to see him this way, in order to ignore its own evil. Why else is he able to kill the king so easily? Banquo, who replies to Duncan's "This castle hath a pleasant seat" by discoursing on the pleasures of birdwatching in Dunsinane, deliberately passes up the chance to tell him about a nearby heath on which he recently heard a rather unsettling prophecy.

The history plays lend themselves particularly well to the Berger approach, since they deal with characters who are trying to tell not only their own histories, but History. While some of the psychological convolutions Berger traces in them might seem overly subtle or cynical, I find these easier to believe because many episodes in the *Henriad* seem to be reruns of episodes from the openly villainous world of the first tetralogy, where the stings and double-crosses rival those of Jonson's comedies. It is generally recognized that the struggle over succession in the plays' public sphere is mirrored in the private one by the struggle between fathers and sons (Henry IV and Hal, Falstaff and Hal, York and Aumerle, Northumberland and Hotspur, Glendower and his son-in-law Mortimer, and—Berger would add—John of Gaunt and Bolingbroke, who feels betrayed by his father's lack of open support). The point about hereditary succession is precisely that it marks the father for death and makes him an enemy of the son who will supplant him. Just as Richard II, who lacks a son, connives in his own deposition so as to transfer as much guilt as possible to Bolingbroke, so the other fathers betray and abandon sons they profess to love, and so (Berger argues in a brilliant *Shakespeare Quarterly* essay published since this book), Falstaff and Hal connive in performing Falstaff's rejection. In the first of the three new essays, "Food for Words: Hotspur and the Discourses of Honor," he shows (with some sympathy) that Hotspur's obsession with honor is a no-win situation: he "stacks the odds against himself and maximizes his commitment to the role of underdog," so that Northumberland's failure to turn up at Shrewsbury can be seen as giving him exactly what he wants (278).

Imaginary Anti-Theatricality 45

The chapter that gives the book its title starts with *All's Well That Ends Well*, ranges widely, but spends much of its time on *King Lear* and the Henry plays. In some ways, the premise enunciated here—"the 'good' characters are those who try to hide their darker purposes primarily from themselves and the wicked are those who try, or pretend to try, to hide them from others" (300)—recalls the neat summary offered in *The Revenger's Tragedy*: "The world's divided into knaves and fools." Yet, when it comes to constructing escape routes from reality, it is hard to say that anyone is a fool. The theatrical convention that forces the good characters to express their goodness aloud merely reveals what, in any case, is true: goodness, like anything else, is a performance. Near the end, the essay returns to *The Merchant of Venice*, takes up the term *mercifixion* (already used in the 1981 essay which opens this collection) and attacks "Christian mercy" itself, a deliberate loading of its victim with obligations that can never be repaid and thus equivalent to the usury for which the Christians condemn Shylock ("Their mercy is revenge—not a gentle rain, but a ton of bricks" [318]). Logically enough, the book's last and longest chapter is on *Measure for Measure*, often seen as a companion study of justice and mercy, which here becomes a travesty of both. Berger's initial comments on the Duke emphasize, much as with Richard II, the elements of comedy, self-contradiction, and self-dramatization that might enrich the role theatrically. Oddly enough, Berger later allows himself to depart from his usual nonjudgmental stance and becomes so condemnatory of the character, whose moral statements he finds merely "pompous," as to overdo Jonson's treatment of Justice Overdo. This essay probably will achieve a more careful integration of the two attitudes in its next revision.

The merit of Berger's view is that he makes the "good" characters more interesting by making them less good. He also validates the playwright. There are many cases in the plays where a character seems to express lofty ideals but to act in a way that contradicts them. At one time, critics were likely to explain this either as a fault in Shakespeare's characterization and plotting or by "convention," the name we sometimes give to something that worries us but which we assume did not worry Shakespeare's contemporaries. Berger, however, locates the contradiction in the characters themselves. This does not mean that he takes the characters to be real people with their own agency, their own unconscious, merely that he sees them as more characterizable, because more language is attributed to them, than the person he scrupulously refers to as "the author of Shakespeare's plays." It is their language that works against them—or, sometimes, not their own language but the language of the play, or of other plays. The reality of the characters is in their language, "and we have to follow the lethal traces down into its burrows and rhizomes" (260). Berger's own delightfully allusive style, which quotes and misquotes freely from the canon, embodies his own principle of redistribution.

Because of his emphasis on language, Berger is generally thought of, and depicts himself, as an anti-theatrical critic. This reputation is largely a myth. It is evident, from the way he writes about the speeches in the plays, that he "hears" them far better than most people. It is not surprising that he should resent the assumption that it takes an expert in stage history to be sensitive to their theatrical quality. I'm not even sure that the subtleties he detects in the text are beyond the possibilities of performance. In his analysis of Hotspur's soliloquy over the letter in 1 *Henry IV* 2.3, he argues that the natural theatrical response to its confident surface bravado runs counter to the one invited by the language, which shows the speaker to be deeply ambivalent about the honor he constantly invokes (282–83). Yet it is not beyond a good actor's ability to bring out—not text and subtext, but both readings of the text. Similarly, Berger's interpretation of *Richard II* is by no means unperformable, and he even uses a bit of theatrical history (the fact that Maurice Evans got a laugh on one line) to support his argument. In fact, whether by coincidence or design, several productions of this play have used insights similar to his. Awareness that the history plays are not just pageants but displays of Machiavellianism in action has been a feature of most good productions in my playgoing lifetime. So has a sense of their metatheatricality. In John Barton's famous Royal Shakespeare Company production of 1973, Bolingbroke came to the prison disguised as a groom and held out the empty frame which had held the glass broken by Richard in the deposition scene; he and Richard looked through it at each other like mirror images. The National Theatre's *Richard II*, which deliberately emphasized a physical resemblance between Fiona Shaw's Richard and David Threlfall's Bolingbroke, embodied something of the self-consciously histrionic "autothanatography" that Berger identifies in the play. Although there is not enough space in the text of *Richard II* for Bolingbroke and Gaunt to play out the troubled relationship Berger imagines for them, several productions of the Henry IV plays have brought out the stresses in the Henry IV–Hal relationship—notably the English Shakespeare Company production, which even featured a punk-rock group called "Sneak's Noise."

With other plays as well, recent productions have experimented with changes of production style to correspond to what they see as discontinuities in the play: costuming comic characters in modern dress while using historical costume for the rest of the cast, bringing the lights up for the Porter's scene in *Macbeth* and letting him play in music hall style to a fully visible audience, or introducing Autolycus with a blast of rock music to contrast with the dignified sound track of the first part of *The Winter's Tale*. The artificiality of the happy ending can be stressed, as when the RSC *Much Ado* with Derek Jacobi and Sinead Cusack made Beatrice and Benedick dance briefly to the strains of a music box. Many productions of *Macbeth* (Polanski's film is an obvious example) have implicated all the play's characters in its evil, and I am sure that I will some day see one in which Banquo's failure to warn Duncan about the witches' prophecy will be signaled, as Berger himself thinks it could be. Much of his argument about *Measure for Measure* has been at least fitfully on display in productions that respond to the comic or sinister potentiality in the Duke—for instance, making Isabella react with outrage when he tells her she will have to explain the bed trick plan to Mariana after he previously had promised to do this himself. Berger's "redistribution," which separates language from the body of its speaker, sometimes reminds me of the Marowitz "Collages"—where, for instance, all the lines in *Hamlet* that offer advice about how to live become conflicting messages addressed to Hamlet himself by a series of self-righteous authority figures.

Oddly enough, moreover, though Berger is more concerned with psychology than history, a historical approach can bring some surprising allies to support his kind of reading. For instance, his abstracting of language from context was the practice of everyone who kept a commonplace book, where passages spoken by heroes and villains alike appear under headings designed to create just the kind of moralizing Berger does his best to demolish here. Then, we assume that all Shakespeare's contemporaries took for granted love between parents and children and would have been horrified by Berger's suggestion that John of Gaunt's attitude to Bolingbroke, like Bolingbroke's to Hal, is "nourished by the desire of immortality, that is, by the fear of death that, projected onto the potential replacement, makes of a 'true inheritor' a true competitor" (151). Yet a poem on the birth of Charles I's eldest son in 1630 began with the ingenious comment that this happy event was potentially tragic because

> each following Birth
> Doth set the Parent so much nearer Earth:
> And by this Grammer, wee our Heires may call
> The smiling Preface to our Funerall.

The author of these lines was, I am glad to say, Henry King.

Perhaps recognizing the random nature of such parallels, Berger usually resists the temptation to seek allies outside the plays themselves. This perhaps accounts for the fact that the most puzzling feature of his work is what Erickson calls its "political" aspect—that is, its implications for the "real" world. To some extent, his dissection of victims' complicity in their own suffering, and the distaste with which he regards "mercifixion" and the "passive aggressive" type, has its counterpart in the popular psychology with which he cheerfully associates himself. Apparently our society is threatened by a dangerous epidemic of people rushing to sacrifice themselves for others and it is the responsibility of the actively aggressive people to keep this from happening. However delightfully written, the unremitting emphasis on the self-deception inherent in all attempts at goodness finally makes one want to ask whether there are no ways of forgiving people without making them feel bad (the Bible calls it heaping coals of fire on their heads). Desdemona's dying "Commend me to my kind lord" and Antony's decision to send after the defector Enobarbus not only his treasure but the words "Say that I wish he never have more cause / To change a master" both have the effect—and may therefore have had the intention—of breaking the heart of the person forgiven. So what should these characters have done instead? (It is surprising that Berger appears to dislike political correctness, since it has a good deal in common with his approach. It judges by results, not intentions, or rather, infers the intention from the result: if you feel that you have been the victim of a racial slur, then you have.) One looks in vain in his pages for any example of goodness that is not in some way vitiated. By way of questioning this pessimism, however, I should like to dwell briefly on one of the few episodes in *King Lear* Berger does not discuss. Just after Gloucester's eyes have been put out, he calls to the absent Edmund to avenge him and Regan gloatingly tells him it was Edmund who betrayed him to her and her husband. Gloucester immediately realizes the stupidity of his own recent behavior. One might expect him to call down vengeance on Edmund and to embrace the juicy role of the doubly betrayed father; one might even expect him, for an encore, to forgive Edmund, Regan and Cornwall. In fact, he never mentions them again. He simply says,

> O my follies! Then Edgar was abused.
> Kind gods, forgive me that, and prosper him.

What kind of evidence are these words giving against their speaker? Perhaps "follies" is a euphemism for sheer stupidity; perhaps Gloucester wants Edgar to prosper so that the good son can take up the role of revenger just offered by mistake to the bad one; perhaps he hopes that by saying these words he can avert Edgar's justified anger, or knows Edgar well enough to guess that he will be delighted to have the opportunity to play Calumniated but Magnanimous Son. Moreover, to call the gods kind, after what has happened, must be either a propitiating lie or a colossal feat of self-deception—which means that Gloucester, by definition, is too unintelligent to be described as self-aware. Berger is well aware that the theatrical experience can work against the "darker purpose" he detects beneath it. I know that it is because I have been so moved by Gloucester's words in the theater that I am desperately anxious to save them from what seems about to happen to them on the page, where, apparently, there can never be speech without shadows.

And yet, if we have to sacrifice the emotional response that depends on a confusion of theatrical behavior with real life, what we may perhaps gain in return is an enhanced sense of the latter. Erickson himself notes the curious contrast between the quirky attractiveness of Berger's manner and the bleakness of his message. One reason, surely, is that he makes (as many of his readers may not) a clear distinction between characters in plays and real people. This is evident both from the number of people whom he thanks in his opening acknowledgments and in what Erickson calls his "intensive engagement with the views of others" (xxxviii), many of whom he knows only as words on a page. Speaking as one of these many others (although the encounter happened in another book), I can vouch for the overwhelming nature of the experience. Most critics who refer to one's work do one of two things: (1) attach it to a lot of other scalps on a string beginning "see also"; or (2) skim it quickly to make sure it does not say what they are about to say, then berate one for not having said it. They are, in short, treating all writers as interchangeable. Berger, on the other hand, engages seriously, as well as playfully, with others and explores implications they probably had never dreamed of.

This is because he knows the difference between real human beings and speech prefixes (as he describes fictitious theatrical characters who come into existence only when imagined by readers or embodied by actors). Much of the behavior he describes in Shakespearean characters would be utterly self-destructive in real life. That's because it is generally disastrous to behave in real life as if one were a character in a play. But Shakespeare's characters *are* characters in a play. To say, for instance, that Macduff is complicit in the deaths of his wife and children is to say that Macduff in his "real" life—that is, as a dramatic character—has more allegiance to the tragic genre than the hypothetically "real" Macduff has to his own family. Surprisingly, the theater can convey even this idea (though, of course, at the expense of other ideas). The Cheek-by-Jowl production of *Twelfth Night* was set in a mental hospital. It depicted Sir Toby, Sir Andrew, and Maria as manic depressives who started crying as soon as they had no practical joke in which to immerse themselves. This emphasis on the extent to which characters themselves have a vested interest in keeping their play going seems to me the best way to understand the concept of "complicity." It has nothing to do with life and everything to do with the pleasure we take in art. One has to be grateful to Harry Berger for insisting on the right to be as intelligent about Shakespeare as he has often been about, for instance, Spenser. Stephen Booth has famously identified as the source of our pleasure in Shakespeare the fact that he makes us feel so intelligent when we read him. The same is true of Berger's criticism.

Recovering the Terror of Trifles

MARSHALL GROSSMAN

> *I know you all, and will a while uphold*
> *The unyoked humor of your idleness.*

WHATEVER IT IS Hal is doing in his doings with Falstaff, Peto, Bardolph, and Poins in the early scenes of 1 Henry IV, his first soliloquy reassures the audience or himself that he will do it only for "a while." Harry Berger reminds us that this "a while"—the lapse of time between the "now" of act 1 scene 2 of 1 Henry IV and, say, the end of 2 Henry IV, when the debt Hal never promised comes due—is mediated by a representation that is both performative and textual (*Making Trifles of Terrors*, 244–45). During and through his verbal performance, the Hal we see or read is at every moment complicated by his and our continual textual and historical reference to Henry V—whose presence is felt sometimes as the Prince imagines him in anticipation, sometimes as anticipated but unrealized by the Prince. At times, the shadow of the King he will become appears without the apparent complicity of the Prince—proleptically, in the mode of "history in the future tense," as Auden characterized the *Aeneid*.

Insofar as the second tetralogy participates, along with *Richard III*, in a legitimating account of the origins of the Tudor dynasty that culminates in a dynastic marriage, the *Henriad*, an identification Berger pointedly adopts, retains formal traces of the dynastic epic epitomized by the *Aeneid*, revived in the dynastic romances of Ariosto, Tasso, and Spenser, and transmuted to supranational ends and ultimate origins by Milton. Shakespeare's "history in the future tense," encompassing the failure of Henry VI and the consequent necessity of a second dynastic marriage—between Henry VII and Elizabeth of York—to establish the Tudors, adds a self-conscious doubling to the generic plot that is wholly characteristic of his structural technique. The doubling (or repetition) of the dynastic plot as a formal structure for reflexive complication in the histories doubles again the use of familial doubling in the same plays—such doubling is obvious in Hal and Hotspur but is now also brilliantly extended by Berger to Gaunt and Bolingbroke, two characters who barely existed as characters before Berger noticed them. More generally in Shakespeare, this reflexive doubling is seen in Lear and Gloucester, Hamlet and Laertes (and Fortinbras)—and then, in the strangely attenuated reemergence of the dynastic plot in the late Romances, with the struggles of Leontes and Polixenes, Alonzo and Prospero resolved through the marriage of their children into a single dynastic posterity.

Berger notes the affinity of the rhetorical weaving of subject positions by this narrative shuttle, in which present actions are given meaning as the effects of a past which has, in turn, been constructed as their cause, and Lacan's passage about discovering oneself in what one will have become, in and through a symbolic order that is always experienced retrospectively:

> For the function of language is not to inform but to evoke. . . . I identify myself in language, but only by losing myself in it like an object. What is realized in my history is not the past definite of what was, since it is no more, or even the present perfect of what has been in what I am, but the future anterior of what I shall have been for what I am in the process of becoming.[1]

I am going to expand this elliptical reference a bit, first in relation to the specifically narrative temporality underlying Lacan's understanding of how the self becomes a subject through the misrecognition of its own desire, and then, with specific (and, I hope, illustrative) reference to Hal's "I know you all" soliloquy in act 1 scene 2 of 1 Henry IV.[2] Doing so will help assess how close Berger has been willing to come to the edge of the "vertiginous vortex of Lacanian conundrums" even at "the risk of being sucked down into those depths and lost forever" (xix), and it will allow me to point—speculatively—in the direction toward which a further collaboration between Shakespeare and Lacan might lead.[3]

In pursuing this line of thought, I shall, for the most part, respect Berger's precautionary good sense and join him in keeping my "appropriations from Lacan as mundane and low-grade as possible." Moreover, I will add to this a working rule of my own: "the most reductive reading of Lacan is—at least for my present purpose—the most useful." Thus, if what I have to say is overly simplistic, its simplicity will at least be self-conscious. I want to think about Hal's verbal evocation of the King he will become and Lacan's familiar remark that "the unconscious is structured like a language" with the aim, eventually, of nudging Harry Berger's characteristically inimitable reading of linguistic complicities toward a consideration of the psychoanalytic transference as a model that may elucidate the performativity of the Shakespearean text; that is, a model which explains what it is the Shakespearean text does in and to its readers, and how it does it. Specifically, transference might suggest how it comes about that these texts enable us—perhaps, force us—to do something ethical with words.

To administer this nudge, I propose to interrogate the specifically textual complexity of Hal's evocation of Henry V by asking again the two questions Harry Berger appropriates from the Nixon impeachment inquiry: "What did the Prince know, and When did he know it?" while recalling Berger's proviso that there is no Prince except as we construct him now and then, here and there.

Berger's allusions are characteristically pointed. The questions, "What did the president know, and When did he know it" were aimed precisely at defining the ethics of the Nixonian text by retrospectively identifying various choices as episodes in an unfolding narrative. The intent of the famous questions was to allow Congress to predicate Nixon's ambiguous words and performance on specific causes and intentions. Once the ethos of the Nixon administration was read out of the actions of the "cover-up"—the inception and, so to speak, paternity, of which was established by Nixon's replayed words in the "smoking gun tape"—it would become possible to read that ethos back into the whole panoply of "White House Horrors" and hold Nixon responsible for them. In a perhaps reversed direction, we are called on to parse the difficult ethos of Prince Harry in terms of when and how he came to identify himself with and as Henry V. Later, in its proper place, it will be necessary to comment on Berger's still more reflexive allusion, at the conclusion of his Henriad essay, to Hitchcock's darkly comic film, *The Trouble with Harry*. Implicating the ethos of the reader in his reading to finally place Harry before Harry, I suspect that this allusion may reveal Harry's "darker purpose," or better, the darker purpose of the Harries.

First, there is more to be said about Harry of Monmouth's Harry. Because Hal (or Henry, or Harry) is made entirely of words, the Prince exists only when he is spoken—either inwardly by a reader or out loud by an actor. In either case, the speaking implies audition. In performance, the Prince is a collaboration of playwright, actor and audience; but, even when read, the Prince is heard as well as spoken, inwardly voiced as the voice of another whom the reader both speaks and hears.[4] This chiasmic exchange of voices in which we lend voice to a fictional character, exchanging his "I" for ours, addresses Cavell's recognition that we must show ourselves to the text.

Writing about *King Lear*, Cavell argues that to "acknowledge" characters as persons, we must become visible to them, "revealing ourselves, allowing ourselves to be seen." What exactly Cavell means by *acknowledgment* is the subject of his long essay on Lear and of much of Berger's elegant "Acknowledgment" of Cavell. I take both Cavell and Berger to mean that we acknowledge characters as persons when we meet them as subjects like ourselves and endow them with supratextual thoughts and experiences, through which they may seem sometimes to know more than they say; sometimes, to say more than they know; sometimes to know more than they are aware of knowing. In acknowledging characters as persons, we necessarily acknowledge ourselves as characters. Cavell says, a bit mysteriously, that to put oneself "in the presence of characters" presupposes discovering that "I am helpless before the acting and suffering of others, but I know the true point of my helplessness only if I have acknowledged totally the fact and the true cause of their suffering."[5] A Lacanian might say, a bit more mysteriously, "I am helpless before the acting and suffering of others, but I know the true point of my helplessness only if I can acknowledge totally the fact and the true cause of the other in which I am," then add: "but, since I can encounter myself only as I am estranged in my speech, I can't." At least for me, this reformulation moves closer to the dynamics of the central issue around which Berger and Cavell circle: when we acknowledge characters as persons by "revealing ourselves, allowing ourselves to be seen," we reveal ourselves to ourselves as characters; we acknowledge our own textuality, when we understand that our subjectivity comes to us by way of a plot. To be a subject, to say "I," is to narrate the story in which one discovers oneself as a character. In short, full subjectivity implies a rhetoric as well as a grammar, and, thereby, a complicity with the symbolic, the language in which the self is always and necessarily to be found—elsewhere. "[I]n psychoanalytic anamnesis, it is not a question of reality, but of truth, because the effect of full speech is to reorder past contingencies by conferring on them the sense of necessities to come, such as they are constituted by the little freedom through which the subject makes them present" (Lacan, *Écrits: A Selection*, 48). In reading Shakespeare, it is not only Hal's "truth" that depends on his ordering of past (and present) contingencies into a language of narrative necessity but, potentially, our own: to the extent that his language—which includes a rhetoric and a grammar—and ours become complicit.

Berger sees Cavell's notion of "acknowledgment" as a reason to privilege reading over performance:

> It is only by taking advantage of the opportunities of the text that we acknowledge "totally the fact and true cause." We may then find that the character is both credited *and* discredited, or we may refuse the language of praise and blame and assert only that the character is responsible, is complicit, in ways that account for and derive from his suffering. Textuality offers us not the answer but the opportunity to struggle against the temptation to use or reduce or praise or blame. In this struggle, the struggle of interpretation, we define the character's personhood over against our own. And we do so in such a way as to preclude our closing the book on the character (68).

I would add that, when we define a character's personhood over against our own, we also define our own personhood over against the character's. What sort of person is Hal? What would Hal think of me?

I am less interested in the rivalry of text and performance than in the underlying processes of identification implicit in Cavell's idea of becoming visible to what are, after all, fictional characters who exist only within us. Berger elaborates the important differences between the Prince performed and the Prince read, but it is a corollary of his own argument that a reading includes a performance and a performance at least evokes a reading. If Berger is right about Shakespeare's thematic anti-theatricalism, and I think he is, then potential performance forms the ground of reading, and reading forms the ground of performance. The creative tension between the two can be appreciated only to the extent that each is haunted by the other. Thus, although the reading I suggest here pertains to text rather than performance, I am less sure than Berger is that it would not pertain to performance as well, and I remain agnostic about Berger's anti-theatrical polemic, which strikes me as rooted very much in a particular critical context. Doubtless, there are distinctions to be drawn between hearing the Prince spoken aloud—on a stage—and hearing him speaking inwardly, perhaps in one's own voice. However, as Lacan points out, "there is no speech without a reply, even if it is met only with silence, provided that it has an auditor" (Lacan, *Écrits*, 40). In performance or in the book, the work of the transference, if it occurs at all, occurs in *ein andere Schauplatz*.

On the textual scene: There is a chiasmic expense of time in the reading of Hal. Like the still frames of a movie from which our eyes and minds construct motion, the words and sentences, of which Hal is made, occur in us; the time of reading mediates to us the fictive time in which Hal becomes Henry. What happens—for text and reader—during this temporal crossover? Using our time to represent to ourselves the "while" that separates Hal from the fullness of his time, we encounter Hal as delinquent, truant from his father's court, ambivalently suspended in the choice of a father or, as Freud would have it, an ego-ideal, between Falstaff—"the latter spring! . . . All-hallown summer!"—whose clock measures time in units derived from bodily appetites: "cups of sack," "capons," and "the tongues of bawds" (*1 Henry IV*, 1.2.158–59; 7–8), and Henry IV, who always knows what time it is, worries about being too late, as Richard II had been in his return from Ireland, or too early, as Hotspur will be at Shrewsbury. The temporal rubbing up of contrary self-representations yields a friction in Hal's character. There is the Prince who knows his comrade idlers and represents his dalliance with them (to himself) as feigned idleness, crafty indulgence—an antic delinquency by which to evade the competition for honor with Hotspur and diminish strategically the expectation of his reign. This version of Hal is close to, but not quite congruent with, the more compactly distant and somewhat cruel experimenter, who uses Francis, the under-skinker, as the subject of an experiment explicitly aimed at the juncture of language, class and the discursive opportunities they provide, and who understands (as Lear would not) that he is separated from Francis only by the wider experience social rank affords. Unlike the addled Lear, he understands this distinction to be instituted by an insurmountable linguistic barrier, not to be overcome by a change of clothes: "That ever this fellow should have fewer words than a parrot, and yet the son of a woman!" The uneasy difference, the dissonance that defines the lability of his character, is that between the Prince who already knows, and therefore is, what he will become and the apprentice Prince who finds the time to be "of all humors" in this "pupil age" (*1 Henry IV*, 2.4.92–98).

Hal represents his whiling away of time in Eastcheap sometimes as the strategic concealment of an enforced royal nature, sometimes as the time in which his true nature will be chosen or created and sometimes as the pupil age in which the future king learns his trade. He directly evokes his future self when he tells an uncomprehending Poins that learning to "drink with every tinker in his own language," he has struck the "very base string of humility" and "that he shall command all the good lads in Eastcheap" when he is King—as we know he will—because they think him "no proud Jack . . . but a Corinthian, a lad of mettle, a good boy" (2.4.5–15). When Hal, role-playing with Falstaff, proleptically assumes his father's state and banishes old Sir John ("I do, I will" 2.4.481), he appears to understand becoming King as becoming his father, and thus reprimanding himself. As he reenacts an inverted version of his grandfather's complicity in the banishment of his own father, some part of him also accepts that in banishing "plump Jack"— both the fat knight and that part of himself that incorporates Falstaff as ego-ideal—he will banish "all the world." What, then, are we to make of the quality of Hal's affection for the idlers of Eastcheap—whom he appears to admire, to loath, and to manipulate to his future advantage—or the drawers, whose company he both enjoys and patronizes with such ironic and perspicacious language?

The assumption of his warlike obligations at Shrewsbury does not make Hal the image of his father either, although we are told that on that day "The King hath many marching in his coats" (1 Henry IV, 5.3.25). Emulating his father's valuation, he eloquently honors the body of Hotspur with his own favor but also eulogizes the undead Falstaff with the admission that he "could have better spar'd a better man" (5.4.104), and—almost but not quite inexplicably—accepts Falstaff's desecration of Hotspur's corpse and with it the code of valor that represents honor as a fungible commodity and covers over as ethos the political necessity for Hal to kill and Hotspur to die. He plucks down Percy and assumes his honors, as he promised his father he would, but only for a while. At the start of 2 Henry IV, it is, comically, Falstaff who strides the field as Percy's nemesis—a lie Hal claims he is glad to "gild," if it will do the fat knight good. These final, ambivalent encounters of 1 Henry IV recall on the field of history the defining moment in the tavern when Hal seems honestly on the cusp of a decision about whether to protect Falstaff or turn him over to the watch, until Falstaff abruptly drops flattery and answers the charge of unknightly cowardice by offering to "become a cart" as well as any man. In the earlier scene, Hal seems to me to be repelled by Falstaff's presumed cowardice, then to be won back by his clever audacity, but also by his assumed willingness to face the sheriff bravely and "as soon be strangled with a halter as another" (1 Henry IV, 2.4.496–99). In the scenes at Shrewsbury, the audacity is confirmed, but so too is the cowardice. Falstaff's corrupt treatment of his conscripted troopers is dark enough to begin to alienate the audience and dramatically prepare us for the Prince's promised rejection of him. Even if the queasy humor of Falstaff leading his "ragamuffins where they are pepper'd" (5.3.36) is discounted as a modern sensibility imposed on an early modern text, the stabbing of Hotspur's corpse is, to say the least, un-endearing, especially so soon after Hal's eulogy establishes the ethos of princely combat. In an odd way, our complicity with Hal in accepting Falstaff's bad behavior at Shrewsbury presages the chill we may later feel when Henry V orders the killing of the prisoners in Henry V, 4.6. The structure of the play seems to prepare everything for Hal to become Henry, but instead Falstaff appears with Hotspur's body, and the newly minted Henry reverts to Hal, setting the stage for Part 2 to repeat the entire pattern of delinquency, military action, and redemption in the fullness of time. It may be tempting to attribute these anomalies to possible exigencies of composition in which the two parts may, at some point, have had more or less independent lives. But such exigencies are irrelevant to the textual unconscious of the text, as we have it.

When we read the Henriad, we confront these various and momentary versions of Hal as a series of dismayingly concordant discordances. We may inscribe his textual self alternatively in a bildungsroman through which Hal transforms himself into Henry V or in a dynastic epic in which he always already figures the fulfillment of a revealed destiny. Mediating or failing to mediate these contradictions is—for a while—how we spend our time, but we will never know Harry all, because no matter what narrative paradigm we use to interpret him there will always be something left over, a superfluity of overlapping signifiers that cannot be resolved into a single plot. It is in this crease or gap in the symbolic that one may sense the presence of the Real, from which derives the tenuous feeling that he—and, therefore, we—are persons. "The Real" is Lacan's designation for that which resists symbolic representation, the unarticulated remainder that is foreclosed from speech. In Shakespearean language, we might say that "the Real" designates something that cannot denote us truly because it passes show. Manifest only as a discontinuity within symbolic representation, the effect of "the Real" is always felt in retrospection, always belated: sensed only in the ripples left on the surface of representation as it disappears.

I think we find something close to the effect of the Real described, again in Shakespearean language, by Theseus in *A Midsummer Night's Dream*:

> The poet's eye, in a fine frenzy rolling,
> Doth glance from heaven to earth, from earth to heaven;
> And as imagination bodies forth
> The forms of things unknown, the poet's pen
> Turns them to shapes, and gives to aery nothing
> A local habitation and a name.
>   (5.1.12–17)

The progression Theseus posits from "things unknown" to imaginary bodies and the symbolic shapes issuing from the "poet's pen" works backwards to explain away the disconcerting evidence of the Dream. Theseus begins with the fairy "bears" of the youths' narrations and turns them into imaginary bushes and to "aery nothing." Not wanting to reveal himself, he refuses to acknowledge the *cause* (in the Real) of the events the youths suffered: "Such tricks hath strong imagination, / That if it would but apprehend some joy, / it comprehends some bringer of that joy" (18–20) and so refuses to acknowledge that he is as they are—subject to the wills of the wisp. But, in the very moment that the *cause* eludes representation and disappears, Hippolyta insists that something remains: something "of great constancy" that is somehow both in and absent from "the story of the night told over, / and all their minds transfigur'd so together" (23–27). This something disappears, yet persists, rather like the hypermetric foot elided, yet marked, by the silent intervocalic v's of "heaven" in Theseus' chiasmus of the poet's rolling eye.

How, then, do we acknowledge Harry and show ourselves? Is Cavell's formulation about Lear pertinent only to tragedy, or must we know our helplessness before Harry's "acting and suffering" by acknowledging "totally" its "fact and the true cause"? It is in response to these questions that I am tempted to inch a step or two closer than Berger to those Lacanian conundrums: "The unconscious is structured like a language" and "transference is the enactment of the reality of the unconscious."[6]

The work of time spent in and on the tension between the competing and contradictory inscriptions of Hal may be illustrated by returning to Hal's first soliloquy to consider the specific linguistic mediations through which Henry V plays over his younger self:

> I know you all, and will a while uphold
> The unyok'd humor of your idleness,
> Yet herein will I imitate the sun,
> Who doth permit the base contagious clouds
> To smother up his beauty from the world,
> That when he please *again to be himself,*
> Being wanted, he may be more wond'red at
> By breaking through the foul and ugly mists
> Of vapors that did seem to strangle him.
> . . . .
> So when this loose behavior I throw off
> And pay the debt I never promised,
> *By how much better than my word I am,*
> By so much shall I falsify men's hopes,
> And like bright metal on a sullen ground,
> My *reformation,* glitt'ring o'er my fault,
> Shall show more goodly and attract more *eyes*
> Than that which hath no foil to set it off.
> I'll so offend to make offense a skill,
> Redeeming time when men think least I will.
> (1 Henry IV, 2.2.195–217, my emphasis)

Following Berger's point about how the distribution and redistribution of bits of language among different characters establish complicities within the text, I want to look at the complicity of the rhetoric and language of Hal's soliloquy in the report Vernon makes of him at Shrewsbury, when Hotspur asks, "how fares the madcap Prince of Wales?"

> All furnish'd, all in arms;
> All plum'd like estridges, that with the wind
> Bated like eagles having lately bath'd,
> *Glittering in golden coats like images,*
> As full of spirit as the month of May,
> *And gorgeous as the sun at midsummer;*
> Wanton as youthful goats, wild as young bulls.
> I saw young Harry with his beaver on,
> His cushes on his thigh, gallantly arm'd,
> Rise from the ground like feathered Mercury
> And vaulted with such ease into his seat
> As if an angel dropp'd down from the clouds
> To turn and wind a fiery Pegasus,
> And witch the world with noble horsemanship.
> (4.1.98–110, my emphasis)

The audience's sense that Vernon reports precisely the sunrise promised in the first act soliloquy is quickly validated by Hotspur's dry response: "No more, no more! worse than the sun in March, / This praise doth nourish agues" (4.1.111–12). Yet one could also imagine alternative scenarios in which we are victims of a deception, in which the Hal of Act 4 is simply a different person who happens to have the same name as the character who spoke the soliloquy in the first act. From within the play, the King almost invites us to suspect as much when he remarks on the tenuous relations of name and person:

> O that it could be prov'd
> That some night-tripping fairy had exchang'd
> In cradle-clothes our children where they lay,
> And called mine Percy, his Plantagenet!
> Then would I have his Harry and he mine.
>
> (1.1.86–90)

His Harry, my Harry—Harry of Monmouth, Harry Bolingbroke, Harry Percy—we are all Harry in this play. Just as the possibility of constructing a story supports our experience of self-identity over time, so the experience of difference within identity, in ourselves and others, supports our ability to read a story. The construction of identity within each of these registers may be more or less successful. Thus, in the case of 1 *Henry IV*, the intervening episodes prepare us for Hal's success at Shrewsbury; our relative comfort in assuming the continuity of his character is reflected in our interest in searching those intervening episodes for clues to its presumed unity. Retrospection restructures the events depicted as a plot with identifiable turning points, decisive choices, crucial traumas, and formative experiences that turn "madcap Prince" into "Feathered mercury. . . . As if an Angel dropp'd down from the clouds." On the contrary, we probably are much less comfortable with, say, the sudden reformation of Oliver in *As You Like It* or, even more tenuously, of Alonzo, Sebastian, and Antonio in *The Tempest*, preferring, in these cases, perhaps to evade the issue of character continuity on the assumption that the author's interest lies elsewhere. Without pausing to cite further examples, I will trust the readers' experience to confirm that identities in the world (as opposed to literature) vary similarly in their ability to attain the "authenticity effect." Recalling Freud's trenchant, clinical observation that hysterics suffer from memories they can't remember—that is, from an inability to situate themselves as the subjects of a coherent history—I will suggest that the linguistic complicities Harry Berger finds distributed among Shakespeare's characters collectively structure the symbolic of these plays—including the "ethical discourses" of sinner and victim Berger identifies—as a series of unspoken reciprocal recognitions, an intersubjective grammar like the one that selects "I" as our name when we are the subject of a verb, "me" when we are its object, and "you" when we are addressed by another. To say, then, that the "unconscious is structured like [*comme*] a language" is to say that the unconscious is structured as a language; it is the set of rules that allows us to recognize ourselves in the Other, as grammatically correct and incorrect—in place or out of place—in the intersubjective structure of our communities of discourse. Most important, it allows us to bind moment to moment in a syntax of tenses that gives us—the sense of self, returned to us from others—duration over time, so that we can both change and remain the same.

Vernon's "gorgeous as the sun at midsummer," delivered in the fourth act of *1 Henry IV*, returns to Hotspur the sunrise Hal had promised in the first; the simile of Hal mounting his horse "As if an angel dropp'd down from the clouds" makes good on Hal's metaphor of the "base contagious clouds." When the Prince's "glitt'ring o'er my fault" returns as Vernon's "*Glittering* in golden coats like *images*," however, things become more complicated and more interesting, because neither "fault" nor "images" provides a sufficiently concrete comparison. Hal's metaphor is clarified by the simile in which it is embedded: his reformed behavior will shine out from the sullen ground of his delinquency as bright metal shines out of a matte background. Vernon's "images" reminds us that both speeches describe—or, more accurately, construct—appearances. Clouds, mists, vapors, images—the language builds through the two widely separated speeches toward Vernon's final verb *to witch* and, by implication, to be bewitched, by the weird sister or night-tripping fairy who says in the Other, which, like his father, is both in him and out, "Prince of Wales thou art [though your father never was] and King Henry thou shall be [though your father is]."

> A mask is never "just a mask" since it determines the actual place we occupy in the intersubjective symbolic network; what is effectively false and null is our "inner distance" from the mask we wear (the "social role" we play) our "true self" hidden beneath it. The path to an authentic subjective position runs therefore "from the outside inward": first, we pretend to be something, we just act as if we are that, till, step by

step we actually become it.... The performative dimension at work here consists of the symbolic efficiency of the "mask": wearing a mask actually *makes us* what we feign to be. In other words, the conclusion to be drawn from this dialectic is the exact opposite of the common wisdom by which every human act (achievement, deed) is ultimately just an act (posture, pretense): the only authenticity at our disposal is that of impersonation, of "taking our act (posture) seriously."[7]

This passage comes from a book that aims to explicate Lacan. I quote it here because I think it also explicates Lacan's collaborator and colleague, Shakespeare.

Transference has a number of related meanings in psychoanalysis, but they all refer to adjustments in the grammar of the language that is the unconscious. Shakespeare's English is profoundly different from the English that King Alfred spoke and significantly different from that of the historical Hal. These changes were not willed. The Norman conquerors did not impose their language on the Anglo-Saxons because they wanted to create the language of Chaucer. The great vowel shift did not occur because someone thought it would be a good idea. Where are the inflectional declensions of yesteryear? Similarly, the language that is the unconscious evolves in response to adventitious, exigent, and contingent experiences—regional accents—and, in not always obvious ways—to the political environment, the communal symbolic in which we must seek ourselves. Transference is the way we think through what we cannot think about, by attaching the emotional import of one set of relations to another set of relations and subtly supplementing their grammar with the impertinencies of rhetoric. When we read Shakespeare, we redistribute his language not only within the community of the plays, but between them and our own; we allow each to "corrupt" the other, and, in this way, we and Harry meet and are changed by having met. This is, I think, why Harry finds that "The only trouble with Harry that really troubles me is Harry's trouble with Harry" (Berger, 250).

So what is the trouble with Harry? His readings are often inimitable, performances, star turns, which limit their theoretical exemplarity and work against his serious ambitions—a conflict perhaps transferred to the tension he feels between text and performance. The reason Harry's readings are inimitable, though, is not just that most of us are not as smart as Harry, or, also and more generally, that we are simply not Harry. It is, I submit, Harry's courage in the transference—his willingness, as it were, to be seen by Shakespeare and to let us see Shakespeare seeing Harry—that *generates* those inimitable readings, that allows him to meld his textuality to a text, re-perform its words and speak from within the Shakespearean symbolic, that makes him so perspicacious and leaves so much working through for the rest of us. Not really wanting to get personal now, I cannot, however, resist adding that the phrase "the trouble with Harry" receives its special resonance from the Hitchcock movie of the same name. In the movie, the trouble with Harry is that Harry is dead but, through a series of screwball circumstances, won't stay buried; so the allusion may point toward Harry's "darker purpose." I will leave aside the relationship of repetition and the death instinct here that might playfully play over his ongoing project of recombining earlier essays into books that make the individual essays new again, and stick more cautiously to Hal and the shadow of death that falls across "I know you all." Banish plump Jack and banish all the world—and that's the trouble with Harry.[8]

Notes

1. Jacques Lacan, *Écrits: A Selection*, trans. Alan Sheridan (New York: Norton, 1977), 86 (as cited in Berger, *Making Trifles of Terrors*, 214).

2. Berger includes remarks on this speech in a recent essay that further elaborates the themes developed in *Making Trifles*. See "The Prince's Dog: Falstaff and the Perils of Speech-Prefixity," *Shakespeare Quarterly* 49 (1998): 40–73.

3. Such a collaboration was most fully explored by Joel Fineman. See especially, "The Sound of O in *Othello*: The Real of the Tragedy of Desire," in *The Subjectivity Effect in Western Literary Tradition: Essays Toward the Release of Shakespeare's Will* (Cambridge, MA: MIT Press, 1991), 143–64.

4. See Harry Berger, Jr., *Imaginary Audition: Shakespeare on Stage and Page* (Berkeley: University of California Press, 1989).

5. Stanley Cavell, *Must We Mean What We Say?: Modern Philosophical Essays in Morality, Religion, Drama and Criticism* (New York: Scribners, 1969), 37–39 and Berger, 68.

6. See Lacan, *The Four-Fundamental Concepts of Psycho-Analysis*, ed. Jacques-Alain Miller, trans. Alan Sheridan (New York: Norton, 1978), 20–23, 149–60.

7. Slavoj Žižek, *Enjoy Your Symptom: Jacques Lacan in Hollywood and Out* (London: Routledge, 1992), 34.

8. This essay materially benefited from the comments of my colleague, Theodore B. Leinwand, whose assistance is gratefully acknowledged.

Reading Harry Berger

Stanley Cavell

Among the advantages to me of working in fields for which I cannot claim professional responsibility is that I do not have to "cover" material which is not pressing me for attention. Among its disadvantages is coming upon work that I might, or should, have found urgent years ago, bettering the ensuing time. Most often it has been friends or students who become concerned to cure my ignorance, but sometimes, I think never more remarkably than in the present instance, a virtual stranger so alertly and generously records a conjunction of interests with work of mine, that notice of it cannot fail to reach me. That the medium of the conjunction is Harry Berger's *Making Trifles of Terrors* is too heartening not to respond to, however incompletely, on so welcome an occasion as the celebration of his work.

It comes at a time in my periodic preoccupations with Shakespeare that has taken me to a late text of Henry James I had not known until this past year, his Introduction to *The Tempest* for Sidney Lee's edition of Shakespeare's *Works* in 1907. I was led to it by my finally getting around to reading through (one of those postponable masterpieces) James's *The American Scene*, published the same year. Each of these texts describes or implies a practice of criticism, particularly, a violence in the practice of criticism as James finds it called for, that I have not heard emphasized by James's readers. From *The American Scene*:

> ... If the *direct* pressure of New York is too often to ends that strike us as vulgar, the indirect is capable, and perhaps to an unlimited degree, of these lurking effects of delicacy. The immediate expression is the expression of violence, but you may find there is something left, something kept back for you, if that has not from the first fatally deafened you. It carries with it an after-sense which put on for me, under several happy intimations, the image of some garden of the finest flowers—or of such as might be on the way to become the finest—masked by an

> enormous bristling hedge of defensive and aggressive vegetation, lacerating, defiant, not to be touched without blood. One saw the garden itself, behind its hedge and approachable only by those in the secret. . . .　　　Penguin Books, Sears ed. (New York, 1994), 141.

The implicit declaration concerning James's writing about his return to America, or sojourn there (to use Thoreau's term at the beginning of *Walden*, the other book about America I find as strange, and similarly strange, as *The American Scene*, their writers making themselves spectrally isolated strangers to their native land) is that its subject is "approachable" only by writing that touches its subject in blood (from the heart, and to wound).

That this necessity is not confined to writing about New York and related scenes but extends to writing about writing, that is, to the criticism of any work art does, receives its declaration in the concluding passage from the *Tempest* Introduction:

> We stake our hopes . . . on indirectness, which may contain possibilities . . . for the Criticism of the future. That of the past has been too often infantile; one has asked one's self how it *could*, on such lines, get at . . . [the man in the artist]. The figured tapestry, the long arras that hides him, is always there, with its immensity of surface and its proportionate underside. May it not then be but a question for the fullness of time, of the finer weapon, the sharper point, the stronger arm, the more extended lunge?

The weapon criticism is evidently to become can scarcely be designed to thrust through a thing and kill the intruder behind it, the objective it is designed "to get at," since that desired target is called by James "the man in the artist." I shall have a suggestion about what that may mean, one to deflect, perhaps, a reflex to reject it as an obviously archaic, not to say superstitious, project. But I should before that say why reading *Making Trifles of Terrors* puts me in mind of James's idea of criticism.

There is, generally, the presence of a complex surface of evocative, conversational prose harboring motives of deadly seriousness about literature that may be described as touching blood, in James's sense of requiring violence to reveal delicacies. More specifically, there is a willingness to invoke what one's contemporaries may take as an archaism, in Harry Berger's case not that of fantasizing a man in the work but of an "interest in returning to a modified character-and-action approach—the approach for which A. C. Bradley is famous or nefarious" (25). Berger raises the stakes of conviction by basing his thought on "the realization that what I thought of characters was both less important and less interesting than what they thought of themselves" (xxi). Doesn't this "realization" just make matters metaphysically worse, increasing the suspicion that what Berger calls characters contain properties that belong only to persons in the world, not to words on a page? Yet two qualms arise about this suspicion: First, it leaves blankly unclear what mistake or confusion is being made in identifying characters as (representations of) persons, so the suspicion is precisely as unclear as whatever the suspicion is directed against. (Is it like the idea that we know something about persons "beyond" their behavior? Or perhaps like the idea that a self is a small person inside the envelope of behavior, or that it is an irreducible something there, as what philosophers used to call a substance? What are these ideas?) Second, if characters are to be so identified (as persons), then, for sure, they are the sorts of things that relate to themselves, for example, think of themselves in various lights. Or are we to doubt our ability to understand other persons as self-reflective? And ourselves?

I understand Berger's return, heightened, to character-and-action study not as metaphysically defiant but as critically definitive, defining a particular practice of criticism. It suggests that the responsible task of literary theory or, say, a philosophy of literature, is not to deny the reading of character on metaphysical grounds (when it is not asserted on metaphysical grounds) but to articulate what the grounds are for the "approach." To take up this suggestion, however, requires taking an interest in one's experience—or, say, one's intuitions—that metaphysical constructions are designed to displace. (If I cannot, in principle, know what another thinks about himself, then it is at most of clinical interest to determine what I think I know about his thoughts.) Criticism such as that at which Berger is a master is meant precisely, if I understand, to entice one to take an interest in his or her experience, to reveal, for instance, one's standing with oneself; and to understand literature (the work art does) as instruction in this enticement.

The experience Berger is punctually drawn to in *Making Trifles of Terrors* is that of what he calls complicities, ones between the characters and their representations of themselves and others, and, ruefully, between oneself, the reader or attender, as participant (through acknowledgment or avoidance) in those complicities. This bears various relations with other understandings of the drive to interpretation, for example, ones that emphasize the necessity for metaphysical suspicion in reading or for tracking specific ideological contracts in what is blindly accepted in a reading. (The affinities between current theories has served typically to feed their enmities, presenting themselves to each other as working in bad faith. Berger, notably and characteristically, refuses this stance, invoking opposing voices out of what strikes me, attractively, as a pedagogical conscience.) I might characterize the depth I find in Berger's practice, motivated by his development of the idea of complicities and their (re)distribution, as one that takes the idea of a contract between reader and text as Rousseau took the idea of contract in characterizing our political relations, namely, as a process defeated in every moment by our private conspiracies, as if the route to the meeting of minds is not through persisting in what we consider our just causes but through recounting our faithlessness to our knowledge of justice.

Naturally, I wonder how Berger's idea of complicity sorts with the idea, as expressed in my essay on *King Lear*, that our avoidances in reading or in attending imply "that we are implicated in the failures we are witnessing, we share the responsibility for tragedy" (*Must We Mean What We Say?*, 282). So that when I find Berger taking exception, in that essay of mine, to, as he puts it, my "assigning guilt a merely ancillary function as a contractive term helping to define the peculiar quality of shame" (xiii), I think to myself, now there is an issue worth engaging. I won't attempt this now, but instead record two smaller reactions, one of instruction and one of suggestion, to indicate the range of reactions I have been enjoying in reading Harry Berger.

Take the suggestive moment first. In "The Lear Family Romance," Berger records his perception of Lear as "sharing in [Goneril's and Regan's] complicity" even in the storm scene (35): "Being turned out in the storm becomes, for him, a triumph. His decision to reject their grudging hospitality ratifies their monstrous ingratitude: 'No, rather I abjure all roofs, and choose / To wage against the enmity o' th' air' (2.4.210–11)." Taking this as Lear's strategy, a circumstance Lear is turning deviously to his advantage, may, not surprisingly (on Berger's account of the reciprocations of reader and character), uncover an, as it were, compensating glint of confession, anyway of self-revelation, in Lear's words. "Wage against" (a turn I had not stopped over in my own essay, if I had noticed its forces) suggests equally the idea of Lear's combating the air and that of taking his chances in it, say, an active and a passive response. But what is it to take either mode of response against "the enmity o' th' air"? Lear utters this before the storm breaks, but we by now may so heavily anticipate the sense of enmity as invoking the famous storm, that "waging against it," if it is not to be taken as already figuring the madness of a King warring against the sea, is realizable either as taking what precautions there are of shelter and clothing or else as exposing oneself to the elements, daring them. Either seems equally passive and active. But maybe its placement before the winds crack their cheeks should prompt us to think of the phrase as naming an enmity of air not as directed from a disturbed sky but as leveled against the mortal's condition of having to live in the medium of air, the necessity of breathing.

In that case, Lear reveals the persistence of his hysteria, his sense of suffocation, well studied by Janet Adelman ("Hysterica passio, down thy rising sorrow" occurs two hundred lines earlier in this scene), now in a form that calls to mind an extraordinary passage from Emerson's "Fate" that I have had occasion to stop over elsewhere:

> We should be crushed by the atmosphere, but for the reaction of the air within the body. A tube made of a film of glass can resist the shock of the ocean if filled with the same water. If there be omnipotence in the stroke, there is omnipotence of recoil.
> Whicher ed., *Selections from Ralph Waldo Emerson* (Cambridge, MA: Riverside Press, 1957), 341.

The context includes "Certain ideas are in the air" (ibid., 350) and "A breath of will blows eternally through the universe of souls in the direction of the Right and Necessary. It is the air which all intellects inhale and exhale, and it is the wind which blows the worlds into order and orbit" (ibid., 342). A lot is going on here, but I isolate just Emerson's impulse to reassure those who present themselves, one by one, to his page that breathing is all right, that we are made for nature after all, nature's inspiration. It is a chance to see why Emerson risks his signature insistence on cheer and joyfulness (so unappetizing to sophisticated ears), to ask what he imagines his readers to bring to the page, let us say, what conspiracies. To cheer them up is to figure them as melancholy (a matter I have harped on in interpreting skepticism); to reassure them that they may safely breathe is to figure that they fear breathing, or fear something about their breath, say, that they (Americans? the Western race? humanity?) manifest symptoms of hysteria. (I think here of a marvelous lecture given by the British psychoanalyst Juliet Mitchell to the Boston Psychoanalytic Institute in 1993, in which she interpreted certain of her cases of hysteria in terms of a fear of death.) I shall not argue that Lear was on Emerson's mind in composing "Fate," but just mention, apart from the pertinence of tragedy to Emerson's subject, that I seem to detect an ambivalent glance at Lear in the adjuration "Let him empty his windy conceits, and show his lordship by manners and deeds on the scale of nature" (ibid., 340). It's as well, for my thinking, to take it that Shakespeare's and Emerson's passages have separately come upon the circumstance of an enmity of breath.

To say what, to my mind, connects the passages, I ask allowance to quote a summary moment from my *Claim of Reason* on the subject of Wittgenstein's exploration of the idea of a private language (351):

> The fantasy of a private language, underlying the wish to deny the publicness of language, turns out, so far, to be a fantasy, or fear, either of inexpressiveness, one in which I am not merely unknown, but in which I am powerless to make myself known [on the following page I include in the fantasy the impossibility of making myself known to myself]; or one in which what I express is beyond my control [which I go on to describe as betraying myself, and as involving fears of attracting suspicion and of being under indictment].

Taking a fear of inexpressiveness as a sense of suffocation, we have the fear of death from breathing presented as a fear of being buried alive within the casing of the body.

If Wittgenstein's idea of the wish for a metaphysical privacy of language confirms the idea, in Lear and in Emerson's "Fate," of the fear of breath as a fear of speech, Wittgenstein's idea receives, in return, amplification from Lear and from Emerson's "Fate," so that the fear of breathing is seen as a projection onto language as a fear of its insufficiency, as if it is language itself that has shrunk from its responsibilities of reference and expression. As if the world and my desires in it are too monstrous for telling, and the burden of language, of bearing meaning, of making myself intelligible, crushes me. The Wittgensteinian connection accents the identity of the discouragement by and with language as a discouragement with the ordinariness of language, with the mother tongue, something I associate—beyond the preoccupations of tragedy—with the seventeenth-century search for a perfect language and with the contemporary invention of opera, one an escape from the necessity of human breath to ratify meaning, the other a sustaining and expanding of that breath.

Corollaries of these ideas have preoccupied me elsewhere, noticing a fear of letting speech come to an end as a fear of death (manifested perhaps in current theories to the effect that one's meaning is always and necessarily deferred, language racing, turning always ahead of oneself), and, opposed to this, reading the form of Wittgenstein's *Investigations* as one in which (as in the sentences of Emerson and Thoreau) language is punctually allowed to come to an end, performing an incorporation of death within speech, learning one's mortality. This has prompted me—since, in Wittgenstein, the end of a philosophical problem is the threading from a maze of disorientation into the order of what Wittgenstein calls the ordinary or everyday—to recognize the ordinary as the recognition of death.

Harking back explicitly to that argument I said was worth having with Harry Berger about the movement in Lear between guilt and shame, I adumbrate the merest suggestion. I was just now emphasizing, from my reading of what I call Wittgenstein's fantasy of a private language, the passive side of the fear, or the fear of passiveness, of something that I suffer or sustain, not something I do or cause. But this fear of inexpressiveness has, as said, a twin in a fear of expressiveness, of what speech exposes me to, of my betrayals of myself (oozing, as Freud puts it, out of every pore of my behavior and my words). Is Lear avoiding something he has done (hence, chased by and chasing guilt [for withholding love]) or something he has not done (hence hiding, brazening out, shame [for avoiding being loved]). Must we choose? Berger, siding with the former, speaks finely of Lear's words as partaking of "the sinner's discourse" (xiii), made most explicit in Lear's claim that he is more sinned against than sinning. Berger challenges Lear's claim there; I share the sense that it should be challenged. I suppose I take Lear's maddened efforts to keep outrunning his knowledge of his wrong in this claim—say, his terror of subjection—as a source and a sign of his shame.

I marked a moment in getting underway, about Henry James's desire to find what he calls the man in the artist, which I must pick up before ending.

An editor of an excellent selection of James's literary criticism (Roger Gard, Penguin, 1987), in the note heading the Introduction to *The Tempest*, speaks of James's long fascination "by the wonder and terror of the problem of how these plays could have come from *that* man—according to Percy Lubbock he referred in conversation to that 'lout from Stratford'" (428). Can it really be that the problem of authorship, let's call it, in an extreme instance, Shakespeare writing *The Tempest*—extreme both in its being this author writing and in its being this author relinquishing writing—the problem, "the eternal mystery," about which James confesses moments "when, speaking for myself, its power to torment us intellectually seems scarcely to be borne" (ibid., 438), is, for James, merely that the person we conjure up from what scraps of evidence exist is historically (socially, psychologically) unworthy of the achievement called Shakespeare's? (Is James merely a snob about writing?) Isn't the torment, instead, that of conceiving how *anyone*, of any comprehensible intelligence, can have accomplished it?

James's Introduction opens with the words, "If the effect of the Plays and Poems, taken in their mass, be most of all to appear often to mock our persistent ignorance of so many of the conditions of their birth, and thereby to place on the rack again our strained and aching wonder . . . ,"—which I do not equate with our ignorance of Shakespeare's birth, but of our ways, in James's phrase, of "get[ting] at" the man in the artist, which is to say, of getting at the art, at *this* way of making something happen, of tracing what imaginably gives birth to what, by using what James calls "indirectness." It is up to us to get "into the right relation" to the independence of the work, which James figures as our "having crossed the circle of fire" (ibid., 429), as if to see the work by its own light. "The finer weapon, the sharper point, the stronger arm, the more extended lunge"—meant to witness birth, not to give death, to trace the proportionateness between the immensity of the surface of the arras and its underside, calling for each other—are to be understood, therefore, as indirect, as the work of penetrative, aversive thinking so often is. The eternal mystery, the persistent cause of our strained and aching wonder, is that this work, in its immensity and hiddenness, is made, however else, and for whatever else, for us, for anyone and no one; that words we have to say to each other can sometimes have this undying benefit for us, that we know how to get across to them, to a relation to them, that keeps them, and leaves them, objects of wonder.

Then why is the indirectness presented by James as violent? I think of it, briefly, in the following way. The sense of the human in the artist is the sense of an other, separate (even while a projection of ourselves), in struggle with the conditions we bring to a work. The work we assign ourselves in entering the object of work, call it the work art does, requires that we risk our current deployment of the criteria in terms of which our words make sense to one another, to struggle to bring them home (in Wittgenstein's persistent image)—for instance, each of the words in "Unhappy that I am, I cannot heave / My heart into my mouth" or "And there is nothing left remarkable / Beneath the visiting moon." The word *Shakespeare* would then name the site or sites of a set of struggles—for some, easily or suavely avoidable, for others, suddenly inescapable. The pertinent suggestion here is one pressed in my *Claim of Reason*, that the discovery and assessment of our criteria of shared judgment is the discovery and assessment of the ordinary, the turning of the ordinary against itself.

On this suggestion the reforged weapon of James's criticism is made to spurn what Emerson calls conformity and what Nietzsche calls philistinism, these passive appropriations (in their respective systems) of power and of will, which block out the future, or, as Emerson likes to say, the new. When, in *The American Scene*, James turns his criticism of the future on the society to which he repatriates himself, his writing takes on a distinctly political mission, where appreciation becomes a figure for consent.

I close by noting—something one might have neglected to show one's thanks for—a moment in which one among Harry Berger's weave of insights has thrown light on a practice of mine, of importance to me, that I have never seen so steadily before. It concerns why I have so often found myself recurring, in uncovering intersections of philosophy and literature, to the genre of drama. Berger speaks of "the crucial difference between performance and text" (68), going on to say (69): "Around the edges of performance, in the uneasiness that accompanies our feeling that we are never hearing all that is being said, the shadow of textuality falls, converting curiosity to anxiety: 'What does your speech import? / I understand a fury in your words, / But not the words.' This shadow invites us to peer into it, to decelerate the language, dislocate it, listen for the meaning in the sound, understand the words beyond the fury." Without denying a syllable of this, I am brought, for the moment, to something like the opposite obligation of perception, one that the genre of drama lives upon, in its condition of parts, the leader of the chorus turning to face the others, the necessity of a speech coming to an end. We exist here in a medium of exchange in which, of all the countless utterances it might have made sense for you to say, it is this that you have said. As Thoreau puts the matter: There never is but one opportunity of a kind. Having your say, you turn sense over to the other. The shadow is silence. Perhaps you shall survive it.

REVIEW ARTICLES

Hen-pecked Husbands and Light-Tailed Wives: The Courts in Early Modern England

S. P. Cerasano

Loreen L. Giese, ed., *London Consistory Court Depositions, 1586–1611: List and Indexes* (London: London Record Society, 1995), 331 pp., £20/$38.00 (cloth).

Laura Gowing, *Domestic Dangers: Women, Words, and Sex in Early Modern London* (Oxford: Clarendon Press, 1996), 301 pp., $69.00 (cloth).

M. Lindsay Kaplan, *The Culture of Slander in Early Modern England* (Cambridge: Cambridge University Press, 1997), 148 pp., $49.95 (cloth).

Jenny Kermode and Garthine Walker, eds., *Women, Crime and the Courts in Early Modern England* (Chapel Hill: University of North Carolina Press, 1994), 216 pp., $45.00 (cloth), $18.95 (paper).

WHEN, IN 1618, the actor-entrepreneur Edward Alleyn totaled up his yearly expenses, he discovered that he had spent just over £65 on legal matters, proclaiming them "the worst of awe [all] ."[1] In comparison with Alleyn's other annual expenses his legal fees were substantial. They totaled ten times the cost of apparel, half the amount laid out for household expenditures, and a third of what it cost to run Dulwich College, Alleyn's combination orphanage-pensioner's home. Yet just as others of his contemporaries Alleyn could not escape the law, neither can scholars studying early modern culture.

The four studies discussed in this essay have been preceded by decades of research into legal history, starting with such comprehensive works as Sir William Holdsworth, *A History of English Law*

(London: Methuen, Sweet & Maxwell, 1903), H. Potter, *Historical Introduction to English Law* (London: Sweet & Maxwell, 1932), and, most recently, J. H. Baker, *An Introduction to Legal History* (London: Butterworth, 1971). The intersection of the law with various government institutions that created and shaped it have also received much attention (see, for example, G. R. Elton, *The Tudor Revolution in Government* [Cambridge: Cambridge University Press,, 1953]). Along the way, studies such as W. H. Bryson, *The Equity Side of the Exchequer* (Cambridge: Cambridge University Press, 1975), J. A. Guy, *The Court of Star Chamber and Its Records to the Reign of Elizabeth* (London: HMSO, 1985), and W. R. Jones, *The Elizabethan Court of Chancery* (Oxford: Oxford University Press, 1967) have begun to elucidate the workings of individual courts. And historians have delved into some specific areas of the legal process. Yet even a glance at H. C. Maxwell-Lyte, *Historical Notes on the Use of the Great Seal of England* (London: HMSO, 1926)—in all of its weighty richness (460 pages)—is a daunting reminder of how complex both the workings of the law and its historical precedents were during the early modern period. Not only this, but such existing scholarship reminds us how far historians still have to go before we enjoy anything approaching a complete understanding of the entire legal system. Any attempt to read through the many books and articles that have already been published would present a monumental task to even the most intrepid reader. Yet what lies ahead for scholars who venture into the area of legal studies is an even more massive undertaking. In large measure, this is because the volume of archival resources is simply overwhelming and often incomplete; and much extant material is virtually unindexed with regard either to persons or subjects (and therefore highly inaccessible). Moreover, despite the attention already paid to numerous aspects of legal history, the workings of various sectors of the legal system remain vague and largely unexplored in any detail.

It is into this morass that scholars wade whenever they attempt to study the law and its influence during the early modern period. However, compounding the previously outlined difficulties is the fact that many historical studies have politely ignored numerous key elements of the legal system. For instance, as several recently published books demonstrate, the role of women remains something of a mystery. Few historians writing in the early years of the twentieth century paid particular attention to female experience, the engenderment of female power within the legal system, or even women's knowledge of the law—all which interest contemporary scholars. Of course, there are exceptions. In *Witchcraft in the Star Chamber* (n.p., 1938), C. Ewen L'Estrange addressed women's actions; however, it is within the larger context of "female-centered crimes"—witchcraft, slander, and theft, as opposed to "male crimes," like treason and burglary—that women traditionally have been studied as actors and agents. It was not until the 1970s that attention was paid more generally to women and the law; and it was not until the 1980s that a surge of interest in women's history encouraged both a greater number of studies and an examination of the theoretical premises on which these histories were built. Thus, recent years have seen the publication of Martin Ingram's ground-breaking study of sex and the church courts (1987), Amy Erickson's enlightening examination of women and property (1993), and J. A. Sharpe's many excellent studies of crime (including witchcraft) in early modern England.[2]

These and other publications form the backbone of what one suspects should be something of a growth industry. Yet it is not, largely because of the methodological restrictions and difficulties I have outlined previously. Consequently, when four books bearing on the law are published within as many years, readers might anticipate a trepidation of the spheres. However, I would be misleading to suggest that suddenly all the relevant intellectual territory has been charted. The four books under discussion here continue the conversation begun by existing studies. Each, within its own interests and dimensions, moves us closer to a more coherent sense of the law. But each also demonstrates, in intentional and unintentional ways, that there is much more to be done.

The index by Loreen Giese and the monograph by Laura Gowing, together with the edited collection by Garthine Walker and Jenny Kermode, share several overarching concerns. Chief among these is that they are self-conscious about the need to map out their territory in a systematic way. For Giese, this takes the form of indexing a significant portion of the London Consistory Court depositions for the years 1586–1611, while Walker and Kermode tackle the problem by drawing together a collection of essays that illustrate a broad spectrum of issues relating to women's experience with the law. Similarly, these authors share an interest in the shaping influences of the law on social mores and, conversely, the shaping of the law by individuals who have negotiated their way through it. Attention is also paid by two of the authors (Giese and Gowing) to a precise jurisdiction—in this case the London Consistory Court.

Moreover, Giese and Gowing (along with Walker and Kermode) share a commitment to understanding more thoroughly the stake that the law held in households and communities; in the case of Walker and Kermode, this quest centers on their particular interest in women (14).

Surprisingly, perhaps, all the works under consideration seem to acknowledge that the law was incredibly fluid during the early modern period, so much so that it increases the difficulty of describing, in steadfast terms, the implications and functions of legal structures within that society. Moreover, more than one of the authors discover that concepts such as "property" and "privacy" are far more ephemeral than we have imagined in the past.[3] Therefore, the works of the authors under examination here finally raise many more questions than they are able to answer. Thus, while such unfinished business opens up new areas of inquiry and encourages future studies, it also goes a long way toward explaining why studies in early modern law are not abounding.

Of all the books under discussion it is Loreen Giese's *Consistory Court Depositions 1586–1611* that advances our understanding of legal history perhaps more than any other, because it opens up the records of a specific court within a particular, well-defined chronological period. The book is volume thirty-two in a series sponsored by the London Record Society, dedicated to the publication of "transcripts, abstracts and lists of the primary sources for the history of London" (332). As such, Giese's volume joins the ranks of those produced by many distinguished archivists and historians, including Betty R. Masters (*Chambers Accounts of the Sixteenth Century*, 1984) and Pauline Croft (*The Spanish Company*, 1973). It also complements Ida Darlington's edition of *London Consistory Court Wills, 1492–1547* (1967), published earlier in the same series.

As an index, the volume offers a meticulous inroad to one of the most significant ecclesiastical courts of the period—the Bishop of London's Court. As such, this is the first attempt to make accessible records that have hitherto been a thicket for researchers. Needless to say, Giese's index will allow scholars to undertake a systematic examination of the Consistory Court during the period between 1586 and 1611. And having this, it should be easier in the future to build on and extend such path breaking research as that produced by Richard Helmholz on marriage litigation and Martin Ingram on attitudes toward sex and marriage.[4] The bulk of the volume consists of the table of depositions which are organized chronologically according to eight types of information: the manuscript item number, date, parties involved, cause, witness, parish or place of witness, occupational status of witness, and age of witness.

The specific twenty-five-year period represented by the volume's chronological limits was chosen because this period showed a sharp increase in the number of cases; it also was a period during which important changes occurred in canon law and in the monarchy. The volume provides as well much useful apparatus. It is fleshed out with an introduction which discusses the Consistory Court during the period under examination. One appendix offers an extensive bibliography of sources pertaining to the ecclesiastical courts and their records; another contains a transcription of Guildhall MS. 25, 188, a table of fees in the London Consistory Court for 1598. From this one can learn what the court charged for the examination of witnesses, the production of copies of depositions, for a license to marry or one to eat flesh in "the time of Lent" (xxxiii, xxxv). Lastly, the editor includes a map showing the parishes of London and Middlesex (2–3). Also important, but easily taken for granted, are four indices at the back of the volume which enable the reader to locate deponents by name, cause, occupation, and place/parish.

Traditionally, the Consistory Court depositions have been cited as providing a particularly rich source of material for the early modern period because witnesses providing evidence often touched on a variety of subjects that bore tangentially on the case at hand. As Giese describes on pages xix–xxv, the causes of lawsuits placed in the Consistory Court concerned a wide range of matters, including defamation, matrimonial adultery, matrimonial cruelty, testamentary disputes, disputes involving tithes, and other matters ecclesiastical (burial, conduct, excommunication, order, upkeep). The rest of the introduction characterizes the ways in which the depositions previously were used by scholars and the procedural inner workings of the court. Despite the fact that many of the sentences have been lost Giese concludes: "those that lack them nonetheless yield valuable information concerning practices and attitudes" (ix).

Yet, regardless of the number of distinguished scholars who have turned to the Consistory Court depositions in order to study the attitudes and opinions of those who offered testimony, it has also been suggested that we should be skeptical about the testimony they contain. Perhaps surprisingly, as Giese reminds us, there are those who would argue that, because the deponents' testimony was recorded by clerks, the depositions were somehow skewed, that they do not somehow represent the "actual voices" of the witnesses (ix, as summarized by Giese).

One scholar who adopts this view is Laura Gowing. In *Domestic Dangers* she asserts:

> The words of litigants and witnesses were also mediated by the men who wrote them down. The registrars and their deputies who were the scribes to the consistory court added to the everyday speech of litigants the conventional legal usages of Latin and English that made up the court's language.... But at the same time, faithful reporting of words was both possible and important.... The clerks' records of witnesses' answers represent, then, a mediated, rearranged, and possibly rewritten version of the real words they heard. (45–47)

For Gowing, this means, among other things, that much formulaic, legalistic language entered the recorded testimony and that third-person pronouns frequently are substituted for what, she imagines, would have been uttered in the first person. While the latter probably is true, however, it is difficult to avoid the contradiction Gowing sets up when she ultimately states that testimony was "rewritten" but that "faithful reporting of words was possible." In the absence of differing versions of the same deposition, it would seem that the insinuation that testimony was "rewritten" (and, potentially, significantly altered) is difficult (perhaps impossible) to support. Also, one wonders how the author would know that "faithful reporting" occurred at all in the absence of some sort of verbatim testimony. And what, finally, does this imply for the legal system as a whole? All the bills and answers, rejoinders and replications that preserve lawsuits were recorded by clerks. But again, to cast doubt on the veracity of their content—in the absence of other types of evidence that would corroborate this view—seems an odd position to defend, especially when Gowing depends on the evidence provided by the Consistory Court depositions to construct her own case.

Fortunately, the author seems to back down from this point as she proceeds with her main business, which she describes as exploring what gender difference meant to early modern people (5). To accomplish this, Gowing concentrates on three types of case: sexual slander, contracts of marriage, and marital separation (12). Chapters include those entitled "The Language of Insult," "Words, Honour, and Reputation," "The Economy of Courtship," "Adultery and Violence," and "Narratives of Litigation." Early on, Gowing acknowledges:

> our idea of the moral standards on which canon law operated in practice needs to be adjusted. Litigation over sex and marriage did not depend on a consistent, homogeneous morality: rather, the rules, principles, and beliefs that women and men spoke of and appealed to suggest a range of moral structures and a degree of flexibility. Nor did these moral principles necessarily accord with either the church's ideal moral standards or any uniform popular morality. Rather, in the various contexts of sex and marriage a mass of ideas, adapted or invented, provided the means by which behaviour might be judged. (10)

Given this, the model of "crisis" so frequently adopted by historians is called into question. Nevertheless, she suggests that gender was "*always* in contest," with gender relations continually being "renegotiated around certain familiar points" (28). But instead of being influenced by periodic social outbursts, cited by historians such as David Underdown, Gowing concludes that "the mental, social, and material worlds of early modern women and men were shaped by an idealogy of gender relations structured around sex and morals that was, in many ways, constant and persistent" (29).

Gowing's second chapter ("Women in Court ") explores the direct relationship between women and the legal system. She writes that the amount of litigation initiated by women in the London Commissary Court was roughly equal to that initiated by male plaintiffs; occasionally, there were three times as many female defendants as male defendants (33). Servants and apprentices are said to make up 16 percent of the witnesses, although they were seldom plaintiffs (48). Throughout the chapter, Gowing informs the reader primarily through the use of statistics; however, at the end of the chapter, she returns to the theme of the unreliability of evidence, asserting that "the narratives of witnesses and litigants were shaped not just by clerks and proctors, but by their narrator's own strategic and unconscious reshapings" (54–55). Again, this seems an odd stance, one that undermines what Gowing is attempting to argue. Although tendencies for error and alteration potentially existed, it would seem as if, ultimately, they are impossible to document. Moreover, the danger is that, finally, the evidence contained in legal proceedings can be wholly invalidated and turned into fiction which, it could be argued, finally bore little relation to the actual gender relations Gowing is attempting to document. The author comes very close to echoing this position when she states:

> The narratives people told at court reflected the stories they already knew. Popular literature featured a series of familiar plots about sex and marriage: women killing their husbands to marry their apprentices, men catching their wives in adultery, handsome young men deceiving old husbands to seduce their wives, and women stealing their husbands' breeches were the stock figures of stories that were collected in printed editions, sung in ballads, and shared orally between men and women. (58)

Other historians might well argue that Gowing has inverted the natural relationship between fiction and archival material, that fiction imitates life, not vice versa. When, for instance, Natalie Zemon Davis wrote of "fiction in the archives," she referred to pardon tales and those who intentionally told them. She did not imply that all testimony in the archives is essentially fiction.[5]

Gowing's "The Language of Insult" (Chapter 3) is a more solid chapter in which she details types of insults, noting that "in the exchanges of slander, both the insulter and the insulted were most likely to be women" (62). Predictably, the terms *whore*, *knave*, and *cuckold* were constant terms of abuse, and they took on many manifestations over time. Hence, the "light-tailed wives" and "henpecked husbands" seemed to become stock characters, whether in lawsuits or in popular literature of the time. Also, whereas bawdry disrupted the usual household order, women gained some of their sway by purposely inverting this order. Insults from husbands could easily be deflected by insults from their wives (85). In addition, "the language of slander offered particular linguistic powers to women, through which they asserted their verbal, physical, and legal agency to judge and condemn other women" (109).

Gowing concentrates on marriage contracts and the litigation surrounding them in Chapter 5 ("The Economy of Courtship"). "Men offered words and gifts with implications," she writes, "[and] women refused, accepted, or gave conditional answers to gain time" (141). The process of gift-giving especially concerns the author because "a set of more material transactions gave premarital commitment an economic context" (159). As a result, women often tried to keep the balance equal, so that the man could not argue later that he gave more than he received (161). The question of timing is raised but never thoroughly explored. Gowing seems to operate on the assumption that most tokens were given before the contract, whereas many were bestowed either at the time of the contract or even afterward.[6]

In Chapter 6, on adultery and violence, Gowing reminds us that women's and men's sexual behavior had different meanings. Essentially, only women could be penalized for extramarital sex and only men could be guilty of violence (180). But men who caught their wives in adultery faced a potentially humiliating dilemma. If they took their wives to court they ran the risk of being made fun of as cuckolds; and these same issues raised others—especially of paternity. However, women, denied the same retaliatory possibilities when their husbands were unfaithful, often resorted to violence, even murder, to settle the score (197–202). This further intensified the rancor between them, as it was even more humiliating for a husband to be beaten by his wife than it was for him to be the cuckold. Consequently, the usual paradigm—men's blows as a response to women's words—was often inverted with serious results. To be taken seriously, Gowing hypothesizes, women's violence had to be lethal (229).

Still, for all of its interest, *Domestic Dangers* is continually undercut by theoretical inconsistencies. Perhaps it is the central section of the book that is the most interesting, that in which the author presents her ideas and allows us to grapple with the evidence she presents for our examination. Not surprisingly, it is here that the reader feels as if he or she is being brought in on the business of thinking along with the author about the central questions of gender issues. Unhappily, it is when Gowing returns to the final chapter ("Narratives of Litigation") that she creates more confusion in raising the specter of untrustworthy narratives, witnesses who shaped their testimony in order to produce stories that could be "plausible and familiar" (232). Again, she states, they must have been influenced by "clerical manipulations [which] must have distorted its [the testimony's] transposition from voice to text" (235) . Yet Gowing fails to explain how the judges utilized such "distorted" testimony in determining the outcome of a case. (It is convenient that few of the rulings for the cases Gowing cites have survived.) Most puzzling, however, is the fact that in the same chapter (and despite the constant reminders that the narrative of testimony is to be treated with wariness), Gowing is ready to argue, with some degree of certainty, that "women and men understood marriage in different terms" (233). If the evidence is as untrustworthy as she so frequently implies, and if testators pitched their stories in the direction of popular myths and stories, as she openly asserts, then, finally, we cannot know at all what the attitudes of men and women were. We are left only with versions of narratives, skewed by clerks and witnesses, that potentially bear little resemblance to actual understandings and attitudes. In this respect the entire approach of looking into legal records is called into question. Are the records of the legal arena necessarily a good source of evidence in this pursuit? (One wonders whether the contentious nature of litigation perhaps invited an extraordinary amount of creative license.) Or must we simply accept them at face value, for the sake of research, and attempt to use them for the information they yield?

Unhappily, and despite the ambition of *Domestic Dangers*, there are other inconsistencies in Gowing's narrative, as well as other historiographical questions raised by her study. For the sake of brevity I cite only two examples. One example of inconsistency is the claim (on page 48) that, in the records of the ecclesiastical courts "women are described by marital status and never by occupation, except as servants." Then, on the following page, Gowing notes that women, "while they often practised their husbands' trades, also mention their involvement in a range of other, often characteristically female occupations." (Giese's index lists many women as midwives, needleworkers, and seamstresses, as well as those who keep alehouses, and so forth.) Also, despite Gowing's professed interest in learning more about both men and women, she draws the overwhelming number of her examples from suits involving women.

In *Women, Crime, and the Courts*, Garthine Walker and Jenny Kermode address many similar questions to those raised by Gowing; however, they have decided to answer them by assembling a wide-ranging collection of essays. It is, overall, a fascinating collection that could easily serve as a foundation course for scholars seeking to acquaint themselves with a range of legal issues and historiographical approaches to women and the courts. A lengthy introduction wisely situates the essays within their different theoretical contexts. The collection is meant to contribute to the creation of "an integrated social history of the period that extends the parameters of the subject while remaining true to its essentially interpretive traditions" (2). The more focused goal, however, is to contribute to a "greater understanding of the role of gender in the construction of ideas and the structures of life" (2). The editors point out that, in the past, "studies of the relationship between gender and social order have adhered to models of transformation or crisis" thus turning women into a "static historical category" (2). Against this tide, Walker and Kermode hope that research into court records will allow them and their contributors to see women differently, as dynamic forces within the "fluid and negotiable relations" that constituted the legal process (3):

> By exploring the dynamics of female behaviour, we dramatically expand our perception of the legal process, of women's engagement with it, and of the gendered attitudes of early modern England. (8)

In contrast to previous studies that emphasize women's vulnerabilities under the civil law courts, Walker and Kermode are quick to point out that "women did engage with the court system, and to an extent made it work for them as plaintiffs" (12).

The essays in this collection are unique in that they extend our sense of women's concerns along with our preconceptions regarding female power and knowledge. We also learn that "women's relationship to property, both moveable goods and land, is far more complex than historians have traditionally assumed." Consequently, "women's rights and their perception of entitlement" extends far beyond property. "Even women accused of witchcraft could both display knowledge of the legal process and demand justice for themselves" (13). As a group, the essays cover an interesting range of topics. Malcolm Gaskill writes on witchcraft and power, concentrating on the case of Margaret Moore (1647); Jim Sharpe complements this with an essay entitled "Women, Witchcraft and the Legal Process." Garthine Walker researches women, theft, and the "world of stolen goods." Martin Ingram contributes an essay on women as "scolds" and their punishment by ducking as a way into the question of gender relations. Geoffrey Hudson considers war widows and the courts in the mid-seventeenth century, while Tim Stretton writes on "Women, Custom and Equity in the Court of Requests." Laura Gowing contributes an essay on women's slander litigation and defamation in the church courts, much of which is repeated in her book *Domestic Dangers*. To be fair, it is impossible to judge the overall quality of a collection of essays written by different authors. Nevertheless, readers will find that the authors included in *Women, Crime and the Courts in Early Modern England* offer numerous engaging insights and contribute importantly to scholarly conversation, if only by raising our awareness of the need for further research.

In addition, the collection opens up significant historiographical queries. For instance, the editors note that, while quantification can be enlightening it can also result in women "being duly counted and discounted" (4). Moreover, they consider the difficulties both of marginalizing female activity when it is sometimes "measured only against male criminality," and the problems presented by considering women's actions in a purely female context. Other historiographic conundrums play around the edges of the introduction (and of various essays within the collection), although not all are probed fully. One I would note is that of the "ordinary person" (occasionally, "ordinary women") which is periodically invoked. For example, the editors note that:

> It is increasingly apparent that qualitative material can tell us far more about the activities and attitudes of *ordinary people* [italics mine] than can aggregates of litigation alone. (5)

Although legal precedent has, for centuries, relied on the concept of the "reasonable man"—primarily as rhetorical shorthand, for convenience in discussing expectations for human behavior—it is difficult to imagine precisely who, historically speaking, this "ordinary person" was. Although it clearly is a shorthand for those weavers and bakers who urged their suits in the early modern courts, we must nevertheless be wary of the perils of employing such a label. Even a glance at the lawsuits adjudicated in any sector—be it a civil law court, church court, or manorial court—indicates that the courts were not segregated by the social position of their litigants. And, whereas some courts earned a reputation as being more expensive than others (the Court of Requests having been dubbed the "poor man's Chancery"), much litigation—by its very nature—ended up involving many ranks and occupations. In his essay on scolding in this volume (48–80), Martin Ingram raises a series of important issues about labeling by historians. In the case he explores, Ingram concludes that it is wise to be wary of any labeling. But additionally, it would seem unwise to assume that during the early modern period, as now, that all litigants were treated equally under the law, or that the knights and yeomen who found themselves in court, along with the tinkers and tallow chandlers thought of themselves as "ordinary people."

In considering the questions raised by the "ordinary person," the reader is drawn back to one striking conclusion in Walker and Kermode's introduction:

> The essays in this book demonstrate how fluid and negotiable relations in early modern England were, both before and during the formal

legal process. The conventional language of social description, predicated upon patriarchal and hierarchical norms, cannot be taken at face value. (3)

One wonders whether the fluidity detected by scholars in the legal process defies the existence of any "ordinary person" (or "usual action") under the law. At the very least, acceptance of the concept of the "ordinary person" would seem open to controversy. By absorbing women into yet another generality, it potentially supports the "patriarchal and hierarchal norms" that Walker and Kermode warn against.

In comparison with the other books under discussion in this essay, it is Kaplan's that does not fit in neatly with the others, despite its title. Consequently, I will rehearse only its major arguments here. Kaplan's purpose is to advance the argument that "slander provides a model crucial for the analysis of power relations between poets and state." Moreover, she argues that "the concept of censorship, currently employed by critics of early modern English literature to discuss these relations, serves rather to limit and distort our understanding" (1) Because she demonstrates these claims in the arena of Spenser's *Faerie Queene*, Jonson's *Poetaster*, and Shakespeare's *Measure for Measure*, Kaplan is interested primarily in the realm of literature and how various authors seemed to "answer" the restrictions placed on printing and printed materials during periods when the state censors seemed most active and vocal.

Censorship, as characterized by Kaplan, appears to be a well-organized, often totalitarian and far-reaching set of strictures. She writes: "the state's own employment of a range of defamatory practices to control, humiliate, or demonize its populace and its enemies implicates it in the very transgressions it ostensibly seeks to silence" (2). However, she concurrently wishes to reject other similarly broad definitions. Kaplan begins her discussion by charting what she feels to be the limitations of the censorship model proposed by former studies, those by Annabel Patterson, Richard Dutton, Janet Clare, and Richard Burt. In particular, Kaplan faults Patterson for adopting a "transhistorical notion of censorship," one suggesting that "all authors in all periods in all countries respond to all political control of writing in a similar manner" (3-4). She finds Clare to be operating under the false assumption that an "all-powerful mechanism of state censorship" succeeded in controlling both "the written products of dramatists" and "their unspoken thoughts" (5). Dutton, she states, is reminiscent of Patterson's model, in which "poetic resistance seems to be precluded by the assumption of compliance with the, albeit fragmented, will of the court" (5). And finally, Burt demonstrates the fluidity of power relations between poets and censors, although—along with the others—he too shares a significant "blind spot": "that censorship is connected in some way to defamation, but the structure, process and significance of infamy remain unexplored" (6). Having performed what she believes to be the necessary "exploration," Kaplan argues that censorship is inadequate as a model for understanding power relations between the poet and the state (8). Yet the sweep of the introductory material is a liability that weakens the entire volume.

Kaplan opens her brief volume (a total 100 pages of discussion) with a chapter entitled "The Paradox of Slander." Here, her major purpose is to set up a simple theoretical and historical framework for the last three chapters, each of which is devoted to a different author. Understandably, within the limits of the twenty pages she allocates for this purpose, Kaplan offers only the barest of outlines regarding the changing definitions of "slander," or "defamation," the workings of the courts and censors, or the public responses to structures. Virtually all she concludes has been written about before. In light of her interests in Jonson, Spenser, and Shakespeare, Kaplan understandably emphasizes the slipperiness of "defamation" as a category of offense and the difficulties this created in prosecuting offenders. As she points out, it was the same "slipperiness" that created "wriggle room" for the authors under examination to respond to what they perceived was a sort of legal and political "double standard" (33). The state could "defame" writers in offering redress for defamation, but authors were subject to having their books burned.

Nevertheless—and perhaps owing to her decision to produce such a modest book—Kaplan, rather, ends up supporting some of the same views for which she faults Patterson and her other predecessors. The generalizations in which Kaplan traffics (one court being pretty much the same as any other)—coupled with her tendency to skip all over the period between the mid-1580s and 1633, in offering examples—predisposes her to engage in transhistorical notions of censorship (and defamation) although the chronological limits encompass a smaller range than that for which she calls Patterson's methods into question. In addition, her introductory chapters are so overgeneralized that, unhappily, many fine points are missed along the way.

Perhaps the most serious of these oversights concerns an important fact Kaplan misses: increasingly, censorship appears to have been a *specific* response to a *specific* moment, one generated as much by readers reading at a particular time as by authors writing or printers making particular texts available.[7] Moreover, censorship practices seem to have differed under one monarch or another; still, much of what seems to have driven censors, in turn, seems mysterious. It has even been demonstrated that censorship occasionally occurred with the full complicity of the Stationers Company, as a means of enforcing trade restrictions and curbing illegal presses.[8] At other times, it appears that the government censored certain texts because it wished to deflect criticism during a particular moment of crisis. This seems especially to have been the case in the convergence of the 1599 ban and the Earl of Essex's unsuccessful war in Ireland.[9] Thus, what was considered "defamatory" at one time might well be ignored at another.

In this context, Kaplan reads Jonson's *Poetaster* (performed in 1601 by the Children of the Chapel) as one in a series of complaints, partly responding to the Bishops' Ban of 1599, which prohibited the publication of specific satires (64, 83). (Throughout the book, she frequently uses the Bishops' Ban as a touchstone of censors' activity.) But the Bishops' Ban seems clearly to have been initiated not by satire in general, but by a response to *specific* books which were subsequently called in by the Stationers Company. (Most of these had been published in 1599 or the year before and so were of immediate interest.) Therefore, it is difficult to interpret such "chronologically localized" activity as a ban on satire in general. As Lorna Hutson points out, long before the late 1590s there was a sense that satire was inherently subversive[10]; Jonson, years later, was clearly using *Poetaster* as a vehicle to address such claims. Nevertheless, the authorized publication of John Weever's *The Whipping of Satyre* and Edward Guilpin's *The Whipper of Satyre*—both in 1601, the year of *Poetaster*'s performance—either makes Jonson appear completely out of step with current practices and complexities or simply, more generally incensed with what seemed to be prevailing attitudes toward satire. There are, as well, other difficulties in attempting to invoke the Bishops' Ban. As with other formal prohibitions, the Ban addressed printed texts, not stage plays. And plays (*Poetaster* and *Measure for Measure* alike) would have had to be licensed by the Master of the Revels for performance and therefore authorized by a state official. Thus, interestingly, of those authors Kaplan explores, it was perhaps Spenser who had the greatest personal cause for offense. Although Kaplan nowhere mentions it, his "Mother Hubberds Tale," having touched off sparks after its publication in 1591, was almost certainly one of those texts called in by the censors.[11]

In addition to the rather benign overview of courts and crimes, the brevity of Kaplan's introductory material makes scant use of some of the richest and most evocative studies already in print. Or, alternatively, one might say that it misses out on some relevant bibliography which, if it had been included, would have given both Kaplan and her readers a more complete picture of the complexity of the legal debate surrounding slander and defamation. Here, I am thinking of Charles Ripley Gillet's essay, "Books which Offended against Morality," which explicitly addresses censorship and the satires.[12] Also curiously absent is Lynda Boose's provocative "The 1599 Bishops' Ban, Elizabethan Pornography, and the Sexualization of the Jacobean State"[13] (along with Clegg's essay on the 1586 decree cited earlier). Taken together, such oversights and generalizations make this a rather bifurcated book which exaggerate both its strengths and its weaknesses.

Given the constraints of space, I have been able to touch only on some points in each of the books under discussion. Readers, however, will learn much from reading and questioning their premises and conclusions. In addition, they will understand more clearly why there is much detailed research yet to be done. In considering future studies more than simply attending to a greater variety of courts and proceedings is required. Historians and literary critics need to work toward a thoroughgoing examination of individual legal arenas, processes, and proceedings in concert with a careful consideration of the historiographical approaches used to interpret the material scholars find in legal sources. Also, they must strive for a more balanced approach. If we are truly interested in learning more about the attitudes of men and women, then examples cannot be drawn wholly from litigation involving either men or women alone. Similarly, we must accept the limitations of extant sources. If the sentences to a particular class of records are missing, it is impossible to fully reconstruct the process of that particular court during the period under study. Finally, we must carefully reconsider such larger concepts as "privacy" and "property," and the ways in which "reputation" became "property." Especially when so many alleged "light-tailed wives" and "hen-pecked husbands" apparently were willing to subject themselves to the vast unpleasantness and expense of the legal system, which—in the name of administering justice—both violated their privacy and revealed all sorts of "property" to the community at large.

Notes

1. George F. Warner, *Catalogue of the Manuscripts and muniments of Alleyn's College of God's Gift at Dulwich* (London: Spottiswoode & Co., 1881), p. 175.

2. Ingram, *Church Courts, Sex and Marriage in England, 1570–1640* (Cambridge: Cambridge University Press, 1987); Erickson, *Women and Property in Early Modern England* (London: Routledge, 1993); Sharpe, *Crime in Early Modern England* (London and New York: Longman, 1984), among others of Sharpe's books.

3. For a provocative discussion that redefines "privacy," see Diane Shaw, "The Reconstruction of the Private in Early Modern England," *The Journal of Medieval and Early Modern Studies* 26, no. 3 (1996): 447–66.

4. Helmholz, *Marriage Litigation in Medieval England* (Cambridge: Cambridge University Press, 1974); Ingram's *Church Courts, Sex and Marriage* is cited in note 2 above.

5. Davis, *Fiction in the Archives* (Stanford, CA: Stanford University Press, 1987).

6. Colin R. Chapman, *Marriage Laws, Rites, Records & Customs* (Dursley, Eng.: Lochin Publishing Company, 1996), p. 79.

7. See, for instance, Cyndia Susan Clegg, "The 1596 Decrees for Order in Printing and the Practice of Censorship," *Ben Jonson Journal* 2 (1995), 9–29, and her more recent book *Press Censorship in Elizabethan England* (Cambridge: Cambridge University Press, 1997), p. 219.

8. Clegg, *Press Censorship*, p. 58.

9. Clegg, *Press Censorship*, p. 202.

10. Hutson, *Thomas Nashe in Context* (Oxford: Oxford University Press, 1989), p. 66.

11. Clegg, *Press Censorship*, pp. 200, 217, 223.

12. Gillett, *Burned Books*, 2 vols. (New York: Columbia University Press, 1932).

13. Boose's essay appears in Richard Burt and John Michael Archer, eds., *Enclosure Acts* (Ithaca: Cornell University Press, 1994), pp. 185–200.

History and Literary History

CONSTANCE JORDAN

David Cressy, *Birth, Marriage and Death: Ritual, Religion, and the Life-Cycle in Tudor and Stuart England* (Oxford: Oxford University Press, 1997), pp. i–xv; 1–641.

Lawrence Manley, *Literature and Culture in Early Modern England* (Cambridge: Cambridge University Press, 1995), pp. i–xvi, 1–603.

LITERARY HISTORY exhibits habits of thought and style as much as does the literature it considers. Early modern literature is particularly notable for its engagement with social and political issues, perhaps because so much of its output was overtly at the service of one or another party or faction. Its history has been similarly focused, especially in the last twenty years. On the one hand, literary historians look for historical data, the material in archives; on the other, we attend to theory, historiography, and anthropology. How they all come together is discretionary, not to say, problematic. In the 1980s, we read the "New Historicism"; now in the 1990s, we read its critique, not to abandon history as much as to reflect on our own historicity.

Assessing the New Historicism, Louis Adrian Montrose has alluded to the need to recognize "the different subject positions from which readers interpret texts and from which they may negotiate or resist inscription into the positions constructed for them by the text they read."[1] His recommendation is apt but challenging: it is never easy to identify the designs a writer has on his or her readers or to know how to respond to them. As readers of early modern literature know well, the study of rhetoric is intended precisely to render writerly intentions undetectable and, in a sense, "artless." Montrose, however, has also discussed what we should find easier to grasp: the elements of a literary criticism that considers both structural relations (between a text and its cultural contexts) and the sequential processes that suggest the terms of its actual production and reception. The historicity of texts and the textualities of histories are thus to be mutually inflected, together to be comprised by the critic's vision and understanding. In this case, historicity is itself broadly construed: it is "the historical specificity, the social and material embedding, of all modes of writing—including not only the texts that critics study but also the texts in which we study them; thus I also mean to suggest the historical, social, and material embedding of all modes of reading" (410). It's worth considering this advice as we sift through the enormous production of critical work in early modern studies, both literary and historical.

The two books under review here provide a rich body of historical commentary from which to sort out the terms of current literary history. They are in some ways polar opposites: David Cressy's magisterial exposition of English *social* life deliberately avoids references to and reliance on the methods of structuralist criticism; Lawrence Manley's brilliant study of London as a *cultural* center generally represents events as characteristic of a signifying system: persons implicated in events tend to be represented less as individuals than as exponents of a style or movement. Cressy gives us a dramatic picture of English life enlivened by the voices of the men and women who wrote of themselves in all kinds of intimate ways. Manley offers us, rather, a perspectivized vision of a community evolving through time and over an ever more extensive locale. Substantively as well as methodologically, each work has much to tell us.

Birth, Marriage and Death: Ritual, Religion, and the Life-Cycle in Tudor and Stuart England might be thought inevitably to have engaged structuralist theory at some level. Analyzing life-cycle rituals, which serve both to harmonize a collectivity and to mark deviance from its norms, it invites thinking about spatial figuration, on centers and margins, on *communitas* and liminality. Yet Cressy admits such structuralist thinking only as it helps us see a "framework"; "applied" to the specificities of historical record it provides diminishing returns and risks, at worst, becoming "boring" (6). Commenting later on the ritual of baptism, he remarks that a social anthropologist might well consider it a "rite of passage" effectively integrating a newborn infant into the religious life of the community. Beyond this generalization, however, "there is little to be gained" from anthropology: "Much more can be learnt by trying to be receptive to difference, by listening to individual stories and by examining particular circumstances as they developed over time" (97–98). Avoiding abstractions, the question becomes one of defining difference as opposed to orthodoxy: that is, I take it, of assuming an ideologically substantive center or *communitas* from or against which to measure degrees of difference or marginality. One could pursue the subject further by distinguishing the concept of difference, which must be systemic, from randomness, which is merely empiric. Cressy's notations of difference are, in fact, deeply significant of various kinds of cultural systems which can furnish a historian interested in structural analysis with a good deal of evidence; it is just that he is not interested in discussing them as such. The merits of his book—and they are many—lie elsewhere: in the careful attention to the voices of individual men and women as they speak of their own experiences, both as individuals and members of a community. Accounts of the reproductive lives of women are analyzed with sympathy for the importance of detail. What becomes apparent through the suggestive exposition of the circumstances and rituals of childbirth, baptism, and churching is the extent to which the collective lives of women, insofar as they actually were separate from the larger society (as in childbirth) or only prospectively distinct from it (as in the ceremony of churching), could constitute what Cressy terms a domain of "mystery" (46), of the "semi-secret" (23, 197), in which one could speak of "charms" (65), and hence also of "unruly" behavior (55). Some of its practices were merely customary: the preparation of the birthing room which had to be dark and warm, the mixing of herbal lotions and drinks, the supplying of clean linen (50–54, 82–84). Others were routinely suspect: some midwives examined the wrinkles in the umbilical cord of a firstborn to know the number of children its mother would have (80). Still others were condemned as frankly superstitious, for example, the Catholic ritual crossing of a newborn infant (81–82). At issue in each case was the status of the sign— the gesture, the object, the word.

 These practices raise questions about the contemporary understanding of the status and function of signs—how and why they had meaning. As Thomas Greene has noted, magical thinking regards the sign it studies or manipulates as continuous with its referent, as in fact transformative. By contrast, in ordinary communication, a sign is devoid of any real connection to its referent and thus simply conventional.[2] Many of the behaviors characteristic of childbirth and the persons participating in this event seem to me to approach transformativity: they could, but do not, necessarily change the circumstances and the situation in which they take place. The question to ask is, How were they considered efficacious? To fold linen in a certain way, to boil up certain ingredients for a "caudle," could be thought of as actions devoid of any meaning beyond their immediate end. At the same time, they could produce a kind of comfort or reassurance that would fill a community with a sense of harmony and well-being. Such an effect is like, but also obviously different from the one hoped for by the openly credulous: to place a coin in the newborn's hand to ward off the devil (82) may induce a certain communal harmony but its principal purpose is to affect the terms of a future life.

Cressy's discussion of baptism (as opposed to childbirth) puts the status of the sign in another, more familiar light. Consider the gesture of crossing the child to be baptized. Catholics thought it transformative; non-conformists condemned it as idolatry (it was not transformative but delusional); and Anglicans considered it memorial (125). In the latter case, it may have been partly transformative, partly not—how much so depended on the importance of memory to the individual worshiper. Early modern English men and women were captivated by these distinctions; a considerable portion of their social and spiritual lives depended on how they understood signs and their significance.

Inevitably, perhaps, rituals restricted to the lives of women provided forms of self-expression that were gender-specific, sometimes indicating resistance to demands or practices thought to be suspect, whether for religious or other reasons. This seems to have been especially true of churching, a religious service required of women after childbirth. Protest could take on comic as well as symbolic aspects: as, for instance, when the wife of Richard Chaw read the minister's part at her own churching; or when "one Essex woman" who went to the service "'disorderly in her petticoat'" and sat "'not in the right seat'" (214–15); or when Elizabeth Shipley refused to wear a veil as she was churched and subsequently was excommunicated (220). Generally, however, Cressy maintains that this service was not oppressive. Discussing the possibility that churching represented "a patriarchal or misogynist instrument for the subjugation of women," he argues that available evidence suggests the contrary: "women normally looked forward to churching as an occasion of female social activity, in which the notion of 'purification' was uncontentious, minimal, or missing" (199). Given the preponderance of evidence, this is a defensible conclusion, yet it may also be only part of the story. What it dismisses is the possibility that churching was an institution dedicated to multiple (and not necessarily consistent) ends. As such, it could have provided both an affirmation of a community of women and at the same time its containment within prescribed limits—a doubleness of function that would have required control by those doing the prescribing (the ecclesiastical establishment), as well as the cheerful acquiescence of those so controlled. One does not have to go to feminism to find a precedent for ambiguities of this kind. The early modern notion of a voluntary servitude describes the position of a subject whose dependency is both coerced and enjoyed.[3] I do not mean to suggest that churching was not fun for women, but rather that it could well have been such and yet have constituted a servitude.

Men also resisted forms of orthodoxy, of course; Cressy has much that is illuminating to say about male and female non-conformists and recusants in general. He makes it clear that the line between custom that was tolerated, and a ritual that was either prescribed or prohibited, was clearly a fine one; *adiaphora*, or religious practices that were inessential to salvation but nonetheless common, were particularly troublesome. A wonderful instance of the worry such practices could cause is to be found in the history of the baptismal font in Durham, whose move to the west end of the cathedral suggested popery to some, piety to others. Not only was the new placement of the font at the west end suspect, the actual ceremony of baptism there was accompanied by music so loud that it was hard to hear the service (146–47). The conflict between those who moved the font and those who opposed the move reveals yet another way in which ritual could take on complex meanings; in this case, they shadowed the status of the minister as performer and the ritual as performative. A case of semiotic overload, the traveling font provoked both a wish for a minister who was correct in his understanding of doctrine and an anxiety that the ceremony itself be truly efficacious—whether those ends were to be achieved by the font in its old or its new place.

Accounts of courtship, marriage, and the rituals surrounding death and burial are equally intriguing; material on these topics has been discussed elsewhere but not often in such compelling detail. Clearly crucial to the communal life of the citizens and subjects of early modern England, ritual could take on many forms, affect many spheres of endeavor, determine many behaviors. It was either religious or secular. As religious, it was either prescribed or indifferent; as secular, it was merely customary. It was either guaranteed or invalidated by tradition; it was ordered by some kind of authority, whether that was old or new. In every case, it had a historical determination; it was not fixed, but changing. Cressy ends his exacting study by observing that further research on the terms of different kinds of life-cycles is needed; it can be expected to demonstrate how "rituals that worked to bind communities together could also be instruments of cultural polarization" (481).

Literary history is as much indebted to cultural studies as it is to social history—the more so, perhaps, when the notion of culture subsumes the terms in which a civilization signifies its values. In one comprehensive view, Manley's *Literature and Culture in Early Modern London* considers the entire, diverse, and vast production of artifacts signifying some aspect of London life during this period. His study is unified by its commitment to structuralist analysis; what is systematic in London life is thus extrapolated from historical data to become his complex subject. Its determinants are the actual social and economic evolution of London from the early Tudor period through the Restoration, on the one hand; and the representation of this evolution in poetry, drama, popular festivals, civic ceremonies, and the literature devoted to celebrating urban life, on the other. The relationship of these determinants reveals continuous change. They shape an environment by "a process of mutual destructuration and restructuration, assimilating the environment to consciousness and action even while consciousness and action are accommodated to environment" (11). The historical setting in which this process takes place is characterized initially by what Manley calls its "neofeudal" and absolutist ethos (18). As London becomes the exponent of a classical and metropolitan culture, however, it is freed from the constraints imposed by local and sedentary conditions, and comes to represent the ubiquitous urbanity of a capital that is also a symbol of the nation as a whole.

This evolution is marked in four phases. First, the city is invented by its citizenry and is thereby distinguished from court and country. Second, it is illustrated by "fictions of settlement" that sketch out its dimensions in ideal forms and patterns. Third, it actually is shaped by the industry of its writers, whether of pamphlets, romances, satires, or drama. And, finally, it is "disseminated" throughout the realm by a return to imaginative projections that are vastly different from the ideal fictions that had earlier given it meaning. The concept most regularly invoked to explain or characterize a historical event or its representation in this history is one taken originally from psychoanalysis: overdetermination (13, 14)—

that is, a causal or circumstantial condition that manifests multiple constitutive elements.

Manley's appeal to the concept of overdetermination complicates his interpretation of his various subjects which are frequently seen in anamorphic perspective, showing a single entity from two different, distinct points of view. Thus, Sir Thomas More's *Utopia* creates the image of a self that is "at once detached from and involved in a dominion represented neither by a royal court nor by an egalitarian city" (37); early modern representations of London show that the "defense of urban power conflicts with an older language of justice . . . even while these languages of justice are transfigured by the new forms of power from which they dissent" (17, 18); *The Faerie Queene* "both marks and narrates a transitional and overdetermined moment in the life of England" (174). Anamorphosis can contract in paradox to represent an ideal and logically impossible perspectivism: the city of Utopia is revealed to be a state both just and tyrannical (32); Spenser's landscape opens to a horizon "in which *eros* and *imperium*, garden and city, may yet paradoxically be one" (194). Such figuration is, of course, the stock in trade of poets; to the extent that literary historians have assumed the languages of fiction it is theirs too. Its usefulness lies in its capacity to communicate complexity, especially in cause and effect relations—what appear to be contradictions are understood to be the occasion not of a self-canceling stasis but a dynamic evolution. It is this sense of an *evolving* condition of being that Manley is most intrigued by and that he conveys most vividly to readers.

London was "invented" by its early Tudor critics, Manley asserts—knowing that "invention" is both the discovery of a thing as yet unknown and the recovery of a like thing once known but subsequently lost. Notable here is More who, in the *Utopia*, instituted a genre of complaint that was, at the same time, a vehicle for the representation of an ideal state, a critical revision of classical republics. Other writers who deplored acquisitiveness turned to pastoral, pointing to the figure of a shepherd-courtier who was both virtuous and urbane; or to romance, celebrating the character of the rich merchant whose morality did the trick of ennobling him and his family. Harder to characterize are the courtly, dramatic, and civic descriptions of the city that appeared later in the century. These fictions were also "actions or practices," instrumental in creating "the mentalities of settlement" (127). Arguing that this process brought into collaborative relations the interests of landed property owners and merchant capital, Manley posits a unified complement of landowning and urban interests—a complement that shaped the character and politics of "the absolutist state."

Recourse to the term *absolute* to characterize early modern English monarchies is likely to be questioned, I think; as Manley relies on it often and in relation to the concept of the "neofeudal," it is worth considering what the idea of an "absolutist state" represents.[4] Since at least the beginning of the Second World War, studies in the history of political thought have described England's monarchy—from the 1400s through the early modern period—as doubly constituted. Prerogative rule was absolute, but the monarch in parliament—the locus of the monarch's more comprehensive power and authority—was supposed to function according to pre-existing law. Its provisions protecting the property of subjects from royal appropriation were identified with those of a feudal state in which the monarch's power and authority over his vassals was limited. A concept of the "neofeudal" can therefore suggest an early modern constitutionalism as much as it can absolute rule.[5] Manley occasionally refers to voices suggestive of constitutionalist norms in London discourse but without specifying their role in shaping the identity of the city (see esp. pp. 133, 157, 185, 197, and 248–49). As the voice of a collectivity, it was, in any case, louder and more insistent than I think he allows. Indicative is Manley's discussion of royal and civic ceremony—which expressed the anti-structural condition" known from Victor Turner's work as "liminality" (214). Although the royal entry typically was staged as reverential, the Lord Mayor's show became increasingly evocative of a "'free'" market ethos and politics (216). The extent to which such an ethos and politics were the pretext for a resistance to extensions of the prerogative is suggested by the history of royal monopolies, a history obviously bound up with the civic culture of London.[6]

A conflation of a politics of absolute rule with a "neofeudal" social structure also underpins the interpretation of *The Faerie Queene*, the most imposing of Tudor "fictions of settlement," notably in Book V. Manley claims that Spenser's notion of Justice corresponds to his "implicit sympathy with the concentrated force of [royal] absolutism" (198); its "theoretical basis is royal prerogative, or equity. . . . By implicitly elevating the new Tudor prerogative courts—Chancery and Star Chamber—over common law, Spenser's allegory translates the *supplement* of Equity in common law into the primary or originary power of the sovereign who rules in God's stead" (201). In other words, the idea of equitable interpretation of the common law is supposed to be transformatively at one with the idea of an absolute monarch whose sovereign authority and power is not only judicial but *legislative*. This translation is seen in the action taking place in Mercilla's palace, where the monarch's "prerogative word" comes to stand for the governments of Faerieland and Britain (203).

Looking at Spenser's text, however, one notes that Mercilla's "word" is not really a word, but a gesture betokening mercy for one whom Justice has condemned, an act encompassed by the prerogative power of pardon (5.10.50). As such, it illustrates the monarch's principal function in late Tudor England—her role as supreme judge. I doubt Spenser intended this "word" to signify a legislative competence; in other words, it was not an index of absolute rule. In fact, it could be argued that by locating the monarch's word in a judicial setting, Spenser was calling attention to the most restricted of prerogative functions, an image in keeping with the notion of a mixed or limited monarchy, rather than an absolutist state. I allude to this little passage not to question that Spenser's politics was generally sympathetic to an autocratic monarchy, as Manley rightly notes on the basis of other evidence, but to suggest how deeply and *subtly* implicated in literary representations of early modern English society was its political order. This history is pervasively inflected by preoccupations with justice and law, with *ius* and *lex*—preoccupations that are registered in many representations of authority and the deployment of its particular powers. Spenser could favor an extension of monarchic prerogative in various ways and yet still be constrained to represent it in its most traditional venue.

The "techniques" by which London was settled in its evolution from a place to a kind of consciousness include the rhetorical styles and forms traditionally represented by didactic and satirical literature, including the drama. The field is therefore a large one. The cultural work performed by various genres is sometimes critical, sometimes constructive, and often both at once. Serio-comic writers like Robert Greene, Thomas Dekker, and Thomas Nashe, promoted an urban morality that was an alternative to tradition; this evolved in time to what Manley terms a "thoroughly modern, though exclusionary, metropolitan mentality" (369). It provoked a reaction that was also, in its own way, a move in the construction of modernity. For Jonson especially, the imposition of difference became important: he and like-minded moralists shared values that specifically were not supposed to be shared by society at large.

By contrast, some satire became morally ambiguous: as writers moved from condemning bad behavior to illustrating dazzlingly successful acts of fraud, their scorn could seem to turn to admiration. At an extreme, the idea of a fake (which presumes the existence of the genuine article) appears to yield to that of an entity which is only "simulated"—that is, which has no correlative in reality. "Simulation ... is a mode of signification governed not by underlying truth but by relationships among signs themselves. Simulated realities are produced from the nuclear, genetic potential of signs," Manley asserts, paraphrasing Baudrillard (385). A case in point is Marston's *SV*, but the cynicism of Donne and others is also at issue. My readerly experience tells me that Baudrillard's category of the simulative is weirdly ahistorical: whatever a writer's intention, it is he or she who puts words on paper, and readers find referents even to wildly fantastic fictions. Imagine the counterfactual: were counterfeit values to be replaced by simulated values (the product of a "genetic potential" of signs), the stage would be set for plays that lacked not actors but playwrights and audiences, the presses would roll with scripts that lacked not texts but authors and readers. Without an agent whose function it is to distinguish the frame of a fiction from the unremarkable limits of life itself, culture would remain without interpretation and, finally, be uninterpretable. A less problematic social criticism is conveyed by Jacobean city comedy and romance which are described as often attempting to resolve the ambiguities of the new and urban morality by the vaporous illusions of romance though with limited success: while "ruthless intrigue" is suppressed by the justice of romance, the justice of romance is shaped by ruthless intrigue (436).

How London acquired its metropolitan, as opposed to its urban character and status in Caroline England, how in fact it came to stand for a national, as opposed to a local and sedentary culture, both concludes and projects forward the development of the city as a uniquely complex sign of the life it contained and supported. During the last half of the seventeenth century, its geographical limits were broached; the West End was created (484); gentry arrived from the country, the country absorbed their urbanity (508); public patriotism yielded to personal sentiment (512); an "imperial urbanism" produced a "national literature" (516–17)—these events are illustrated in the work of Herrick, Jonson, Davenant, Randolph, Habington, Cowley, Waller, Dryden, and Denham. The aspect of London's character that was manifest in its theatricality, its reliance on a ceremonial order to justify facts on the ground, as it were, is recast and reformulated to evoke the notion of the metropolitan. Its rationale reconceptualizes the notion of place as a specific geographical locale, London: as that city became a metropolis and indeed cosmopolitan, its community became identified by communication (531).

Place was rethought in terms essentially incompatible with geography. For cavaliers as well as for Puritans, where one stood was a matter for metaphor; that "place" signified conviction, integrity, personal liberty. More important, what was created was a sense of place as pervasively virtual, nowhere yet everywhere. Analogous to the place of the theater, which depends on assent to the experience of the virtual, the place of politically disparate Londoners thus became a space unified by its common denominator, its quality of being effective rather than actual. The principal catalyst in this transformation of sensibility was the disturbance occasioned during the Interregnum and later by the dissent of various groups: Puritans, Baptists, and Independents, both religious and political. To these were added men and women returning to London from the "Howling wildernesse" of the New World, conditioned by an experience of the limitless that made the virtual seem more real than the real (537). Their sense of geographical place was consistent with their sense of social place: the notion of a "people" comprehended as it had not done earlier a collectivity fashioned to speak with a single voice taking precedence over "All Formes of Lawes and Governments" (542). Opposed to sedentarism, advocates of an "absolute natural right" were confronted by a countervailing argument for preserving a "'civil right'" and a "permanent fixed interest'" (the words Ireton's [564]), and the evolution of a politics of ubiquity suffered a reality check. It cannot be said, however, to have lost its appeal. Its poetic expression, always inflected by a liberty imagined as subject only to a divine and transcendent ruler, was Milton's *Paradise Lost*, whose "indifference to place" was indebted to the "matrix of metropolitan culture out of which that thought arose" (568).

The achievement of *Literature and Culture in Early Modern London* is prodigious, consistently intelligent, and unlikely to be countered soon. As a reflection on its subject, it bears careful reading—I can think of no structuralist study of this period that so diligently encompasses such a range of topics with a comparably profound critical sensitivity. As a model of literary history, however, it may prove difficult to follow. Structuralism and its reflex in deconstruction tend to suppress evidence of agency. The interest of "reading"

London, of interpreting its signifying systems, is indisputable; but literary history is also about the men and women who created the stuff so systematized, whether they were writers or the anonymous sponsors of civic art and ceremony. Increasingly, it is even about those who did not think they were creating culture but whose words survive in narratives of everyday life. As New Historicism has developed self-reflexively to promote an understanding of culture as both a subject to be constructed and an image of that construction, its progress has been marked by attention to difference, as well as to differential systems. Literary historians need to consider both: the datum of record and its systematic transformation over time.

Notes

1. Montrose, "New Historicisms," in *Redrawing the Boundaries: The Transformation of English and American Literary Studies*, ed. Stephen Greenblatt and Giles Gunn (New York: The Modern Language Association of America, 1992), 392–418, 394.

2. Thomas M. Greene, "Language, Signs and Magic," in *Envisaging Magic: A Princeton Seminar and Symposium*, ed. By Peter Schäfer and Hans G. Kippenberg (Leiden, New York, Köln: Brill, 1997), 255–72.

3. The classic text is Etienne de La Boètie, *Discours de la Servitude Volontaire*, c.1550, ed. Simone Goyard-Fabre (Paris: Flanknation, 1983).

4. See especially, Glenn Burgess, *Absolute Monarchy and the Stuart Constitution* (New Haven: Yale University Press, 1996).

5. An obvious resource is J. G. A. Pocock, *The Ancient Constitution and the Feudal Law: A Study of English Historical Thought in the Seventeenth Century* (Cambridge: Cambridge University Press, 1957). See also, Charles Howard McIlwain, *Constitutionalism Ancient and Modern* (Ithaca: Cornell University Press, 1940); and Margaret Atwood Judson, *The Crisis of the Constitution: An Essay in Constitutional and Political Thought in England, 1603–1645* (New York: Octagon Books, 1971).

6. On monopolies, see David Harris Sacks, "The Countervailing of Benefits: Monopoly, Liberty, and Benevolence in Elizabethan England," in *Tudor Political Culture*, ed. Dale Hoak (Cambridge: Cambridge University Press, 1995), 272–91.

ARTICLES

Mingling Vice and "Worthiness" in King John

Robert Weimann

With the advent of Marlowe the aims of representation in the Elizabethan theater were sharply redefined. As the prologues to *Tamburlaine* suggested, the dramatist literally felt authorized to "lead" the theater to a new horizon of legitimation, one against which the hero could more nearly be viewed as a self-contained "picture." Such a portrait would "unfold" the scene "at large"; the character "himself in presence" would dominate the performance. This at least is how the Prologue to *The Second Part of Tamburlaine the Great* proceeded to elucidate the uses of "this tragic glass" in the earlier Prologue:

> But what became of fair Zenocrate,
> And with how many cities' sacrifice
> He [Tamburlaine] celebrated her sad funeral,
> Himself in presence shall unfold at large.[1]

As promised on the title page, the heroic character's "presence" continued to be felt in "his impassionate fury." As Richard Jones, the printer, assumed in his Preface to the Octavo and Quarto editions of 1590, these fruits of a literary imagination would have appealed "To the Gentlemen Readers and others that take pleasure in reading Histories." Moving easily from stage to page, these eminently readable representations, forthwith available in print, recommended themselves in terms of what "worthiness" the "eloquence of the author" could profitably deliver to a gentle preoccupation with "serious affairs and studies." The flow of authority now seemed to be not simply from text to performance, but—an even closer circuit—from the dramatic writing—via the printing—into the studies of those familiar with "reading Histories." Or so at least Jones, a not entirely unbiased observer, would have it. London theater audiences, even when hugely thrilled by Edward Alleyn's portrait of Tamburlaine, appeared to take a different view, even when what they "greatly gaped at" did not find its way into the printed text.

Here, to recall the partisan position Jones betrays in his Preface provides us with an illuminating foil against which to read the treatment, between Marlowe and Shakespeare, of how comic or grotesque "jestures" were mingled, or otherwise, with the "worthiness of the matter itself." In Marlowe's plays it was possible, at least in print, to view serious matter as incompatible with such "graced deformities" as performances on public stages entailed. Participating in the countermanding flow of authority, even snatching part of it for himself as a discriminating reader, the printer, apparently without intervention on the part of the dramatist, saw fit radically to cancel out the most gaped-at elements of performance. Since, obviously, the latter were viewed as having no authority of their own, the tragical discourse was not to be contaminated by "some fond and frivolous" traces of mere players; these needed to be refined out of existence, as befitted "so honorable and stately a history."

Unfortunately, we can do little more than conjecture Marlowe's perspective on the issue of this cultural difference in question, even though, of course, we recall the dismissal of jigs and "mother-wits" in the Prologue to the first part of *Tamburlaine*. But then we have Shakespeare's own word that the difference between the worthy matter of history and the "unworthy" stage of its performance was perceived, and that it loomed large, in the theater of the Lord Chamberlain's men as well. Only, as I have suggested elsewhere, the prologue to *Henry V* was designed both to expose and to appropriate the gap between noble matter and its common staging, to "digest" the use and "Th'abuse of distance." No doubt, Shakespeare, in a different manner, sought to grapple with the cultural divide—in a manner that was so much closer to the matrix in which the stamp of his own life and work was cast.

There was then, in both Marlowe's and Shakespeare's theater an awareness of this "distance" between the represented locale in the world-of-the-play and the location of playing-in-the-world of Elizabethan London. Implying a difference of not only geographical and spatial but also temporal and social dimensions, this distance must have affected, as well as reflected, the enabling conditions under which to mingle the tradition of Vice and the "matter of worthiness." In Shakespeare's playhouse, the distance was between "this unworthy scaffold" and "so great an object" (*Henry V*, prologue, 10–11) in the emergent discourse of history. If the gulf between them was generic as well as cultural, it provided a challenging threshold that had to be crossed both ways. Performers in a mere "cockpit," precisely because they could not traverse the "vasty fields of France" (11–12), had to assimilate the worthy matter of history in their own terms. In doing so, they, as it turned out, had a way of metamorphosing certain discourses into deformity, "minding true things by what their mock'ries be" (4.0.50).

At this point, our recourse to the theater of Marlowe helps throw into relief how, on the "unworthy scaffold" of both *Richard III* and *King John*, it was possible to assimilate cultural difference in and through an unfixed space for (dis)continuity between dramatic text and performance practice. Introducing the performative energy of the old Vice into the "tragic glass" of history and personality, the dramatist's idea was *not* to eliminate these "fond and frivolous jestures" from the realm of "serious affaires and studies" but, as it were, to digest the distance between them. The project was not to accept but to transgress and so reform the socially sanctioned boundary endorsed by Jones between those "graced deformities" and the "worthiness of the matter itself." Thus, the protagonist in *Richard III*, in his hybrid mingling of Vice and "worthiness," could absorb significant 'deformity' in the very image of the tragic hero. Reducing any unnecessary "digressing" in purely presentational practice, this vicious protagonist, in a grim version of frivolity, was "himself in presence" designed to "unfold at large" the play in question.

However, in *King John* (1596)[2] the mingling of Vice and "worthiness" achieved a bewildering new turn, one that, in the assimilation of contrariety, was potentially even more experimental and, from a providential point of view, much less reassuring than *Richard III* and the entire first tetralogy. It is true, *King John* does project, through the stamp of a non-vicious protagonist, the frivolous figuration to the point of its containment: Faulconbridge is made faithfully to rehearse most of the attributes of the Vice, only to go beyond them. But in doing so, he reaches out, with a remarkable twist, for something new. He seeks to redeem the unbridled energy of the valiant performer on behalf of his arduous task in the building of, historically speaking, an anachronistic image of the nation-state. Along these lines, Faulconbridge may even be said somewhat to anticipate the more highly qualified appropriation of the Vice figure in *Hamlet*, where, partially, memories of this figure are infused into an antic, mad version of "graced deformities"—one that was motivated by a desire to scourge the world and "set it right." In the tragedy, the very gap between madness and "matter," frivolity and "worthiness," was projected as part of a composite structure, in its own way constituting "two meanings" in one play. Whether or not in the wake of this operation the tragic glass of Renaissance subjectivity cracked and the "unmatched form and feature" of Renaissance "youth" was "blasted with ecstasy" (3.1.168) or, as in Richard Gloucester's case, "curtailed of this fair proportion" (1.1.18), the result was unprecedented and paradoxical to the extreme. Decorum, discretion, and the kind of authority that was postulated in the worthy discourse of princely conduct was confronted with its own "great disgrace," as that was folding out from *within* "so honourable and stately a history."

The strategy of integration between the uses of rhetoric, eloquence, and representation in writing and the inscription therein of an excessive and 'ecstatic' type of performance practice was not, of course, confined to history plays such as *2 Henry VI*, *Richard III*, and the two parts of *Henry IV*. But here, and this marks the mingling of Vice and "worthiness" in *King John*, the aim was not to abandon "worthiness" in the discourse of history; rather, the nonhumanist tradition, with its mad, frivolous performative was effectively inserted into these literate images of high Renaissance endeavor. In the language of Marlowe's prologues to *Tamburlaine*, the self-contained "glass" of representation, the unfolding "presence" of the hero's own "picture," the *locus* of his "stately tent" and station were churned by an alien energy, a leavening of kinetic force and otherness quite unknown to neoclassical poetics and rhetoric.

Thus, through the assimilation of an eccentric source of performative energy, the matter of representation itself was turned into a vehicle of cultural contrariety. To have, as in *Richard III*, a martial hero, but to have him "rudely stamped" (16) made it feasible on the stage to unfold "th'abuse of distance" from within the act of performance. The distance in social station and language use between the mirror of a Renaissance prince and the cultural practices of Elizabethan players (by many regarded as vagabonds and beggars) came to fruition when the fearsome Duke shared out the indiscretion in his triumphant, gleeful display of how to sue a royal "wench;" when the Prince himself began to moralize two meanings in the twinkling of his eye, in one word, one gesture, one grim jest; and when, in the greatest of tragedies, the most venerably overweening of royalty himself turned mad beggar. Thus, in the mingling of Vice and "worthiness," there accrued a site for "bifold authority" (*Troilus and Cressida*, 5.2.147) in the matter of representation itself. Such mingle-mangle made it impossible to have things as they should be. To have the "glass of fashion and the mould of form" (*Hamlet*, 3.2.152), the image of a worthy hero, "himself in presence," blasted by "ecstasy" implicated (when read as 'ex-stasis') the disruption of "stasis" if the latter can be defined as a "state of equilibrium or inactivity caused by opposing equal forces" (Webster) .

If, in this context, decorum and discretion were undermined, one of the reasons was that their deformation was inseparable from the performative resilience in the legacy of the Vice. This legacy, as Alan Dessen has shown, was well remembered, at least up to 1610, in the Elizabethan theater.[3] Remarkably, the memory of it resonated with a sense of the Vice's duplicity and "impudence." For the comic and the serious descendants of the Vice to "mistake the word" (*The Two Gentlemen of Verona*, 3.1.283), to "play upon the word" (*The Merchant of Venice*, 3.5.43), and to "moralize two meanings in one word" was to do and "to gainsay" the distortion, to accomplish and then to deny the deformation. But such disavowal, always duplicitous in an ambidextrous manner, was conspicuous for its performative zest that made the impudent game irresistible in the first place. Almost certainly we have an echo of this in Leontes' words:

> I ne'er heard yet
> That any of these bolder vices wanted
> Less impudence to gainsay what they did
> Than to perform it first.
>
> (3.2.54–57)

As Blakemore Evans annotates the passage, "Less" here stands "where a modern ear expects 'More'," intensifying the "wanted.") The element of "impudence"—going, as im-pertinence or nonpertinence, against the grain of the "necessary question" in representation—must have been close to what "performant function," in Jean Alter's sense, there was in juggling. Thus, as late as in Ben Jonson's *The Staple of News* (1626), "the old way" of the Vice is remembered "when *Iniquity* came in like *Hokos Pokos*, in a Juglers jerkin, with false skirts."[4] Here as elsewhere, memories of the Vice are closely related to the presentational practice of jesters and jugglers.

In this direction, Faulconbridge's residue of jesting and presenting, compounded as it is with "worthiness," serves as both leaven and lever for a theatrical treatment of history. His attributes of "impudence," bastardy, dispossession, and opportunism were symptomatic of how the unsanctioned world of cultural "deformities," always already "unmeet for the matter," could actually be made integral to it. In his figuration, there was a determined attempt to be aware of, and yet use (and abuse), the "distance" between the placid Renaissance mirror of nobility and the highly nonstatic site of kinetic energies in performance. The idea was to explore the frivolous, fond, deforming, and unsettling contours of this site from within the uses of "this tragic glass" itself.

Going further than any other adaptation of the figure called "Vice" in Tudor drama, Faulconbridge ended up by suspending his initial dispossession and apartness. In *King John*, the process of adaptation was not marked by the absence in a Renaissance figure of nobility of "this fair proportion"; there was no ungentle hunchback that irrevocably conveyed a "misshapen" (1.2.250) character's sense of being socially apart. Whereas in Richard Gloucester's case this apartness was given, at least up to his self-directed coronation, Faulconbridge determines not to stand apart but in his own way to meet the madness of the world, the rule of commodity itself. Henceforth, the Vice cannot serve the alien energy of otherness, when "there is no vice but beggary" (2.1.597). Thus, in this "worshipful society," time-serving is the watchword:

> For he is but a bastard to the time
> That doth not smack of observation—
>
> (1.1.207–8)

But "observation" as a servile, sycophantic complaisance is entirely compatible with an altogether different "inward motion" or inclination "to deliver" a purgation or, at least, some "poison for the age's tooth." Thereby, the grounds of apartness are finally surrendered when the "inward" impulse is to be, rather than "a bastard to the time," its true child and agent.

At this point, the footsteps of this "mounting spirit" (1.1.206) potentially begin to lead away from what was the material correlative in theatrical space, the *platea*-function, of Faulconbridge's initial position in the play. It is true, the force of this "inward motion" continues to be at least partially intercepted by his lingering resistance to closure, reaching out into the epilogue-function of his concluding speech. Still, the absorption of the Bastard by the discourse of historiography seems undeniable when compared with related adaptations of Vice. In most cases, the images of isolation or apartness were distinctly accompanied by, hence interactive with, the allotment of a material, unenclosed downstage type of performance space. It was in this decentered space, "aside" from the central action, that a surplus of awareness and audience rapport would redeem or at least set off self-isolating illegitimacy and all kinds of social, lineal, racial, and economic apartness. Thus, Aaron in *Titus Andronicus* tends to "speak aside" (3.1.187–190, 201–4; 4.2.6, 26). His position of difference was borne out by a site symbolically encoded by his "slavish," "servile" memories and his blackness, coupled with a fierce desire for self-liberation:

> Away with slavish weeds and servile thoughts!
> I will be bright, and shine in pearl and gold.
> (2.1.18–19)

In Iago, the sense of being underprivileged, even dispossessed and cheated, dramatically affirms (and, to a degree, motivates) stringent apartness in his plans for evil manipulation. His sardonic signature tune, "Put money in thy purse" (*Othello*, 1.3.341–43, 345; etc.), effectively recalls the chorus-like refrain of the old Vice, even when it symbolically associates the absence of material means, an awareness of the hardness of things, the need to make ends meet. In an altogether different vein, Edmund, the illegitimate son of the Earl of Gloucester, more brutally a "whoreson" (*The Tragedy of King Lear*, 1.1.23), feels 'branded' in his relation to the legitimate Edgar:

> Why brand they us
> With 'base,' with 'baseness, bastardy—base, base'?
> (1.2.9–10)

Such iteration resounds with a sarcastic crescendo of exuberant energy and inversion when delivered as in affirmation of the "lusty stealth of nature" and other sources of "fierce quality" (11–12). Thus, the enforced apartness of the underprivileged is turned into a resilient site of aggressive mobility on which the peculiar mingling of vice and virtue, à la Faulconbridge, is consistently deferred.

Not unlike Richard Gloucester, Edmund presents himself as overcharged by something deeply anomalous; each is responding excessively to a particular social or psychological logic, which response requires scheming, counterfeiting, and evil gaming. There is a need for all of them, and Iago especially, to be double-faced; the native art of counterfeiting thrives, even culminates, in a great density and mobility, an ecstasy, as it were, of performative practice. In all these figurations, a strong performative exceeds rational or socially responsible motivation to the point that, as in Aaron, Gloucester, and Iago, it celebrates itself as a motiveless malignity that, ultimately, is unaccountable (as well as self-defeating) in terms of any mirrored locus of verisimilar action.

As against the resolute malignity in these descendants of the allegory of evil, Bastard Faulconbridge has a far more checkered genealogy and serves a new hybridity of functions.[5] The thoroughly experimental note in his amalgamation of Vice and worthiness emerges when his deliberate time-serving turns out to be "honest" in that it does not go hand in hand with strategies of deceitful counterfeit but, rather, a brash, undisguised stance of sarcasm. At the same time, the complicity of scourge and minister was so adapted that the performative surplus of vicious speech and "jesture" could, in the course of the play, be domesticated and at least partially harnessed to the representation of bravado and virility in the service of the nation-state. Without altogether surrendering the boisterous quality of his early irreverence, Faulconbridge, once turned into a represented agent of courageous patriotism, ends up bastardizing his own hybrid extraction.

Thus, the conflation of Vice and worthiness is turned into a potent and profoundly ambivalent site on which the strong performative of popular playing and the Renaissance discourse of Machiavellian politics are made to interact. This interaction culminates in the speech on "commodity" where the contrarious dramaturgy in the figuration of the Bastard—presentational and representational—culminates in a strange contradiction between the unveiling language of the commentator and the complicity of the participant. The speech is significant because contrariety itself is projected into both the theme and its ironic treatment, when Faulconbridge addresses

> [. . .] that same purpose-changer, that sly devil,
> That broker that still breaks the pate of faith,
> That daily break-vow, he that wins of all,
> Of kings, of beggars, old men, young men, maids,
> Who having no external thing to lose
> But the word "maid," cheats the poor maid of that,
> That smooth-fac'd gentleman, tickling commodity,
> Commodity, the bias of the world—

Mingling Vice and "Worthiness" in King John 117

> The world, who of itself is peized well,
> Made to run even upon even ground,
> Till this advantage, this vile-drawing bias,
> This sway of motion, this commodity,
> Makes it take head from all indifferency,
> From all direction, purpose, course, intent—
> And this same bias, this commodity,
> This bawd, this broker, this all-changing word. . . .
> (2.1.567–82)

Here, the Bastard, alone on stage, face to face with the audience, provides a sample of that "abundance of superfluous breath" (2.1.147) which is part of his overcharged articulation. At the same time, such superfluity is the mark of both the "disorderly motion"[6] in the play's imagery and that "vast confusion" (4.3.153) in the play at large that results from the attempt "To tug and scamble, and to part by th' teeth / The unowed interest of proud swelling state" (4.3.146–47). The speech, therefore, addressing the political economy of self-interest on almost every level, focuses on a crucial point of realignment. It is the point where the historical "matter of worthiness" is unravelled through *and* in commotion and commodity. The Bastard, viewing "the battlements" of Angiers "As in a theatre" (2.1.375), grasps "commodity" as "the bias of the world." In other words, covetous self-interest is metaphorically defined in terms of a slanting sport of bowls where the "off-centered weight" of "a wooden ball,"[7] thanks to a piece of lead—the "bias"'—"Makes it take head," or rush from, a straightforward trajectory toward a curved course. The Bastard's version of "how this world goes" (*King Lear*, 4.5.150–51 [quarto text]) maps an oblique path, a direction marked by an asymmetrical play that perfectly links up with the representation of a decentered motion in the world-picture. As against "all direction, purpose, course, intent," this "sly devil," "this vile-drawing bias" obtains as an "all-changing word." Turned into a transitive/intransitive language, this word in the mirroring picture is swayed by a motion that is out of control, beyond all "indifferency."

Since Faulconbridge himself is a self-styled "devil" (or at least "One that will play the devil"—135), he himself fully participates in the rush from "indifferency," from settled meanings and balanced purposes. Disordered motion itself is shared out between his own sense of "Legitimation, name, and all is gone" (1.1.248) and what contingency is contained in the world of the play at large. In other words, by recognizing the world as a place of disorder ("Mad world, mad kings, mad composition!" [561]), the bastard's own eccentricities seek to comply with the absence of "direction, purpose, course, intent." Here, his own mad, illegitimate make-up can fully participate, even achieve a representative function. In other words, Faulconbridge serves as both a medium of revelation and a source of contamination vis-à-vis the absence of genuine "worthiness" in the matter of history.[8]

Thus, revelation, insight, knowledge, and form itself all help define the deformation, and vice versa, just as "indifferency" (or impartiality) helps constitute a notion of partiality. The Bastard, in exploiting the instability of his own (re)presentational position, is free to quibble himself out of having to make a choice: the "sway of" motion is such that, playfully, his open hand is stretched out "When fair angels would salute my palm" (591)—the currency of commodity conflates heavenly bliss and possession of metal coins called "angels."[9] "And why do I rail on this commodity?" The answer provided marks the point where, in his own complicity, the Bastard taunts the audience, inviting them to share a "tickling" disillusionment about the commodification of politics. Here and elsewhere, the sarcastic descendant of the Vice can easily perforate closure. Serving as a liminal medium, his eccentric position—one not at all lost in the locus of historical narrative—can convey more knowledge about the playworld than its own representations are made to contain. Faulconbridge, through his irreverence, is instrumental in shaping an awareness that helps penetrate the surface of the Elizabethan discourse of order and degree.

In his hybrid figuration, the legacy of the Vice is unmistakably revitalized. The opening scene of *King John* shows Faulconbridge as a "rude man" (1.1.64) and "madcap" (84), an "unreverent boy" (227) with "country manners" (156). His use of language is thoroughly indecorous, marked by an inordinate amount of colloquialism (" 'a pops me out / At least from fair five hundred pound a year," 68–69). His impertinence first emerges vis-à-vis Queen Eleanor, in his literal refusal to respond to what Hamlet in his advice to the players calls the "necessary question" of the scene, that is, her points and questions in dialogue. Thus, his 'reply' to the Queen's gracious offer is remarkably far from the purpose of *her* playing and meaning.

> *El.*   I am thy grandame, Richard, call me so.
> *Bast.*   Madam, by chance, but not by truth; what though?
>   Something about, a little from the right,

Mingling Vice and "Worthiness" in King John 119

> In at the window, or else o'er the hatch.
> Who dares not stir by day must walk by night,
> And have is have, however men do catch.
> Near or far off, well won is still well shot,
> And I am I, howe'er I was begot.
>   (168–75)

His response is such that "quite athwart / Goes all decorum" (*Measure for Measure*, 1.3.30–31). Like Mischief, the Vice in *Mankind*, who assumed the role of an impertinent "wynter-corn thresscher,"[10] the Bastard is at pains to underline the rusticity of his language and imagery. As a "good blunt fellow" (71), his idiom is as proverbial as—in confronting the court—completely devoid of discretion. Answering the queen, he reproduces a series of homely allusions and commonplaces that, resisting the representation of courtly meaning, come close to signifying a "wild of nothing [. . .] / Express'd and not express'd" (*The Merchant of Venice*, 3.2.182–83). His answer to Queen Eleanor is, in both senses of the word, impertinent because, in its impudence, it refuses to acknowledge pertinent, that is, referential uses of dramatic dialogue. His words preclude the illusion of dramatic dialogue as a dramatic representation of actual exchange and communication. But, although his reply is, in the full senses of these words, scandalous and offensive, none of the courtly characters seems to mind. It is spoken, as it were, out of hearing, as if spatially remote from the locus of courtly manners and "worthiness." No less strange is his persistence in thoroughly irrelevant sexual innuendo, as when in eight lines (140–47) he manages to convey six or seven obscene puns, among them "tail" for "tale," "hour" for "whore," "case" for "vagina." If anything, these quibbles serve to sustain his distance from the language of dramatic verisimilitude and courtly decorum. Going hand in hand with his highly performative penchant for a self-displayed style of role-playing, these uses of language presuppose a verbal, social, and spatial apartness from the sites of authority customarily represented in the dominant discourse of Renaissance conduct.

Thus, the Bastard stands for a remarkable freedom to (re)moralize meanings in the play's thematic concern with sin, social mobility, and primogeniture. Unashamedly punning, he freely celebrates his own bastardy ("Now blessed be the hour, by night or day, / When I was got . . ." (1.1.165f). He is prepared to "thank" his mother "for my father:"

> And they shall say, when Richard me begot,
> If thou hadst said him nay, it had been sin.
> Who says it was, he lies, I say 'twas not.
>
> (274–76)

Downright denial of "sin" here is part of a complex figure of inversion. The difference between vice and virtue, strictly implemented in allegorical uses of language, is suspended: the meaning of "sin" (in relation to its contemporary referent) is de-moralized. The cultural semiotics of rupture is such that semantic stability, the preordained standards in signification, can effectively be upset, together with what authority might sanction stability in the representation of sexual and marital relations.

Hence, Bastard Faulconbridge serves as a theatrically effective vehicle of de-moralizing and remoralizing meanings in one word. His language is full of those "frivolous jestures, digressing . . . far unmeet for the matter," which Marlowe's printer saw fit to omit. If, fortunately, these were not obliterated in the textual history of *King John*, the main reason is that these "graced deformities" were so written into the text of historiography as to affect its direction from within. Faulconbridge does not need to "speak more than is set down" for him—the play text itself provides space and idiom for continual impertinence. Almost unlimited in its heterogeneity, this text, through having absorbed a perfectly eccentric potential for performative practice, might very well claim to serve more than one purpose of playing.

Thus, the Bastard, up to a point, retains his capacity for playing with the difference, in dramaturgy, between presentation and representation. As his own show master, he can assimilate a *platea* type of space in which to exercise his remarkable skill for a display of more than one role. What he does may not exactly be classified as "some necessary question of the play," but it is both an entertaining display of histrionic competence *and* an exquisite, meaningful making of images that participate in the staging of his own upward mobility and "conversion":

> Well, now can I make any Joan a lady.
> "Good den, Sir Richard!"—"God-a-mercy, fellow!"
> And if his name be George, I'll call him Peter;
> For new-made honour doth forget men's names;
> 'Tis too respective and too sociable
> For your conversion. Now your traveller,
> He and his toothpick at my worship's mess,

Mingling Vice and "Worthiness" in King John

> And when my knightly stomach is suffic'd,
> Why then I suck my teeth, and catechize
> My picked man of countries. "My dear sir,"
> Thus, leaning on mine elbow, I begin,
> "I shall beseech you"—that is question now;
> And then comes answer like an Absey book:
> "O sir," says answer, "at your best command,
> At your employment, at your service, sir."
> "No, sir," says question, "I, sweet sir, at yours";
> And so, ere answer knows what question would,
> Saving in dialogue of compliment,
> And talking of the Alps and Apennines,
> The Pyrenean and the river Po,
> It draws toward supper in conclusion so.
> But this is worshipful society,
> And fits the mounting spirit like myself;
>
> (1.1.184–206)

This, indeed, is excellent game when an actor/character goes out of his way to stage a one-man show, using as his dialogic agents Question and Answer to catechize, as in an "Absey book" on social difference, the elementary principles of upward mobility and haughty condescension. This, surely, is a satirical image and, hence, a representation of upstart behavior, no doubt inflecting the extraordinary late Elizabethan welter of classes and values. But, at the same time, this is not exactly a representation of character; although himself an upstart, there is no implication that this is, in any reliable sense of the word, in character with, or a characterization of, Philip Faulconbridge.

Even as he says, "now can I make any Joan a lady," the purpose of playing behind this speech is more impertinent than this.

> A foot of honour better than I was,
> But many a many foot of land the worse.
>
> (182–83)

With these quibbles (and they immediately precede this speech) the Bastard, as it were, plays himself out of the constraint of a purely self-referential application of meaning. Conflating the "foot" of his status or degree with the "foot" or simple measurement of material space, he can convey a sense of the limits of "honour" through its complicity with "land" and its capacity for commodification. Thereby, the play on the signifier signals an awareness of, and betrays a distance to, the purpose of his own playacting, the mimicry of a self-conceited upstart.

Thus, throughout the first part of this speech, Faulconbridge serves not so much as one represented but one who is doing the (re)presenting. The speaker does not so much map his own potential course of action but, more provocatively, mimics the abject arrogance of the nouveaux riches or, even, those that make up "worshipful society" (205). Again, the twist of the word "worshipful" displays a strongly performative gesture of impudence. There is an element of exuberance in what the performer behind the Bastard performs. One needs to imagine the irresistible gusto of a play-acting that invites spectators step by step to attend to the taunting "Now" (190), the gesticulant "Thus" (194), the caustic "And then," and the "conclusion so" (204). Note the dazzling quality of performed action, the affably maintained relish of superiority, a stance best expressed in the subtext of the French analogue *suffisant*, when his "knightly stomach is *suffic'd*" and "Thus, leaning on mine elbow, I begin . . ." The gloating here is that of the performer more than of the performed. All this adds up to a stunning theatricality that resides in the act of delivery, the self-supporting presentation, by which the speech is zestfully turned into a histrionic display of the first order. Thereby, the player, far from identifying with the displayed, can knowingly exhibit what competence, skill, and mastery go into the playing of this play in miniature.

In this remarkable interplay between "author's pen" and "actor's voice," the circulation of authority in Shakespeare's playhouse comes full circle. The playwright, by appropriating the scenario of a zestful display of the player's skill, so adapts it to his larger theme and representation that, at the height of histrionic virtuosity, the focus remains on the "necessary question of the play." The "Law of writ" is clearly in evidence; its controlling instance here is more sustained than, by comparison, in the performant function in Q1 *Hamlet*. But, while authorial authority effectively prevents these "frivolous jestures" from being "unmeet for the matter," the playwright follows, rather than dictates, the player's craftsmanship. The script, far from seeking to displace the player's appeal, actually helps mediate the performer's own authority and competence. His calculated presence, therefore, is not administered by or, simply, superimposed on the writing; the player's act of presentation is just there—an enabling, formative condition of how playacting before us is inscribed into the text. Thus, while the "author's pen" throughout is in the "actor's voice," that voice finally helps to find, and decides on, the form, genre, and scenario of what we have before us.

Even so, the presentational *gestus* remains strictly limited. Even before the text provides a cue for the performer to withdraw behind the character's persona, the remarkable élan in this playing with a difference peters out with the "dialogue of compliment." Thereafter, the descendant of the Vice—so far, close enough to the "old Vice"—appears to maintain his credentials strenuously through a proverbial reference to travel and traffic. Faulconbridge hearkens back to the Vice's penchant for boundless movements, as when—one case among many—Hickscorner, in his nonsensical travelogue, listing no less than thirty places, claims to "have ben in many a countre."[11] But except for the pungent use of the rhymed couplet (citing "the River Po, / [. . .] in conclusion so"), the reference to a self-fashioning "mounting spirit" with a Renaissance sense of "myself" (1.1.206) remains a somewhat questionable, lame transition to the stirring verse of

> For he is but a bastard to the time
> That does not [smack] of observation—
> And so am I, whether I smack or no;
> And not alone in habit and device,
> Exterior form, outward accoutrement,
> But from the inward motion to deliver
> Sweet, sweet, sweet poison for the age's tooth,
> Which though I will not practice to deceive,
> Yet to avoid deceit, I mean to learn;
> For it shall strew the footsteps of my rising.
>
> (1.1.207–16)

The use of "bastard" in this new context serves an inversionary function. If, as Faulconbridge's rise and service in the play attest, illegitimacy is at best an untrustworthy signifier, the question here is raised as to what—after "Legitimation, name, and all is gone"—in fact constitutes legitimacy or, in modern parlance, authenticity. The answer, despite its cynical overtones, points in a direction Bacon first attempted to formulate.

> And with regard to authority, it shows a feeble mind to grant so much to authors and yet deny time his rights, who is the author of authors, nay, rather of all authority. For rightly is truth called the daughter of time, not of authority.[12]

Hence, Faulconbridge's resolution "to deliver / [. . .] poison for the age's tooth" serves as a double-edged weapon. Its twofold function neatly divides between vicious time-serving (unprincipled, like the old Vice) and virtuous service to one's time, and place, and country. For the Bastard is prepared, with Bacon, not to "deny time his rights"; not to serve authority as perennially given but to follow a better criterion of "truth," one that is the "daughter of time." Nor will he himself "practice to deceive"; rather, he will "learn" to "avoid it," even though, as a true child of the age, he will not desist to feed the appetite for "observation" or obsequious flattery.

Even in this pragmatic agenda for practical self-help in response to the fashion of the times, the Bastard does not quite slough off the "sweet poison" of vicious ambivalence. As "mounting spirit," he is prepared to "smack of observation," that is, to see through flattery and tolerate the motions of obsequious practice. Having affirmed a highly precarious identity, however, he is at once ready to juggle with what provocative 'meaning' his own status of "bastard" has so far projected. Now "a bastard to the time" is used disparagingly; the natural and the metaphorical uses of the word are played with. Similarly, the connotations of "smack" (to have a taste or trace of something) are promptly exploited with punning on "smoke" (the spellings were not yet distinguished). Paradoxically, though not perhaps fortuitously, this "mounting spirit" can, in one line, relish a licentious release of his first-person singular; as Honigmann reads: "And so am I, whether I smoke or no."[13]

Again, the punning ("smack"/"smoke"), together with the ambiguous use of "observation" (where, in each case, vital awareness of the senses is invoked) establish a pattern of play and instability between signifier and signified. Representation is paltered with, meaning remains elusive or is encoded ambiguously, when the alternative to *not* being a "bastard to the time" can, in Braunmuller's edition, positively be rephrased as "a legitimate or successful participant in current affairs."[14] Here, if anywhere, is a half-hidden clue to how the new sources of authority—those which in Bacon's phrase, do *not* "deny time his rights"—are vulnerably exposed. When all is said and done, the distinction is at best relative between time-serving and service to one's time and place in a contingent world. At this point, the Bastard's vulnerability anticipates a great predicament in modern, even postmodern notions of political practice.

The Bastard's speech, read as a whole, reveals the full dynamic, but also the impromptu nature of the experiment, in the Shakespearean transmutation of the Vice. Up to a point, the figure constitutes a thoroughly performative force disrupting closure and decorum, an unprincipled agency of duplicity, neatly derived from a hybrid ancestry conflating allegory and farce. In this popular Renaissance adaptation, however, a new commingling of worthiness and Vice, a new hodge-podge of ideology and skepticism tends to supersede the older conflation with its binary order of vice and virtue. It is through a new, duplicitous perspective on legitimacy and authority that, as in the different uses of "bastard" itself, the "fond and frivolous jestures" of the irreverent juggler are domesticated in a seminal representation of the unruly self in "worshipful society."

At this point, the new departure rehearses and yet leaves far behind the anti-allegorical potential of the Morality play. As can be seen in *The Tide Tarrieth No Man* (1576), the early modern loosening of fixture in the semiotics of allegory went hand in hand with new "contrarious" openings in the strategy of dramatic representation. In early modern narrative the largely immutable gap (an "abyss,"[15] Walter Benjamin called it) in allegory between figurality and meaning gave way to a dynamic, often ironic, highly mobile, non-dualistic relationship between signifier and signified. As I have shown elsewhere, in Erasmus, Rabelais, Sidney, and Nashe, the gap between what was said and what was meant began to be filled by a dance-like movement between closure and rupture.[16] Similarly, in medieval drama, the structure of allegorical personifications had remained fixed in its dualism as long as the principle of psychomachia was strong enough to marshal a moral universe in terms of a strictly controllable, consistent order of fixed values. But then the performative energy of the Vice by itself tended, at least partially, to transform and empty out from within the element of correspondence between these oppositions and their allegorical extensions. Shakespeare, already taking for granted the suspension of metaphysical dualism in allegorical drama, uses a thoroughly secularized, revitalized version of the Vice as a visceral kind of leavening by which to expand the gap between what was said and what was meant.

In *King John*, this gap, as never before, is projected into a strangely groping, troublesome representation of the world and the self. Part of our difficulties with the play lies in its movement by fits and starts, the absence in it of any easily discernible design. But this crisscrossed movement, and the Bastard's response to it, must appear deliberate as soon as we recognize, in Walter Cohen's pointed phrase, that "the logic of the plot is to undermine logic, to frustrate expectation, to reveal the uncertain relation between intention and outcome in a world that offers only fragments of an overarching religious consolation for the frequent futility of human endeavor."[17] If, throughout the play, the 'meaning' of events remains more or less puzzling, the uses of characterization respond in kind. As in the Angiers sequence, the marching to and fro of two kings and their armies almost paradigmatically establishes an order that brings forth Nothing. As elsewhere in the play, the purposive activities of characters, their grand schemes and strategies, are strangely thwarted, even pointless. As Emrys Jones notes, in "such sequences as this, activity itself seems to be mocked: The great ones, who posture on the stage of the world, and who think themselves free and self-determining agents, are incapable of achieving anything."[18]

Once the world of the play comes to resemble a game marked by pointless fits and starts, the gap between what is said and what is done (and what is meant) becomes constitutive of a new type of (dis)order in both language use and emplotment. Here, the pervasive infiltration of contingency is crucial, in that it affects both resolution and motivation, action and events. Between them, the high Renaissance "mould of form" (*Hamlet*, 3.1.153), the mirror of proportion, "modesty," and discretion, the image of what should be, are all lost sight of. As a ruthless alternative, the awareness of futility and contingency enters into an alliance with the compromising (though not, in itself, compromised) pragmatism of the first-person singular. In its opportunistic, ambivalent response to "commodity," the emerging self-conscious "I" is fairly remote from the high Renaissance image of man and the idealizing postulate of a consortium of speaking and doing. As an illegitimate offspring and anomalous commentator on an unprincipled society, the Bastard is locked in between criticism and commodity, his own self serving as an unadulterated vessel of both contrariety and opportunity, one deeply torn between serving the times as well as his country *and* playing the game of "I am I" (1.1.174), as these times go.

Against this larger constellation, it should come as no surprise that the emergent first-person singular actually thrives in a context marked by reckless self-reliance, bodily energy, nonsensical speech, and a cultural semiotics of unsettling instability in relations of words, deeds, and meanings. Here, we cannot but recall Richard Gloucester's "I am myself alone" (*3 Henry VI*, 5.6.83), with its early linkage between socio-spatial distance and a downstage sense of theatricality ("as if the tragedy / Were play'd in jest by counterfeiting actors"—2.2.27–28). This linkage, I suggest, provides a seminal site wherever in the figure of the Vice-descendant theatricality and apartness come together. There is a paradox in this conjuncture between the *platea*-associated vehicle of evil sport and (traditional) game, on one hand, and the socio-spatial isolation as conducive to a (modern) sense of emergent selfhood, on the other. The contradiction in question, however, is of great consequence as a site on which, in Shakespeare's theater, a unique shaping power is at work in aid of a newly unstable perspective on a 'forlorn' relationship between the world and the self. Again, this power is best adumbrated where "deformity" (even in the shape of "commodity") works, contradictorily, as both source and outcome of untold dramatic energies. Thus, "deformity" can "mock," invert, and help

> To disproportion me in every part,
> Like to chaos, or an unlick'd bear-whelp
> That carries no impression like the dam.
> (3 *Henry VI*, 3.2.160–62)

There is a similar formlessness, an unshaped "bastard" fold in Faulconbridge's unstable makeup, similar to those bear whelps that, in Elizabethan lore, were believed to be born as formless lumps, only later to be licked into some shape. Although the Bastard is exceptional in that—unlike Richard Gloucester—he makes good, his point of departure is not totally unlike that of the latter in 3 *Henry VI*.

> And I—like one lost in a thorny wood,
> That rents the thorn, and is rent with the thorns,
> Seeking a way, and straying from the way,
> Not knowing how to find the open air
> But toiling desperately to find it out—
> (174–78)

Although, of course, the analogy between Faulconbridge and Gloucester has obvious limitations, both characters exemplify a strenuous need to perform, "toiling desperately" to play a role, "to find it out," and, for better or worse, to take up arms against a thorny world. Both share a moment of "vast confusion," as in the Bastard's anguished outcry,

> I am amaz'd, methinks, and lose my way
> Among the thorns and dangers of this world.
> (4.3.140–41; 152)

The echo—losing one's way among thorns—may perhaps be fortuitous, but the sentiment points to a new, intense and mutually painful interaction between the self and the social, culminating in an aggressive endeavor that "rents the thorn" even while the intervening medium itself is "rent" by "thorny" circumstances that tear and split whatever identity or agency is at work here. It is some such disillusioned sense of being "lost" in a role-playing game of apartness that serves as an important matrix for exceptional uses of selfhood. The Bastard in *King John*, exemplifying these uses, harps on the first-person singular. As Honigmann has shown in his edition of the play, with Philip entering early in Act I, "the pronoun I is used fifty-eight times, fifty-one times by Faulconbridge" (6). There is a connection, it seems, between the Bastard's self-reliance and his insecurity in the wake of his release from lineage ties and bonds of family and fealty, from "Legitimation, name, and all." Such release is especially strong where a lusty spirit—Richard and Edmund, no less than Faulconbridge—feels himself authorized to realign "Exterior form" and "inward motion" and—in doing so—suspend another chain of predesigned correspondences. Hence, the Bastard's impertinent "And so am I, whether I smack or no" points in a direction where the stubborn sense of an unrelenting, pushing self outrageously asks to be admitted to the ranks of "worshipful society." It is as if "degree, priority, and place," together with "proportion, season, form" (*Troilus and Cressida*, 1.3.85–86) and, of course, discretion and decorum need to be discarded before the new self with its "appetite [. . .] seconded by will and power" (121–22) can take over.

Thus, in a virulent context of verbal, moral, sexual, and social disruption, the memory of the Vice spawns a reckless type of subjectivity:

> And have is have, however men do catch.
> Near or far off, well won is still well shot,
> And I am I, how'er I was begot.
> (*King John*, 1.1.173–75)

The complicity between age-old topsy-turvydom and threefold iteration of the first-person singular is remarkable. Unleashing the ties to the preordained meaning of his one-time iniquity, the descendant of the Vice turns his sardonic sense of sublunary relations to (another pun) the sexually charged praise for an accurate shot. As is the case with Edmund, the private "stealth of nature" and the social cast of contingency are lusty bedfellows, especially when it comes to populate the world with "rising spirits." Somewhere between "outward accoutrement" and "inward motion," but certainly along the complex cultural semiotics residing in the site of their male-gendered interaction, the early modern dramatic male-gendered self emerges—snatching, against "the plague of custom," for himself status and privilege.

The reasons why Shakespeare, in marked contrast to his probable source play, The Troublesome Reign of King John, saw fit to introduce as catalyst into his play a figure as sourceless as the Bastard[19] are worth pondering. To judge by his dramatic function, Faulconbridge, though positively moving toward taking the lead in the struggle for the early modern nation-state, cannot be subsumed under the discursive design of historiography. It seems that Shakespeare's mode of assimilating on "unworthy" scaffolds "the worthiness of the matter itself" called for a strong performative with which effectively to contain the elements of closure and homogeneity that patterned the discourse of history. The dramatist did so, even when, according to recent revisionist readings of Holinshed (those of, for instance, A. R. Braunmuller, Larry S. Champion, and above all, Annabel Patterson), the latter was, politically speaking, far from univocal.[20] Clearly, the Bastard, at least in the early parts of the play, is made to perform at the frontiers of historiographical representation. In Braunmuller's phrase, he "is both a reader of the text of history and part of that text." As a "reader," he is someone who, again from a distance, seeks to appropriate for himself, and make sense of, the "text of history." As "outsider to many of the play's overt concerns—law, family, politics—he embodies the playwright's own practical need for an analytical consciousness and offers a focus for unifying disparate, uninterpreted events."[21]

We do not need to dismiss the Bastard's structuring function in the play text to realize that this cannot be the exclusive *raison d'etre* behind his adaptation. While the unifying and the unified quality of the Bastard's function can be exaggerated, the important point is that Shakespeare's response to the problems of dramatizing the "worthiness of the matter itself" in Tudor historical discourse called for a theatrically effective, at least partially countervailing medium, for which the hybrid descendant of the Vice offered itself. There must have been an intriguing connection between the memory of the extra-dramatic function of the Vice as leader, director, and master of ceremonies on the "unworthy scaffold" and the need to dramatize, revise, and reauthorize in a post-Reformation context the text of a particularly remote chronicle history. It may well have been the need for the sheer power to enliven and perform things; the "terrific energy," in Michael Goldman's words, of an actor/character who "both is and is not himself";[22] the conjuncture of a presentational and representational gestus; the inscribed penchant for both mobility and (in)stability; in a word, the principle of contrariety itself, which predestined a bastard figure like Faulconbridge—"an old-young, legal-illegal, royal-common, male-female oxymoron"[23]—for this function.

The Bastard, of course, is not the only agent in the play who helps rewrite and reread a remote past in the light of Elizabethan concerns. Critics have drawn attention to the astonishing degree to which historical narrative is manipulated in order to underline a groundswell of analogies between the reign of John and that of Elizabeth I. But on top of the inevitable anachronism in the composition of the play, the Bastard serves as a vital medium in the conflation of past significance and performed meaning. As Emrys Jones persuasively argues, the Bastard—standing "with one foot in history, the other in myth"—appeals "to a deep layer of audience-memory"; through him, "Shakespeare makes his audience reach back into *its* past for an idea of someone larger than life yet life-size." Along these lines, the Bastard, acting "as a critic and commentator," even serving as some "spectator-surrogate," is "both inside and outside society, just as he is both inside and outside the play."[24]

Such anachronism, in conjunction with a stance of liminality, marks the Bastard's protean function in the play. Simultaneously, he can provoke and proscribe, instigate and decry, tempt and denounce, as he does in his speech on "Sweet, sweet, sweet poison" (itself an oxymoron) and "Mad world, mad kings, mad composition." His double-dealing culminates in the "wild counsel" to unite with the enemy to destroy the object of rivalry, and then, "That done, dissever your united strengths" so as to attack each other (2.1.372–95). In other words, the Bastard—precisely because he erupts into the play as someone from without the text of historiography—can be used as an "artificial person"[25] who "himself," but in the absence of a stable self, "shall unfold at large" the dramatized matter of chronicle history. Here, in conclusion, to quote again from Marlowe's prologue to *2 Tamburlaine*, is to suggest the scope, but also the irresistible sweep in the Bastard and his performing gestus: spanning both the fond "conceits" of "rhyming mother wits" and the "tragic glass" of early modern selfhood and contingency, Faulconbridge can draw on an incommensurable font of contrariety and thereby reject the early Marlovian alternative, with its arrogant claim to "lead" spectators away from greatly gaped-at actors' voices and bodies. The Bastard can serve as a catalyst of diverse assimilations precisely because he is at the point of intersection where the language of representation and the medium of presentation (and theatrical self-assertion) interact and through this interaction mutually transform one another. As "the worthiness of the matter itself" and the agents of production and reception engage one another, the mingling of Vice and history is one way of sounding the use and abuse of distance between dramatic representations and the circumstantial world and validity of their transaction.

Notes

I wish to thank William West for extremely helpful comments and suggestions on this essay.

1. Christopher Marlowe, *Tamburlaine the Great*, ed. J. S. Cunningham, "The Revels Plays" (Manchester: Manchester University Press, 1981). This is the text from which I continue to cite Marlowe's prologues and Richard Jones' preface. In what follows, my main text is, unless otherwise noted, *The Riverside Shakespeare*, ed. G. Blakemore Evans (Boston: Houghton Mifflin, 1997^2).

2. In the present context, the question of the date of *King John* is important, in that it implicates *The Troublesome Reign* as, possibly, a text, independently adapted for performance, even a politically motivated "propaganda piece," though "not exactly a bad quarto" (L. A. Beaurline). But in my approach I reject this all-too tempting scenario and follow the traditional dating, despite E. A. J. Honigmann's and Beaurline's not unpersuasive argument in favor of 1590/91. Cf. *King John*, ed. Honigmann, "The Arden Shakespeare" (London: Methuen, 1954), esp. xviii–xxv, liii–lviii; *King John*, ed. Beaurline, "New Cambridge Shakespeare" (Cambridge: Cambridge University Press, 1990), 194–210; cit. 206). For a recent debate on the question—crucial in dating the play—whether or not *The Troublesome Reign* preceded *King John*, see Sidney Thomas, in *Shakespeare Quarterly* (37 [1986], 98–100) and the exchange between Honigmann, Paul Werstine, and Thomas, ibid., 38 (1987), 125–30, on the interpretation of "documentary links"— mainly, a stage direction—in establishing precedence. See also, Guy Hamel, "King John and The Troublesome Raigne. A Reexamination," in *King John. New Perspectives*, ed. Deborah T. Curren-Aquino (Newark: University of Delaware Press, 1989), esp. 41, 58, note 2; and Brian Boyd, "King John and The Troublesome Raigne: Sources, Structure, Sequence," in *Philological Quarterly* 74 (1995): 37–56. In the question of sequence, A. R. Braunmuller's consideration that the better stylistic, metrical, critical, and historical circumstantial evidence is in favor of *King John* postdating *The Troublesome Reign* seems to me, if not ultimately the last word, the most persuasive answer we have. See *The Life and Death of King John*, ed. Braunmuller, "The Oxford Shakespeare" (Oxford: Clarendon Press, 1989), 15.

3. See Alan C. Dessen, *Shakespeare and the Late Moral Plays* (Lincoln: University of Nebraska Press, 1986) 18–23; 137–38; 162–63, who lists "a wealth of allusions to the Vice" (21).

4. Second Interlude, 14–15; see *Ben Jonson*, ed. C. H. Herford, Percy and Evelyn Simpson, 11 vols. (Oxford: Clarendon Press, 1925–52), 6:323.

5. On the genealogy of the Bastard, see *King John*, ed. John Dover Wilson (Cambridge: Cambridge University Press, 1936), xxxix–xli; Honigmann, Arden edition, xxii–xxv; as well as other editors. Further, Richard Levin, "King John's Bastard," *The Upstart Crow* 3 (Fall 1980): 22–41. What deserves to be underlined is the multivocal nature of the Bastard's presence in the play, as discussed by Michael Manheim, "The Four Voices of the Bastard?" (*"King John": New Perspectives*, 126–35). In the present context, however, the most consequential division in his "purpose of playing" is between his presentational and representational cast—conveniently summed up by Alexander Leggatt as "an unmistakable amalgam of participant and commentator" ("Dramatic Perspective in *King John*," *English Studies in Canada* 3 [1977]: 15–16). On the seminal dimension of the Bastard, see Emrys Jones, *Scenic Form in Shakespeare* (Oxford: Clarendon Press, 1971), esp. 99–101,185–86, 239–42.

6. See James E. May, "Imagery in Disorderly Motion in *King John*: A Thematic Gloss," *Essays in Literature* 10 (1983): 17–28.

7. Here, I use L. A. Beaurline's paraphrase, *King John*, 98 (line 574).

8. Christopher Z. Hobson, "Bastard Speech: The Rhetoric of 'Commodity' in *King John*," *Shakespeare Yearbook* 2 (1991): 95–114.

9. See *King John*, ed. Braunmuller, Appendix C, 286–89.

10. *The Macro Plays*, ed. Mark Eccles, EETS, 262 (London: Oxford University Press, 1969), 155, l. 54.

11. *Hyckescorner*; cit. *Specimens of the Pre-Shakespearean Drama*, ed. J. M. Manly, 2 vols. (Boston: Anthenaeum Press, 1987), 1:396; cf. ll. 309–25.

12. Francis Bacon, *The New Organon*, ed. Fulton H. Anderson (New York: Liberal Arts Press, 1960), 81.

13. *King John*, ed. Honigmann.

14. *King John*, ed. Braunmuller, 132.

15. Walter Benjamin, *Gesammelte Schriften*, ed. Rolf Tiedemann and Hermann Schweppenhauser (Frankfurt: Suhrkamp, 1974), 1.1:342; in the German original, the "abyss between figurate being and meaning" (my translation) is, literally, an *Abgrund*.

16. Weimann, *Authority and Representation in Early Modern Discourse*, 133–59.

17. Cohen, Introduction to *King John*; cf. *The Norton Shakespeare*, Stephen Greenblatt, gen. ed. (New York: Norton, 1997), 1015.

18. Jones, *The Origins of Shakespeare* (Oxford: Clarendon Press, 1997), 249.

19. See, however, Jacqueline Trace, "Shakespeare's Bastard Faulconbridge: An Early Tudor Hero," *Shakespeare Studies* 13 (1980): 59–69, where she says, "Shakespeare's Faulconbridge, originating in the figure of Philip of Cognac from Holinshed's *Chronicle*, developed from the dramatist's acquaintance with the Henrician Faulconbridge so closely associated with the antipapal policies of the Tudor princes" (68). But, then, the significance of these sources poses troublesome questions.

20. See Braunmuller, "*King John* and Historiography," *English Literary History* 55 (1988): 309–22, who finds that both "Shakespeare and Holinshed wrote confusing texts because each believed that confusion was not sedition" (318). As no one else before, Annabel Patterson has shown "the surprising commitment of the *Chronicles* to the underprivileged, the demotic, the untitled"; *Reading Holinshed's "Chronicles"* (Chicago: University of Chicago Press, 1994), xv.

21. *King John*, ed. Braunmuller, 697–71.

22. Goldman, *The Actor's Freedom: Toward a Theory of Drama* (New York: Viking Press, 1975), 7, 11.
23. *King John*, ed. Braunmuller, 72.
24. Jones, *Origins of Shakespeare*, 249, 252, 247.
25. This recalls J. Leeds Barroll's *Artificial Persons: The Formation of Character in the Tragedies of Shakespeare* (Columbia: University of South Carolina Press, 1974)—a phrase that appears especially felicitous in view of the hybrid construct that is the Bastard's character. In this direction, we do well to ponder on the warning contained in Steve Longstaffe's essay, "The Limits of Modernity in Shakespeare's *King John*," *Shakespeare and History*, ed. Holger Klein and Rowland Wymer (London: Edwin Mellen Press, 1996), 91–118.

The Language of Treason in *Richard II*

Dermot Cavanagh

I

Postwar criticism of *Richard II* characteristically has addressed its portrayal of "the secularization of politics . . . paralleled by the commercialization of the word."[1] The play is often perceived as describing the transition from a medieval political ethos to early modern conditions. In depicting the violent extinction of Plantagenet monarchy, *Richard II* also distinguishes the ascendancy of Lancastrian pragmatism, setting a "divinely sanctioned monarch against Machiavellian 'new man' whose power resides exclusively in his own will."[2] In particular, the language of *Richard II* has been identified as expressing this shift from a world which assumes political values are divinely ordained, to one dominated by the functional pursuit and maintenance of power. In James Calderwood's influential account of "the fall of speech," the play represents "the surrender of a sacramental language to a utilitarian one in which the relation between words and things is arbitrary, unsure and ephemeral."[3]

However, increasingly telling questions have been raised concerning the adequacy of this interpretation of the play and the kinds of political recognition it advances. Joseph A. Porter reminds us that there are a variety of idioms in *Richard II*, which qualify any reception of, and identification with, the monarch's: "What falls after all, is only Richard's speech—his conception of language—not as he [Calderwood] would have it, 'Speech' itself."[4] More recent criticism has been similarly attentive to the range and ambivalence of *Richard II*, as well as its sympathy for the language and values of those who challenge the integrity of Richard's "sacramental" speech and bring about his deposition. The play's notable utility for the Essex rebels has inflected historicist readings of its theatricality as demystifying, subverting dominant conceptions of political obedience.[5] From this perspective, *Richard II* is held to envision the "medieval past not as a lost world of symbolic unity but as the scene of a continual struggle between aristocratic and constitutional liberties and a monarchy that kept trying to appropriate public resources for its private interests."[6] The stress on parliament as the context for the deposition scene, as well as its striking absence from the three Elizabethan quartos of the play, has been interpreted by Cyndia Susan Clegg, as endorsing "an authority over the monarch far more consonant with resistance theory than with the government's understanding of parliamentary authority."[7]

Such distinct critical emphases are expressive of the ambivalence created by the play's opposing perspectives, and these can be analyzed in terms of their shared concern with defining treason. Any political reading of *Richard II* involves an evaluation of treachery, emphasizing either Richard's or Bolingbroke's betrayal of fundamental obligations; the play foregrounds this issue. In *Richard II*, "treason" and cognate words appear with greater frequency than in any other Shakespeare play, and its principal conflict might well be characterized as a struggle over the authority to define the offense.[8] In a play peculiarly devoid of realized action, its language is dominated either by the attribution or the evasion of the stigma of treachery; virtually every significant dramatic episode is constructed around purported breaches of trust, and most characters are depicted as implicated in or, at the very least, reacting to such violations. Specifically, formal accusations of treason provide an induction into the distinct regimes presided over by Richard and Bolingbroke, and the adjudication of these helps decipher their respective strategies of governance, as well as the forms of opposition they arouse. The drama culminates, of course, with the defining actions of high treason: the deposition and assassination of a monarch.

What is distinctive to *Richard II* is not simply the centrality of treachery to its political exchanges, but the inquisitiveness with which competing formulations of the offense are considered. However vehemently treason is ascribed within the play, evidence is rarely constituted in a definitive way. Thus, Bolingbroke and Mowbray charge each other with treachery without the audience being able to judge who is telling the truth. Later in the play, Richard's adherent, Aumerle, is, in turn, accused of treason against Bolingbroke in a manner that is equally difficult to appraise. Moreover, such ambiguities over identifying the figure of the traitor are accompanied by uncertainties in defining treason. It can thus be depicted as the violation of honor and fealty (as Bolingbroke forcibly asserts in the play's opening) or, primarily, an offense against the king's person and will (as King Richard and, later, the Bishop of Carlisle believe). It can be apprehended as a violent action or as a form of corrupt speech (as Mowbray argues in his defense against Bolingbroke, a view adopted by his opponent as he assumes the crown). The play's structure is reflexive and dynamic, rather than being organized in a sequence or in terms of a definitive historical transition; it is through the shifting configuration of treason thus generated that some of *Richard II*'s most daring political speculations can be discerned.

Rather than expressing either a singular or a antithetical conception of treason, *Richard II* is characterized by a relational or, more accurately, dialectical approach, in which treason is viewed as dependent on modulations in authority, finding meaning only in relation to the sovereignty it would help establish or undermine. If opposition to King Richard is "gross rebellion and detested treason" (2.3.108)—and Richard, of course, will see himself in his resignation of the crown as "a traitor with the rest" (4.1.248)—once Bolingbroke is crowned, opposition to his rule is, in turn, no less treasonous: Aumerle is, even to his father, guilty of "foul treason" (5.2.72).[9] Betrayal appears not as an incontrovertible act which distinguishes the faithful subject from those doomed by their corrupt ambition, but as a far more conditional offense. By locating its attributions of treason within mutating historical circumstances, the play elucidates the political conflicts intrinsic to such allegations. Repeatedly, treachery is defined in the struggle to constitute or diminish authority, and by the language used to substantiate this; as such, it can be modified, contested, and redefined in relation to varying claims of legitimacy. One can conceive of the play's "ambivalence," then, in the terms suggested by a recent analysis of the dialectical method of Machiavelli's writing: as engaged in an "internal critique of positive claims to authority."[10]

One obvious influence on, and context for, these fluctuations in the play's representation of treason lies with its major source, the 1587 edition of Holinshed's *Chronicles*. In reinterpreting the inclusiveness of Holinshed—as well as the work's organizing commitments to constitutional government and an ethic of civic prudence—Annabel Patterson argues that a form of "early modern relativism" emerges in its account of the historical formation of treason, an attitude symptomatic of its "critical perspective on 'Law' as a set of socially and politically constructed rules, rules that particularly at this stage in history were subject to sudden and continuous change."[11] This helps in both identifying and interpreting one of the most noticeable features of Holinshed's treatment of the turbulent reign of Richard II: how treason is made to accommodate changes in the disposition of power, rather than embody a consistent concept of justice.

In its detailed narration of the struggle between royal and baronial parties, the attribution of treason and the resistance it provokes help structure Holinshed's account: it is the instrumental means by which factional ascendancy is secured and (temporarily, at least) maintained. The text, however, is notably reluctant to denote any stable conception of treachery; it is, consistently, a matter of perspective. This is expressed in Holinshed's recurrent citation of treason accusations with an accompanying phrasal qualification: "whom they called traitor," "those whom they reputed to be traitors," "whom he tooke to be plaine traitors," "traitors (as they tearmed them)."[12] Here, treason is situated rhetorically, located in conflicting and partisan attempts to validate authority.

An economical example of Holinshed's pragmatic view of treachery is demonstrable in the account given of the events that lead to Richard's attack on two pivotal figures in the baronial opposition: the abduction and covert assassination of the Duke of Gloucester, which so substantially informs the action of Shakespeare's play, and, simultaneously, the trial and execution of the Earl of Arundel. In 1388, the king dissolves a statutory council of state, which maintained an "ouersight under the king of the whole gouernment of the realme" (2:776), imposed on him by his magnates. Richard and his advisors exert extraordinary pressure on a council of judges to have those responsible for this body deemed treasonable and to agree on an elaborate defense of the king's prerogative: "it was demanded of them how they ought to be punished that interrupted the king so, that he might not exercise those things that apperteined to his regalitie and prerogatiue. Whereunto answer was made, that they ought to be punished as traitors" (2:782). In response, the baronial party "gathered their power togither, determining to talke with the king with their armour vpon their backes" (2:784). They demand, by issuing a feudal challenge, the expulsion of those advisors who are responsible for such a treacherous abuse of legal process, insisting Richard "take awaie from him such traitors as remained continuallie about him. . . . And to prooue their accusations true, they threw downe their gloues, protesting by their oths to prosecute it by battell" (2:787). Despite his initial acquiescence, the king continues to conspire against the lords and succeeds in having Gloucester forcibly removed from the realm and assassinated (2:836–37) and secures a trial, in parliament, of the Earl of Arundel for treasonably taking up arms against his authority. When the king's favorite, Bushy, articulates the "demand" of the Commons that Arundel's guilt be punished, his mordant reply provokes the same theatrical display of outraged feudal honor deployed earlier against the king's favorites:

> The earle turning his head aside, quietlie said to him; "Not the kings faithfull commons require this, but thou, and what thou art I know." Then the eight appelants standing on the other side, cast their gloves to him, and in prosecuting their appeale (which alreadie had beene read) offered to fight with him man to man to justifie the same" (2:841).

What is noticeable in this treatment of treason is its reversibility; the same ritualistic means of proving the offense can be used either for or against royal power. Arundel (as well as Gloucester) can appear as agents in the definition of treason and as traitors. For Holinshed, betrayal can be both a corruption of the law that should protect subjects or an encroachment upon the royal prerogative; any consensus over what is unpardonably illicit is not secured. Treachery is a medium in which antagonistic interests are expressed, and it provides a language in which particular claims of authority are made to appear provisional. As Arundel's case demonstrates, the discursive status of the offense means it can be exposed as partial and contingent. Holinshed's text is alert, even in a sardonic manner, to the interests that inform public speech, political displays, and legal procedure. None of the latter is free of political mediation, a feature which is registered most powerfully, in that both the object and the nature of treason can be redefined in the enforcement or modification of sovereignty. Significantly, this is equally true at all stages of the historical process he represents; there is no palpable sense of a transition between distinct modes of authority. For Holinshed, treason is given static form alone according to the needs of specific circumstances. It is this conception of the offense that has significant consequences for the dialectical construction of *Richard II*. This relationship between the language of treason and the dynamics of authority is equally integral to Shakespeare's play; its implications merit detailed scrutiny.

II

At the opening of *Richard II*, an explicitly feudal discourse is established in the attempted trial by combat between Bolingbroke and Mowbray who perceive treason in terms of the obligations, and rights, of subjects in relation to the code of honor. It is this that Richard abrogates by correlating treachery with his own person and will. This monarchical conception of treason, however, is revised by those opposed to his rule; moreover, an audience learns quickly of the cynical pragmatism with which Richard exploits the judical and other prerogatives of his office (1.4). This modified evaluation of the sovereignty of the king's speech is rendered distinctively through the play's treatment of betrayal, especially in relation to Bolingbroke who, on his illicit return to the realm, deploys a tactical language in which the distinctions between treasonous and loyal sentiments are no longer clear. Bolingbroke's flexibility of speech proves his political versatility, yet the rhetorical maneuvering it demands is also subjected to critical examination and not only as a dilution of his earlier commitment to honor. In its later phase, the play demonstrates that his usurpation fosters the subsequent prosecution of treason committed in words, an offense with which he had earlier been charged, as much as in actions: this definition finds new significance in the light of Bolingbroke's own actions. Rather than arrange its conflicting registers of speech in a hierarchy, *Richard II* stages these as mutually qualifying. Each figure who claims political credibility and, ultimately, authority, derives this from the ascription of treachery; however, the rhetorical status of such claims are simultaneously perceived in terms of an alternative conception of betrayal.

From the outset, *Richard II* depicts a struggle concerning the power to define treason, and an argument is rehearsed over the principles it validates.[13] Significantly, in the conflict between Bolingbroke and Mowbray, any affiliation with a controlling viewpoint, including that of the crown, is obstructed, in that the appellants are opposed on broadly equal terms. Moreover, informing this irresolution in discerning the traitor is a far more profound inability to identify the nature of treachery. The dissension of the appellant knights is based on an expressed commitment to chivalric honor, which the king perceives as superseded by his own person; their competitive behavior embodies the "moral autonomy" of the honor code Mervyn James has made familiar in leaving "little room for the concepts of sovereignty, or of unconditional obedience."[14]

We can see this schism in the definition of treason emerging in the king's opening query to Gaunt, regarding Bolingbroke's motivations:

> Richard. Tell me, moreover, hast thou sounded him,
> If he appeal the Duke on ancient malice,
> Or worthily as a good subject should
> On some known ground of treachery in him?
> Gaunt. As near as I could sift him on that argument,
> On some apparent danger seen in him,
> Aim'd at your Highness, no inveterate malice.
>
> (1.1.8–14)

The king is already sensitive to Bolingbroke's sense of principle: the phrase "ancient malice" is dismissive both of an enduring feud with Mowbray and of its archaic expression. For Richard, the worth of "a good subject" is determined by his attitude toward treachery; and Gaunt, intriguingly, is unsure of his son's status. Here, as in the following scene, Gaunt expresses a conception of social relations familiar to Tudor sensibilities, in that betrayal is conceived of primarily as an intended assault on the king. This emphasis on the monarch's person as the supreme object of treason had long been ascendant in legislation; yet, in *Richard II*, the language of betrayal is not concentrated wholly on the king.[15]

The chivalric fervor with which Bolingbroke expresses his sense of profaned honor signifies his sense of treachery; any defilement of the privileges intrinsic to nobility is treason; even the mute element of blood speaks, or cries, with the force of scriptural injunction to avenge the injustice and dishonor committed by the murder of Gloucester. Mowbray:

> ... like a traitor coward,
> Sluic'd out his innocent soul through streams of blood,
> Which blood, like sacrificing Abel's, cries
> Even from the tongueless caverns of the earth
> To me for justice and rough chastisement;
> And, by the glorious worth of my descent,
> This arm shall do it, or this life be spent.
>
> (1.1.102–8)

There are unchivalrous connotations, of course, in the offenses attributed to his enemy: Mowbray has misused the public purse, embezzling for "lewd imployments" money intended for military pay and, in a wild accusation, has engineered all the conspiracies "for these eighteen years / Complotted and contrived in this land" (1.1.95–96). However, aside from such self-interest, cowardice and lack of knightly largesse, the core act of treason is Mowbray's desecration of blood for which the right of redress is claimed.

Bolingbroke does present his indictment of Mowbray as "a traitor and a miscreant" as an act of protective loyalty toward his king. The monarch and the realm must be protected from such a dangerous subject; this care issues from "the devotion of a subject's love, / Tend'ring the precious safety of my prince" (1.1.31–32). Yet, the rhetorical opportunity this affords him for a charismatic assertion of his own dynastic authority diminishes this care as a central motive; Bolingbroke acts under the sacred obligations entailed "by the glorious worth of my descent." His words are spoken under the hearing of God, rather than the king, and their truth will be testified to in a providential verdict elicited by his own will:

> ... for what I speak
> My body shall make good upon this earth,
> Or my divine soul answer it in heaven.
> . . . .
>
> With a foul traitor's name stuff I thy throat,
> And wish—so please my sovereign—ere I move,
> What my tongue speaks my right drawn sword may prove.
> (1.1.36–38; 44–46)

The fact that Richard's desires are here reduced to a parenthesis is consistent with Bolingbroke's acting as both the bearer of proof and the instrument of retribution. There is audacity in the correspondence drawn between the words he uses and their validation in the justice his body will enact.

Mowbray also addresses treason as a violation of honor. For him, it is Bolingbroke's speech that enacts this violation. In insisting that the allegations are made by a "slanderous coward," Mowbray indicts his opponent's words as issuing "from the rancour of a villain, / A recreant and most degenerate traitor" (1.1.143–44). Again, the physicality of the language is striking, as well as the forcible manner in which aristocratic honor is to be vindicated independently through the trial by combat. Mowbray will "prove myself a loyal gentleman / Even in the best blood chamber'd in his bosom" (1.1.148–49), a demand that outweighs the king's command:

> Myself I throw, dread sovereign, at thy foot;
> My life thou shalt command, but not my shame:
> The one my duty owes, but my fair name,
> Despite of death, that lives upon my grave,
> To dark dishonour's use thou shalt not have.
> I am disgrac'd, impeach'd, and baffl'd here,
> Pierc'd to the soul with slander's venom'd spear,
> The which no balm can cure but his heart-blood
> Which breath'd this poison.
>
> (1.1.165–73)

Here, Mowbray further intensifies the personal dimension of betrayal in his sense of the spiritual peril consequent upon obliterated knighthood. Similarly, Bolingbroke insists that he cannot obey Richard's command to forego resorting to arms against Mowbray; this would be a "deep sin", an injustice done to honor which he is obliged to rectify regardless of the king's will (1.1.187–95).[16]

Clearly, Richard is alert to the political implications of this shared language which transcends his own entitlement to obedience. This is apparent in his implied admonition to Bolingbroke as "our subject" (1.1.115–23) and in his reaffirmation of his "sceptre's awe" by countermanding the trial by combat. The king is determined to subsume the role of providence and resolve the issue of treason within his own judicial prerogative. Moreover, he offers a scathing commentary on chivalric justice and the equivalence it draws between honor and treachery. For the king, the "rites of knighthood" are merely an imposture, animated by a mixture of "eagle-winged pride / Of sky-aspiring and ambitious thoughts, / With rival-hating envy" (1.3.129–31). Richard perceives their martial display as a regressive and sectarian indulgence which threatens:

> To wake our peace, which in our country's cradle
> Draws the sweet infant breath of gentle sleep;
> Which so rous'd up with boist'rous untun'd drums,
> With harsh-resounding trumpets' dreadful bray,
> And grating shock of wrathful iron arms,
> Might from our quiet confines fright fair peace,
> And make us wade even in our kindred's blood—
> Therefore we banish you our territories.
>
> (1.3.132–39)

Richard insists on his possession of the kingdom—"our fields"; "our fair dominions"[17]—construing its welfare as that of an infant threatened by the clangor of feudal violence. The peace of the realm is individuated physically, and it is this which can be made subject to assault and betrayal. Richard's identity is symbiotic with that of his kingdom as the object of treason, and the king rebukes the knights as subjects whose primary duty is to obey his will.[18] The obsolescence of their conception of treachery is forcibly demonstrated, both in the peremptory sentences of banishment and in the arbitrary revision of Bolingbroke's exile, eliciting his stunned recognition of the power of words issuing from "the breath of kings" (1.3.213–15). Richard, then, initiates a process of great significance for the play: by displacing the authority that the appellant knights claim through treason, he establishes a critical perspective on the interests with which it is informed.

It is integral to the play's "internal critique" of authority, however, that the legitimacy of Richard's appropriation of treason is, in turn, qualified by those who dissent from it. Opposition to the monarch is not conflated with treachery; indeed, *Richard II* extends considerable latitude to those who perceive the king's actions as a destructive repeal of custom. The ethos whereby fealty and honor are primary forms of social obligation allows assumptions regarding obedience to be revised when it is the king who is responsible for their violation.[19] In the exchange between Gaunt and the bereaved Duchess of Gloucester that precedes the planned trial by combat, Gaunt's insistence on the submissiveness owed "God's substitute" must withstand powerful criticism from an alternative understanding of loyalty. For the Duchess, Gaunt's noble blood should reveal that his "patience" is equivalent to "pale cold cowardice," excusing Richard's involvement in her husband's assassination and inviting future annihilation (1.2.25–36). In another compelling metaphor of personification, the Duchess envisages Edward III's bloodline as a dynastic tree being "hack'd down," its destruction that of a living identity: "Yet art thou slain in him" (1.2.25).

Finally, Gaunt himself testifies to this understanding of Richard as betraying the values from which his royal authority is drawn. From Gaunt's historical perspective of an England governed by "true chivalry," it is the king who appears dishonorable and alien, enslaved to Italianate fashions, the flattery of favorites, and his own corrupt will. In the growing intensity of this condemnation, Richard's "England" is depicted as engaged in the conquest of itself, a paradox whose dreadful implications demands opposition (2.1.57–68). The culminating moment in Gaunt's verbal assault on Richard's status comes in his direct challenge to his continuing legitimacy:

the heroic spirit of Edward III is invoked as desiring the king's deposition even before his accession to the throne (2.1.104–8).[20] In a crushing formulation, he asserts that Richard has now effectively deposed himself—"Landlord of England art thou now, not king, / Thy state of law is bondslave to the law" (2.1.113–14)—a statement whose treasonous implications the king immediately recognizes (2.1.115–22).[21] Gaunt continues to subject the king's actions to corrosive rhetorical scrutiny, climaxing with the monstrous image of his pelican-like consumption of the slaughtered Gloucester's blood, "tapp'd out and drunkenly carous'd." After Gaunt's death, York continues this critique of Richard's entitlement to the throne, given his betrayal of "customary rights," embodied in Richard's confiscation of his brother's estate, and the discord this will arouse among "well-disposed hearts": "And prick my tender patience to those thoughts / Which honour and allegiance cannot think" (2.1.207–8).

York's desperation at reaching the limits of his fealty, at being brought to the brink of treason, brings us to a key episode in the play's developing concern with the effect of political crisis on existing social duties. The insecurity *Richard II* cultivates over a reliable definition of treachery is augmented when those opposed to the king's will further complicate attitudes to the offense by a subtle process of verbal arbitration: it is this that allows for the dissent repressed by York's sense of "honour" and "allegiance." In contrast to the often stark and declarative language that accompanies the play's earlier antipathies, Bolingbroke and his allies develop an equivocal mode of speech which can be adjusted tactically. Again, an awareness of the influence exerted by treason on the play's representation of conflict is useful in identifying how much verbal expedience is required to evade its ascription. Rather than establish feudal disenchantment as the principal challenge to Richard's betrayal of his office, the play attends, increasingly, to the strategic composition of language.

In the first stirrings of resistance against Richard, it is significant that—in the hostile reactions of Northumberland, Ross and Willoughby to Bolingbroke being "Bereft and gelded of his patrimony"—there is a growing sensitivity to the political implications of words:

> Ross. My heart is great, but it must break with silence,
> Ere't be disburdened with a liberal tongue.
> North. Nay, speak thy mind, and let him ne'er speak more
> That speaks thy words again to do thee harm.

> Will. Tends that that thou wouldst speak to the Duke of
> Herford?
> If it be so, out with it boldly man;
> Quick is mine ear to hear of good towards him.
>
> (2.1.228–34)

Once agreement has been reached to speak securely, their grievances can be rehearsed against the king's arbitrary rule and the consequent vulnerability of "our lives, our children, and our heirs" to factional whim. The dangerous logic of this critique of the "degenerate king" as a thief and a tyrant leads to a number of tactics to sustain both critical reflection and the actions that might accompany it. Thus, Northumberland's news of Bolingbroke's imminent return at the head of an armed party is introduced tactfully:

> ... even through the hollow eyes of death
> I spy life peering; *But I dare not say*
> *How near the tidings of our comfort is.*
>
> (2.1.270–72; italics added)

If Richard's regime is equated implicitly with death, this demands that the possibility of "life" be embraced; but, again, the consequences of such a choice are presented indirectly. Ross urges Northumberland to disclose his knowledge in terms of their shared desires; hence, it has the quality of thought, something unspoken: "Be confident to speak, Northumberland: / We three are but thyself, and, speaking so, / Thy words are but as thoughts; therefore be bold" (2.1.274–76). Richard's betrayals are used to sanction the development of a flexible idiom in which inhibitions against open criticism of the king are overcome. Richard, however, is not to be resisted explicitly: the effect of Bolingbroke's return is conveyed conditionally through discreet metaphors of freedom restored, guilt exposed, and honor renewed:

> If then we shall shake off our slavish yoke,
> Imp out our drooping country's broken wing,
> Redeem from broking pawn the blemish'd crown,
> Wipe off the dust that hides our sceptre's gilt,
> And make high majesty look like itself . . .
>
> (2.1.291–95)

This attentiveness to the accommodation of words and loyalties to new circumstances is present in Northumberland's elaborate compliment to the returned Bolingbroke's "fair discourse" (2.3.2–

18), a homage that is amply repaid: "Of much less value is my company / Than your good words" (2.3.19–20). It is striking that Bolingbroke's speech is now denuded of chivalric fervor and is characterized by politic insinuation. Those who rally to his cause are greeted warmly with oblique hints of the material advantage that will accrue from their loyalty (2.3.45–67). Of course, the perspective from which Bolingbroke's return to the realm, and his defiance of the king, are perceived as treachery does not disappear from the play. It is reintroduced punctually with York's angry imputation of his "gross rebellion and detested treason" (2.3.108). York's attack on his nephew's resort to arms is met by Bolingbroke's claim of a new status as the wronged "Lancaster" and an appeal to his uncle's sense of the outrageous violation of family honor: "I am a subject, / And I challenge law" (2.3.132–33). Bolingbroke's strategy is typified by this pragmatic arbitration; he does not formulate an alternative conception of treachery so much as amend York's dogmatism by revealing its limitations in the present context—a mitigation adapted, persuasively, to the needs of both his supporters and his opponents.

Bolingbroke proves expert in complicating the judgments made concerning his actions. In the dispatching of Bushy and Greene to execution, he takes pains to "unfold some causes of your death" to legitimize his assertiveness. The transgression against chivalric honor incurred by his dispossession is stressed, as well as his protective care for the monarch. The tacit implication, however, is that they are guilty of treason to Bolingbroke as instruments of Richard's corrupt will. The personal judgment they are subjected to enhances his right and status as "a prince by fortune of my birth, / Near to the king in blood" (3.1.16–17).[22] Again, Bolingbroke's speech is equivocal in having an implicit, but not exclusively critical, potential. Northumberland's "uncrowning" of the king in his curt reference to "Richard" (3.3.5–14) may betray many of the attitudes of those loyal to him, but such indiscretion is entirely alien to Bolingbroke's political tact. His public standing is increased by the use of suggestion: just as the king once sabotaged Bolingbroke's authority by superseding his chivalric entitlement to dispense justice, so "Lancaster" rhetorically depletes Richard's authority by tempering the monarchical concept of treason. In a remarkable speech, Bolingbroke delegates to Northumberland an address to Richard in which he uses the formulation "King Richard" on five occasions (3.3.31–67). At the outset, this testifies to the "allegiance and true faith of heart" that governs his loyalty to "his most royal person." Yet, this seemingly sacrosanct pledge is immediately qualified: it is contingent upon the repeal of his sentence and the restoration of his lands. What accompanies this is a threat of violence, the collocation of force with persuasion in Bolingbroke's political lexicon; his "stooping duty" is delivered alongside the retribution he will visit in a "crimson tempest" on the "fresh green lap of fair King Richard's land." In an informal coda, Bolingbroke engages in what appears to be an elaborate parody of Richard's imminent metaphorical projection of the "thund'ring shock" that should accompany their encounter:

> Be he the fire, I'll be the yielding water;
> The rage be his, whilst on the earth I rain
> My waters—on the earth, and not on him.
> March on, and mark King Richard how he looks.
> (3.3.58–61)

The profane potential of these words is given more implication by the seditious pun on "rain"; notably, Bolingbroke's response to the king's appearance is equally divested of reverence:

> See, see, King Richard doth himself appear,
> As doth the blushing discontented sun
> From out the fiery portal of the East,
> When he perceives the envious clouds are bent
> To dim his glory and to stain the track
> Of his bright passage to the occident.
> (3.3.62–67)

This satirical account of Richard's poetic, and political, self-conception dispenses with the king's charisma.[23]

The ambiguous implications of Bolingbroke's address help establish the grounds for his ascendancy; his strategic refusal to behave as a unified political subject makes manifest that absolute claims of authority can be subject to qualification and change.[24] Again in *Richard II*, the kernel of this strategy is formed by its relationship to treachery. Bolingbroke's linguistic cunning allows him to rebut Richard's charge, "That every stride he makes upon my land / Is dangerous treason" (3.3.92–93). By maintaining, principally through Northumberland, that his wants have a strictly limited scope—his own "infranchisement" and the restoration of his "lineal royalties"—Bolingbroke manages to assert simultaneously his own royal blood and his sense of justice, with what degree of good or bad faith, it is impossible to evaluate. Although Richard longs to "send / Defiance to the traitor, and so die" (3.3.130–31), his bitter resignation to "come at traitor's calls" recognizes the power of "King Bolingbroke."

III

As several have established, Shakespeare's interest in treason is intrinsic to his understanding of the distinctive practices of early modern authority. Historical study has demonstrated that treason statutes, and the trials and executions that accompanied them, were carefully regimented by Tudor governments: as many defendants pointed out, their prosecution acted to confirm an already assumed guilt.[25] The public exposure of the traitor was expected to reveal an adherence to the heinous beliefs itemized in the treason act of 1571: "that the Queene . . . is an Heretyke Schesmatyke Tyraunt Infidell or an Usurper of the Crowne" (13 Elizabeth c. 1). In the ritualized judgment and punishment of treason against the monarch, and in the citation of such procedures and their assumptions in other settings such as the theater, the populace were encouraged to absorb antipathies and inhibitions. However, there were significant debates in Tudor culture concerning both the impartiality of treason trials and the adequacy of the law itself, disputes whose implications are absorbed by both Holinshed and Shakespeare's play. In particular, there were marked differences concerning the status of verbal and written expression as proof of a treasonous temperament, the "transgressive imagining" Karen Cunningham has detailed as an innovatory mode of interpreting political betrayal.[26] Current critical thinking has interpreted treason not simply as a matter of external juridical control, but as a discourse that sought to influence political consciousness: "a tranquil and orderly society seemed to depend not merely upon the 'outward observance' and 'external conformity' of its subjects, but upon their 'heartfelt love' and 'sincere conviction'."[27]

Certainly the legislative pursuit of the "imagining" of treason had material effect on the conduct of late Elizabethan treason trials, where the majesty of sovereignty was testified to in the prosecution of words that might impede its prerogative. A representative case, proximate to Shakespeare's play, is the arraignment of Sir John Perrot, the Lord Deputy of Ireland in 1592.[28] This precisely reproduces the prohibitions against injurious forms of political reflection and expression, the treasonous "Pryntinge Wrytinge Cyphryng Speache Wordes or Sayinges," prohibited in the 1571 act. Perrot is "not charged with not executing her majesty's commandments, but with contemptuous speeches used against her majesty in the matter" (1319). His offense is proved by hostile interpretation of his irreverent words and the debased imaginings they express: "which imagination itself was in itself High-Treason, albeit the same proceeded not to any overt fact: and the heart being possessed with the abundance of his traitorous imagination, and not being able so to contain itself, burst forth in vile and traitorous Speeches, and from thence to horrible and heinous actions" (1318). As one witness defined it: "he spoke as though the kingdom were his own, and not the queen's" (1319).

Such a politically charged legal process, however, was subject to challenge. Catholic polemicists are an especially rich source of criticism of Elizabethan legal policy toward treason, as Curt Breight has noted.[29] An apposite example would be Cardinal Allen's parodic citation of the terms cited by Tudor treason law as, in fact, evidence of the truths the government sought to extirpate from public discourse: "she [Elizabeth] ys so notoriously knowne, termed and taken for an heretike, as well at home as abrode, that she was glad to provide by a special acte of parliament, that none should call her heretike, Schismatike, Tyrante, usurper, or infidell, under pain of highe treason."[30] The capacity to question the interests informing prosecutions for treason was widespread. Camden, for example, provides important evidence of a contemporary capacity to demystify the treason trial; his account of Perrot's indictment emphasizes how partisan motivations could operate under the guise of justice. Sir Christopher Hatton and a circle of Perrot's adversaries at court "laboured tooth and nayle to put him from his place, as a man over-proud. And so farre was the matter brought, that when they found an informer or two in *Ireland*, though *Hatton* were now dead, they called him in the moneth of April to his tryall, *Burghley* Lord Treasurer labouring to the contrary."[31] Even in the most carefully orchestrated arraignments, there could be volatile moments where the crown's evidence could be disputed by a competing account of its distorted and malevolent character. Essex questioned the motivations of those proceeding against him, accusing Cecil of treasonable sympathies for a Spanish succession: "I can prove thus much from sir Robert Cecil's own mouth; that he, speaking to one of his fellow-counsellors, should say, That none in the world but the infanta of Spain had right to the crown of England." The proof for Cecil's disaffection is based on verbal testimony, but a witness promptly testifies that he "never did hear Mr Secretary use any such words," and the distinction between treasonous and loyal speech is reaffirmed to Cecil's satisfaction: "The difference between you and me is great; for I speak in the person of an honest man, and you, my lord, in the person of a Traitor."[32]

In *Richard II*, language is consistently adduced as evidence of a character's treasonous disposition, from Richard's opening inquiry to Gaunt concerning his son's motivations; but the play is equally attentive to the historical and political necessities which accompany this. Even in the feudal atmosphere of the play's early scenes, Bolingbroke is accused of treacherous speech by his opponent, although the proof of this is to be decided in combat. However, there is a distinctive emphasis on the apprehension of verbal treachery that arises from the means Bolingbroke uses to assume the throne. Again, treason is identified as the key medium through which sovereignty is expressed (as well as challenged); the accession of the new king is commingled with that of Aumerle for the assassination of the Duke of Gloucester. Unquestionably, there is intention in this: reopening the circumstances surrounding Gloucester's death further besmirches Richard's authority and uncovers the corruption Bolingbroke has been impelled to contain. That the once-reviled Bagot is the chief—and, presumably, suborned—witness is another indication of the purpose of these events.

Bolingbroke initiates the proceedings against Aumerle:

> Now, Bagot, freely speak thy mind—
> What thou dost know of noble Gloucester's death,
> Who wrought it with the king, and who perform'd
> The bloody office of his timeless end.
>
> (4.1.2–5)

Significantly, the accusations that follow have little of the earlier chivalric insistence on the dishonor intrinsic to specific actions. The testimony is not simply evidence of a treasonable assault on a member of the royal family, but proof of his disloyal temperament. Bagot, and subsequently the appellant knights, recount their recollections of what Aumerle said:

> My Lord Aumerle, I know your daring tongue
> Scorns to unsay what once it hath delivered.
> In that dead time when Gloucester's death was plotted,
> *I heard you say* "Is not my arm of length,

> That reacheth from the restful English court
> As far as Callice, to mine uncle's head?"
> Amongst much other talk that very time
> *I heard you say that you had rather refuse*
> *The offer of an hundred thousand crowns*
> *Than Bolingbroke's return to England—*
> Adding withal, how bless'd this land would be,
> In this your cousin's death.
>
> (4.1.8–19; italics added)

Bagot's indictment resembles the protocols of the Elizabethan treason-trial: the reckless words of the accused prove his malicious ambition. Strikingly, given the character of Bolingbroke's earlier political strategy, Aumerle's treachery is proved by his equivocal language, his use of words which are an implicit claim of kingly stature and which culminate in the compassing of Bolingbroke's death.[33]

Despite Aumerle's attempts to discredit Bagot, he is repeatedly confronted with hostile accounts of his disloyal conversations and those of his confederates:

> By that fair sun which shows me where thou stand'st,
> *I heard thee say, and vauntingly thou spak'st it,*
> That thou wert cause of noble Gloucester's death.
> . . . .
>
> As I intend to thrive in this new world,
> Aumerle is guilty of my true appeal.
> Besides, *I heard the banished Norfolk say*
> That thou, Aumerle, did'st send two of thy men
> To execute the noble Duke at Callice.
>
> (4.1.35–37; 78–82; italics added)

Again—it is not simply what Aumerle, or Mowbray, is accused of saying—but also the "vaunting" manner in which it was spoken. It is difficult, however, to identify conclusive proof in this; the rhetorical nature of the allegations is palpable. Surrey, an apparently reliable witness, was also "in presence" during the disputed conversations; he testifies for the accused, and we have no evidence to evaluate the rival claims. Instead, the issue of Aumerle's treachery is displaced by the Bishop of Carlisle's shocking intervention to insist that the real enactment of treason has just been witnessed in Bolingbroke's sudden decision to "ascend the regal throne" (4.1.114–49). Carlisle reaffirms the political proprieties of speech—"I speak to subjects, and a subject speaks"—and the ordained hierarchy that has been violated by the deposition of "the figure of God's majesty." Carlisle's rival testimony continues to envisage what cannot be seen directly in his prophecy of the "tumultuous wars" that subsequently consume the kingdom, a form of seditious speculation which results in his immediate arrest for treason.

To help interpret this melee of accusation and counter-accusation, it is important to register again the investigative nature of *Richard II*'s treatment of authority. The play is alert to the origins of Bolingbroke's action against utterance as those of a protagonist inured to the adaptation of principle to necessity. Such a perspective sheds light on the new king's use of contrivance to consolidate his power, a tendency that is notoriously visible in Richard's subversive self-deposition. This scene is laden with inference concerning the imperative for an orchestrated spectacle compressed in Bolingbroke's terse instructions to: "Fetch hither *Richard*, that in common view / He may surrender; so we shall proceed / Without *suspicion*" (4.1.155–57; italics added). Again, there is a significant emphasis on verbal testimony; Richard's public resignation of the crown should naturalize Bolingbroke's authority by infusing it with both inevitability and rectitude. This tactical production of a criminal self is, of course, drastically undermined by Richard's poetic intensification of the deprivation to which he is being subjected and by his competing use of equivocal speech to imply that political interests exist within judicial procedures. Contrary to his penitent demeanor in Holinshed—where he reads out and signs, in public, the statement of his own deposition[34]—Richard refuses to confirm the legal forms that would guarantee his own subjection by using Bolingbroke's tactics of self-abnegation and indeterminate statement:

> Mine eyes are full of tears, I cannot see.
> And yet salt water blinds them not so much
> But that they can see a sort of traitors here.
> Nay, if I turn mine eyes upon myself,
> I find myself a traitor with the rest.
> For I have given here my soul's consent
> T'undeck the pompous body of a king;
> Made glory base, and sovereignty a slave;
> Proud majesty a subject, state a peasant.
>
> (4.1.244–52)

The groundlessness of Bolingbroke's authority appears in the absurdity with which the deposed king expresses his new loyalty (4.1.218–22). Richard divulges his understanding of the actual treason being committed: the "truth" of the scene is shown to be composed in the interests of new-made sovereignty. Partly, this is established by the historical process the audience has witnessed in the play with its conflicting formulations of treason. Bolingbroke's accession has been predicated on a reappraisal of social obligations that demonstrate his entitlement to act as a self-constituted source of authority. The consequence of this is that "King Bolingbroke" constrains the same kind of politically destabilizing speech which might qualify his own entitlement to power, specifically the use of insinuation to disclose the pragmatic origins of his jurisdiction (and which is deployed with such dialectical force by Richard).

Richard's coded ridicule is reinforced within the play by a new strain of absurdity in its closing phase. As a number of critics have argued, there is a strong taint of the ridiculous over Aumerle's involvement in the conspiracy against Bolingbroke.[35] Of course, it is the treason committed by Richard's imprisonment and killing that distances an audience from Bolingbroke's "new world." The sinister allusion that secures Richard's death embodies the same tactics of intimation that secured his authority. Just as Bolingbroke deployed a versatile political register in achieving power, so the play arouses a similarly fluid range of reactions to that authority. It is precisely this latitude that treason is being mobilized to regiment, but it is vulnerable to the conditional political insight that brought it into being. As the drama proves, such practical deliberation can also decipher the limitations, discontinuity, and defectiveness that validated its own ascendancy.

Still, in important respects, the foiling of Aumerle's plot is a tribute to the success of Bolingbroke's kingship and its impressive combination of toleration with force. Yet, there is a double-edged aspect to this. Partly, the incongruous nature of the conclusion is reinforced by its fugitive resemblance to the play's opening events: the accusations that accompany the preparations for Aumerle's trial by combat are also followed by an act of dispossession that questions the monarch's legitimacy, and this incurs another conspiracy against the king. The play appears to visit Bolingbroke with the return of intractable political problems. In light of the new king's earlier concern with the symptomatic appearance of disloyal expression, it is significant that Aumerle's offense is committed and betrayed by a piece of writing. Similarly, the scale of his treason is diminished by its manifest lack of sophistication, and its crassness is emphasized by its discovery in the York household.

This diminution in the efficacy of treason is connected both to the practice of Bolingbroke's sovereignty and the historical conditions that underpin it. York's impulse to betray his own son is a signal, in however serio-comic a fashion, of a compulsive loyalty derived from highly unstable circumstances. It is this which revokes his earlier allegiances both to Richard and to kinship and honor. Clearly, it is fundamental to Bolingbroke's success that he has transcended existing obligations and impressed on his new subjects the necessity of conformity to his will and maintenance of his favor. In identifying the recapitulation of events and situations in the play, it is significant that York's protective loyalty to the king is now expressed by both informing upon and then demanding the death of his son.[36] However, York's eloquent compassion for Richard in his public humiliation is juxtaposed to his abrupt, even insensate, commendation of the necessity that dictates they have become Bolingbroke's "sworn subjects" (5.2.37–40). The apprehension of Aumerle's conspiracy by his father continues to plot a dynamic relationship between treason and sovereignty as political quantities prone to alteration. More pressingly, there is an increasingly debased quality to the formation of loyalties. The obligation demanded by the new regime—embodying the easily recognizable injunction that to fail to report treason is itself treason—is rendered as disturbing and divisive and the reductive conception of honor to which York appeals has a similarly degraded aspect: "Mine honour lives when his dishonour dies, / Or my sham'd life in his dishonour lies; / Thou kill'st me in his life—giving him breath, / The traitor lives, the true man's put to death" (5.3.68–71). Such a tortuous set of paradoxes and inversions in the language of treason register the degree to which loyalty derives from a circumstantial historical process whose fluctuations are embodied in York.

In his final (as well as first) soliloquy, the imprisoned Richard II reflects on the extraordinary displacement that has deprived him of power. He summons up habits of thought that appear convincing, only to expose their partiality and limitation. Given the brute reality with which deposition has contradicted his own self-conception as a monarch, the king explores how any settled physical state can be overturned and how any process of thought is self-deceiving to the extent that it ignores the possibility of negation. Just as his ambitious fantasies of escape are canceled by the prison walls, so even "thoughts of things divine, are intermix'd / With scruples, and do set the word itself / Against the word" (5.5.12–14). Of course, the Duchess of York has just used the same phrase in berating her husband's cynical use of the term *pardon* to prevent the bestowing of pardon on Aumerle: "That sets the word itself against the word!" (5.3.120). This verbal formulation describes the subtle and pervasive dramatic process by which apparently self-consistent terms and concepts are qualified and divided against themselves in *Richard II*. As Richard acknowledges in the moments prior to his death, there is a painful correspondence between sovereignty and treason, as if one condition produces the other which haunts and dispossesses it: "Sometimes am I king, / Then treasons make me wish myself a beggar, / And so I am" (5.5.32–34). In a macabre, destructive way, treason and sovereignty depend on and describe each other, and such proximity is most strikingly manifested in rendering the other provisional: if a king can become a beggar, Richard has witnessed how a traitor can become a king. Like its soliloquizing protagonist, *Richard II* seems drawn to such paradoxical and inquiring modes in its consideration of political values, especially as they are established and contested through language. There is no starker instance of the questions the play has raised concerning the authority treason threatens and locates than in its final paradoxical spectacle of the new and treason-tainted king confronted by the body of the betrayed and the betrayer.

In a recent essay, David Norbrook argues that criticism of *Richard II* should attend more carefully to the motivations of the Essex conspirators and their revival of the play on the day before their rising: "the 1601 performance was a significant pointer to elements in the play's political rhetoric."[37] In conclusion, it is worth pursuing briefly this suggestion to reflect on the play's concern with treachery in relation to the rebellion with which it has long been associated. To modern sensibilities, the inclusiveness of the text, and the demands it makes for complex modulations in emotional and political response, render it a bizarre choice either for incendiary propaganda or for ideological material likely to strengthen rebellious resolve. If Mervyn James is correct, *Richard II* could hardly have offered the inspiration provided by John Hayward's *The First Part of the Life and Reign of King Henry IV* (1599), where "history became a field for the play of the heroic energy of the autonomous political will, seeking to dominate events by its command of the politic arts."[38] If the temperament of Essex has been accurately evoked—"a confused jumble of fears, rages, sly plottings and crude irrational outbursts of emotions, culminating in the tragic and dismal fiasco of the 8 February rebellion"[39]—it may be misguided to impute, either to the Earl or his circle, any subtlety of interest, beyond that of an apparently successful deposition, in the spectacle of Shakespeare's play.

However, if the interest of Essex and his followers in the history of Richard II is undoubted, their attitude toward it is less clear. When the Earl accused Robert Cecil of supporting a Catholic succession, he implied Cecil's sympathy for Robert Parson's notorious tract *A conference about the next succession* (1595). Parson's key argument for the Spanish claim was based on the legality of Richard II's deposition, and, hence, the primacy of the Lancastrian line, an argument Essex repudiates as treasonous.[40] As Paul Hammer points out, an emphasis on the military complexion of the circle has tended to simplify its nature, primarily by obscuring the Earl's erudition. His following was renowned as a center for intense, if hardly disinterested, scholarly inquiry, centered upon an "intellectually high-powered" secretariat, "a remarkable concentration of scholarly talent."[41] In this ethos, a more sophisticated rationale might be admitted for the conspirators' interest in Shakespeare's play, especially its disputative stance toward treason as a category relative to authority. The earl's complaint that his reputation was distorted by "the false glass of others' information"[42] certainly resonates with *Richard II*'s concern with the ensnarements of treason for public figures and the politically charged dynamics by which reputations are divested of, as well as invested with, integrity. Moreover, even the play's dialectical openness may have appealed to their demand for the right of unprejudiced judgment, an impartial appraisal of the often complex and misunderstood realities that could be obscured by the rhetorical flare of treason allegations. The fullness and lucidity with which *Richard II* considers the intensive political mediation intrinsic to the attribution of treason may have been the source of a more complex interest from the Essex circle in the fate of both its protagonists.

Notes

1. James L. Calderwood, *Metadrama in Shakespeare's Henriad: Richard II to Henry V* (Berkeley and Los Angeles: University of California Press, 1979), 32.

2. Barbara Hodgdon, *The End Crowns All: Closure and Contradiction in Shakespeare's History* (Princeton: Princeton University Press, 1991), 130.

3. Calderwood, *Metadrama*, p. 6.

4. *The Drama of Speech Acts: Shakespeare's Lancastrian Tetralogy* (Berkeley and Los Angeles: University of California Press, 1979), 43. For a similar critique of Richard's language, see Ronald R. MacDonald, "Uneasy Lies: Language and History in Shakespeare's Lancastrian Tetralogy," *Shakespeare Quarterly* 35 (1984): 22–39, esp. 22–30.

5. See, for example, David Scott Kastan's influential "Proud Majesty Made a Subject: Shakespeare and the Spectacle of Rule," *Shakespeare Quarterly* 37 (1986): 459–75. For a critique of such approaches, see Leeds Barroll, "A New History for Shakespeare and His Time," *Shakespeare Quarterly* 39 (1988): 441–64.

6. David Norbrook, "The Emperor's new body? *Richard II*, Ernst Kantorowicz, and the politics of Shakespeare criticism," *Textual Practice* 10 (1996): 329–57, 348–49.

7. "'By the choise and inuitation of al the realme': *Richard II* and Elizabethan Press Censorship," *Shakespeare Quarterly* 48 (1997): 432–48, 444.

8. "Traitor" occurs twenty-eight times in *Richard II*; there are thirteen uses of "treason." *Henry V* also has thirteen instances of the latter, although ten of these are concentrated in the "traitor's scene," 2.2. A number of recent essays have analyzed Shakespeare's interest in what one critic terms the "vast discourse of treason that became an increasingly central response to difficult social problems in late Elizabethan and early Jacobean London"; Curt Breight, "'Treason doth never prosper': *The Tempest* and the Discourse of Treason," *Shakespeare Quarterly* 41 (1990): 1–28, 1. For a range of recent discussions of Shakespeare's treatment of the motif, see Craig A. Bernthal, "Treason in the Family: The Trial of Thumpe v. Horner," *Shakespeare Quarterly* 42 (1991): 44–54; Karin S. Coddon, "'Suche Strange Desygns': Madness, Subjectivity, and Treason in *Hamlet* and Elizabethan Culture" in *Hamlet*, ed. Suzanne L. Wofford (New York: Bedford, 1994), pp. 380–402; Karen Cunningham, "Female Fidelities on Trial: Proof in the Howard Attainder and *Cymbeline*," *Renaissance Drama* NS 25 (1994): 1–31; Nina Levine, "Lawful Symmetry: The Politics of Treason in *2 Henry VI*," *Renaissance Drama* NS 25 (1994): 197–218. The most comprehensive historical account remains John Bellamy's *The Tudor Law of Treason* (London: Routledge & Kegan Paul, 1979); the same author provides further useful context in *The Law of Treason in the Later Middle Ages* (Cambridge: Cambridge University Press, 1970). See also, Lacey Baldwin Smith, *Treason in Tudor England: Politics and Paranoia* (London: Jonathan Cape, 1986); and G. R. Elton *Policy and Police: The Enforcement of the Reformation in the Age of Thomas Cromwell* (Cambridge: Cambridge University Press, 1972), 263–326. Mark Nicholls has produced some interesting recent analyses of the political conspiracies and treason-trials that accompanied James's accession to the English throne; see "Two Winchester Trials: the Prosecution of Henry, Lord Cobham, and Thomas, Lord Grey of Wilton, 1603," *Historical Research* 68 (1995): 26–48; "Treason's Reward: the punishment of conspirators in the Bye plot of 1603," *Historical Journal* 38 (1995): 821–42. His conclusion in the latter, 842, is conceived narrowly: "treason remained a personal crime, committed by individuals with often the pettiest, most idiosyncratic of motives—on occasion, indeed, with no perceptible motive at all."

9. All citations of *Richard II* refer to the Arden edition of *King Richard II*, ed. Peter Ure (London: Methuen, 1961).

10. Victoria Kahn, *Machiavellian Rhetoric: From the Counter-Reformation to Milton* (Princeton: Princeton University Press, 1994), 5.

11. Patterson, *Reading Holinshed's Chronicles* (Chicago: University of Chicago Press, 1994), 159. This comment is part of a valuable analysis of treason law in

relation to the significant, if highly anomalous, trial in 1554, of Sir Nicholas Throckmorton, 154–83.

12. These and all subsequent quotations are from *Holinshed's Chronicles*, ed. Henry Ellis, 6 vols. (London, 1807–8; repr. New York: AMS Press, 1965). These phrases occur on 2:738, 784, 791.

13. For an analysis of the blend of deference and aggression intrinsic to the judicial combat and its significance for Elizabethan concerns with the native rights of the nobility, see Richard C. McCoy, *The Rites of Knighthood: The Literature and Politics of Elizabethan Chivalry* (Berkeley and Los Angeles: University of California Press, 1989), esp. 1–27.

14. Mervyn James, "English politics and the concept of honour, 1485–1642," in *Society, Politics and Culture: Studies in early modern England* (Cambridge: Cambridge University Press, 1986), 308–415, 327.

15. Its most influential formulation is located in the famous statute of 1352, the progenitor of all subsequent legislation: "When a Man doth compass or imagine the Death of our Lord the King, or of our Lady his [Queen] or of their eldest Son and Heir" (25 Edward II 5 c. 2). The act was revised, audaciously, under Cromwell's auspices for Henry VIII in 1534, to emphasize the harm to majesty incurred by hostile "imagining"; those who "malicyously wyshe will or desyre by wordes or writinge, or by crafte ymagen invent practyse or attempte, any bodely harme to be donne or commytted to the Kynges moste royall personne" (26 Henry VIII c. 13). It was this thesis of treason that became the period's dominant formulation, and which was absorbed into the major component of Elizabethan legislation in 1571. For a historical analysis, see Bellamy, *Tudor Law*, esp. 31–34 and Elton, 263–92; for interpretations of its significance for Shakespearean theater, see Cunningham and Katharine Eisaman Maus, "Proof and Consequences: *Othello* and the Crime of Intention," in *Inwardness and Theater in the English Renaissance* (Chicago: University of Chicago Press, 1995), 104–27.

16. Robert Bartlett observes how the medieval trial by combat was a medium in which political differences between the aristocracy and the monarchy were expressed: "There are, then, signs in this period of a clash between rulers seeking to limit the duel and aristocracies jealous of their judicial authority and individual honour," *Trial by Fire and Water: The Medieval Judicial Ordeal* (Oxford: Clarendon Press, 1986), p. 126. Ute Frevert develops this point in ascertaining the political significance of the duel for the feudal aristocracy in ways pertinent to the play: "Instead of regarding their own honour as a mere derivative of that honour which was personified by the prince as ruler and master, the sense of honour of the aristocracy retained a residue of habitual freedom and self-determination, to which they lent expression by engaging in duelling," *Men of Honour: A Social and Cultural History of the Duel*, trans. Anthony Williams (Cambridge: Polity Press, 1995), p. 15.

17. Joseph Porter is acute on Richard's tendency to refer to his own public self when apparently speaking of collective issues: "throughout the play Richard generally uses 'we' to mean a public identity which exists in the perception, consciousness, and thought of his audience—that-which-is-perceived, as it is perceived by the public"; *Drama of Speech Acts*, p. 31.

18. Compare the insistence of the 1352 treason act: "that ought to be judged Treason which extends to our Lord the King, and His Royal Majesty" (25 Edward III 5 c. 2). Claire McEachern's remarks on the utility of personification in Elizabethan political discourse are also useful in interpreting "a vocabulary of the monarch's private identity in the service of corporate identity," "Henry V and the Paradox of the Body Politic," *Shakespeare Quarterly* 45 (1994): 33–56, 37.

19. Obviously, the early phase of the play is alert to the importance of political divisions within medieval society. Peter G. Phialas emphasizes the significance of Edward III's kingship as a contrast to Richard's corruption of the office; "The Medieval in *Richard II*," *Shakespeare Quarterly* 12 (1961): 305–10. More recently, Graham Holderness has argued that the play depicts the distinctive political ethos of feudal society, defining the traditional social values violated by Richard as "a feudalism given cohesion and structure by the central authority of a king bound to his subjects by the reciprocal bonds of fealty"; *Shakespeare Recycled: The Making of Historical Drama* (Hertfordshire: Harvester Wheatsheaf, 1992), p. 64.

20. In terms of the 1352 treason act and subsequent Elizabethan legal practice—see below, note 28—such speculation could amount to a traitorous 'imagining' of a harmful act against the monarch, a feature that confirms Gaunt's break with orthodox loyalties.

21. As has been observed, this is a powerful constitutional statement of the necessity for a law-centered monarchy where it is the law from which the king's power derives and he is to rule according to it; see Donna B. Hamilton, "The State of Law in *Richard II*," *Shakespeare Quarterly* 34 (1983): 5–17.

22. In an (unconscious) acknowledgment of the equivocal implications of this scene, Leonard Tennenhouse asserts that Bolingbroke "arrests Bushy and Green on charges of treason for assaulting the king's [that is, Richard's] body"; see his *Power on Display: The politics of Shakespeare's genres* (London: Methuen, 1986), 80. The rhetorical emphasis, however, is undoubtedly on their offenses against Bolingbroke. Tennenhouse's general observation on the political process represented in Shakespeare's history plays helps illuminate Bolingbroke's attitude toward treason: "Together these chronicle history plays demonstrate, then, that authority goes to the contender who can seize hold of the symbols and signs legitimizing authority and wrest them from his rivals to make them serve his own interests"; *Power on Display*, p. 83.

23. The political implications of Bolingbroke's equivocal speech may well have carried more charge to an Elizabethan audience; Steven Mullaney discerns a widespread cultural sensitivity to ambiguous speech—"the figure of treason itself"—as symptomatic of a politically disordered subject; see his "Lying Like Truth: Riddle, Representation and Treason in Renaissance England," *English Literary History* 47 (1980): 32–47. Patricia Parker makes a similar argument in interpreting the "motivated rhetoric" of, among other texts, Thomas Wilson's manual of logic, *The Rule of Reason* (1551): "The 'doubtfulnesse' of words—their capability of being 'twoo waies taken'—not only undermines reason's 'rule' but may lead to specious and politically dangerous "consequentes" based on the transport of words outside an acceptable range of regulated meaning" Parker, *Literary Fat Ladies: Rhetoric, Gender, Property* (London: Methuen, 1987), 100.

24. The relationship between Bolingbroke's making relative static assumptions and the command this demonstrates can again be illuminated by analogy to the form and content of Machiavelli's writing, interpreted by Victoria Kahn as a "sophisticated rhetorical strategy, the aim of which is to destabilize or dehypostatize our conception of political virtue, for only a destabilized *virtù* can be effective in the destabilized world of political reality"; *Machiavellian Rhetoric*, p. 25.

25. See, for example, Mary, Queen of Scot's shrewd observation on the prejudicial nature of her trial: "being already condemned by forejudgings, to give some shew and colour of a just and legal proceeding," William Cobbett and Thomas Howell, eds. *Cobbett's Complete Collection of State Trials* (London, 1809), 2:1169–70.

26. Cunningham, "Female Fidelities on Trial," esp. 2–4.

27. Maus, "Proof and Consequences," 24.

28. Subsequent quotations are from *State Trials* 2:1315–34. For an insightful account of the legal procedures involved in proving treacherous interiority, see Karen Cunningham, "'A Spanish heart in an English body': The Ralegh treason trial and the poetics of proof," *Journal of Medieval and Renaissance Studies* 22 (1992): 327–51.

29. Breight, "Treason doth never prosper," 3–5.

30. *An admonition to the nobility and people of England and Ireland* (1588), sigs. A5ᵛ–A6ʳ. For a detailed study of Elizabethan Catholicism, see Peter Holmes, *Resistance and Compromise: The Political Thought of the Elizabethan Catholics* (Cambridge: Cambridge University Press, 1982), esp. 129–65.

31. *The historie of the princesse Elizabeth* (1630), trans. R. Norton, sigs. Eee3ʳ⁺ᵛ.

32. *State Trials* 2:1351–52.

33. W. F. Bolton notes that Aumerle's figurative response to Bagot's accusation—"mine honour soil'd / With the *attainder* of his slanderous lips" (4.1.23–24; italics added)—refers to the legal consequences of accusation (that is, the extinction of rights and capacities that followed the sentencing of a traitor). see, "Ricardian Law Reports and *Richard II*," *Shakespeare Studies* 20 (1988): 53–66, 59–60.

34. *Holinshed's Chronicles*, 2:862–63.

35. Sheldon P. Zitner, "Aumerle's Conspiracy," *Studies in English Literature, 1500–1900* 14 (1974): 236–57. John Halverson argues that the tone of the whole play is more satirical and absurd than has been registered; "The Lamentable Comedy of *Richard II*," *English Literary Renaissance* 24 (1994): 343–69.

36. In relation to the unsettling effect of this, compare Craig Bernthal's perceptive remarks on the conflict over treason between Thumpe and Horner in *2 Henry VI*, as embodying "the disquieting reality that people are not safe to speak their minds even in their own homes, that loyalty to the family and loyalty to the state are in fact at odds, and that, while a state cannot exist without stability in the family, the state's very efforts to purge itself of treason could undermine the harmony of family life and, in the long run, the state itself"; "Treason in the Family," p. 50.

37. "'A liberal tongue': Language and Rebellion in *Richard II*," in *Shakespeare's Universe: Renaissance Ideas and Conventions*, ed. J. M. Mucciolo (Hants: Scolar Press, 1996), 37–51, 38. Norbrook reexamines the Essex circle's interest in the play's aristocratic constitutionalism and "the slow and painful process of formulating opposition"; "Liberal Tongue," p. 41.

38. "At a Crossroads of the Political Culture: The Essex Revolt, 1601," in *Society, Politics and Culture: Studies in Early Modern England* (Cambridge: Cambridge University Press, 1986): 416–65, 421.

39. Robert Lacey, *Robert, Earl of Essex: An Elizabethan Icarus* (London: Weidenfeld and Nicolson, 1971), 261–62.

40. In "'By the choise and inuitation of al the realme': *Richard II* and Elizabethan Press Censorship," *Shakespeare Quarterly* 48 (1997): 432–48, Cyndia Susan Clegg discusses the implications of Parson's treatise for the play, esp. 437–42.

41. Hammer, "The Uses of Scholarship: The Secretariat of Robert Devereux, Second Earl of Essex," *English Historical Review* 109 (1994): 26–51, 31.

42. Cited in Penry Williams, *The Later Tudors: England, 1547–1603* (Oxford: Clarendon Press, 1995), 372.

Women's Letters and Letter Writing in England, 1540–1603: An Introduction to the Issues of Authorship and Construction

JAMES DAYBELL

> I say she never did invent this letter;
> This is a man's invention, and his hand.
> (Shakespeare, *As You Like It*, IV.3.29–30)[1]

IN RECENT YEARS scholars working on women's writing in Renaissance England have sought to study a wide range of texts produced by women alongside and in addition to the more formal genres of writing such as poetry, plays, and translations, of which letters are merely one example.[2] Indeed, attempts to establish a corpus of material written by women have moved away from a concentration on published works and increasingly made use of manuscript sources.[3] This is in part because there is little evidence of actual female publication, at least until well into the seventeenth century.[4] It also results from the fact that attention has begun to be focused more appropriately on the different arenas of female activity, for example the court, the law courts and more especially the household, with references to the various types of writing that were produced by women within these contexts. Furthermore, the collapsing of the boundaries in terms of what constitutes a "literary" text has led to the consideration of more material forms of writing such as household accounts, recipe books, religious meditations, letters, diaries, autobiographies, depositions, petitions, and even needlework.[5] In each case the precise form of writing brings with it its own idiosyncrasies; its own set of rules, methods, and conventions of textual production; and its own set of problems for interpretation. This article is concerned with the methodologies relating to women's letter writing in the period 1540 to 1603, for which I have gathered approximately 2,500 individual letters, written by some 650 women. More specifically, it will explore the way in which letters were constructed, that is who wrote them, how they were written and ultimately surveying the extent to which they can be seen to represent a female authored text. It will also argue for the acceptance of a relatively broad definition of women's authorship. Furthermore, the sheer volume of letters available must surely call for a reassessment of the sixteenth century as a period of literary production for women, but one in which the issue of female literacy is more problematic than has hitherto been assumed.

A significant proportion of the women's letters during this period were in fact written by an amanuensis, or bear the signs of having been written by more than one person. This issue of "mediated" writing, questioning as it does modern definitions of authorship and textual production is one that has concerned literary scholars of the late medieval and Renaissance periods.[6] Social historians too have encountered similar problems in their use of depositional evidence where the voice of a female deponent is muffled by legal and bureaucratic procedure.[7] However, as far as I am aware, the full impact of the ways in which letters were constructed, the input that an amanuensis might have had, the constraints imposed by a lack of epistolary privacy, and the self-censorship this would have led to, has not yet been studied. Clearly, the mechanics of letter writing are of fundamental importance when looking at a range of interesting issues relating to women's writing and their lives. These include women's persuasive and rhetorical skills, the degree of confidence and authority that they displayed, self-fashioning and the creation of personas, empowerment and female agency, as well as the intimacy and emotional content of social and family relationships. In sum this article seeks to assess the varying input of women in the writing of their letters and the extent to which these letters can be considered as either personal or spontaneous.

At the heart of this analysis are the questions of who physically wrote the letters and how to decide whether a letter was written in a woman's own hand or in that of an amanuensis. That is, whether the main body of the letter was actually written by a woman, or whether she merely signed it. The former is referred to as a holograph letter, whereas the latter is known as an autograph letter. Unfortunately, the task of establishing a holograph hand is often a matter of some subjectivity and one that is made all the more difficult by a number of factors.[8] First, there is no such thing as an identifiably female hand, despite the fact that some time before 1600, italic appears to have been established as the preferred hand for women.[9] The professional penman Martin Billingsley, writing at the beginning of the seventeenth century, recommended that women be taught to write in italic. He expressed the view that italic

> is conceived to be the easiest hand that is written with Pen, and to be taught in the shortest time: Therefore it is usually taught to women, for as much as they (having not the patience to take any great paines, besides phantasticall and humorsome) must be taught that which they may instantly learne: otherwise they are uncertaine of their proceedings, because their minds are (upon light occasion) easily drawne from the first resolution.[10]

Italic appears to have been used by many women by the end of the sixteenth century and was the hand adopted by a number of court women from as early as the 1530s.[11] However, throughout most of this period, its popularity among women was limited; until the 1570s at least, it was largely a fashionable accomplishment for a learned minority. What is more, by 1590 it was becoming increasingly popular among men of the nobility and gentry. In short, the use of italic was less a guarantee of a writer's gender than of their class and high literary ability.[12] In practice women wrote a variety of scripts throughout the whole of this period, including cursive and secretary. Indeed, the copybooks which begin to be published from about 1570 onwards provide a number of hands that women would have had the opportunity of mastering.[13]

Another factor making the identification of a holograph letter more problematic is the fact that a woman's hand may not always have been consistent. Differences in an individual's hand were caused by numerous conditions, including the speed of writing and the cut and quality of the quill used.[14] Variations in style may also have occurred over a period of time. Lady Elizabeth Russell's handwriting changed with age, from "the schoolgirl copybook style of her twenties to the large and shaky script of her last years."[15] Additionally, certain women appear to have been capable of writing a number of hands which they used for different types of document.[16] Indeed, the letters of Lady Arbella Stuart show how she used two separate hands for different occasions. Her familiar letters and the rough drafts of her court letters were written in an informal italic hand, whilst in the presentation copies of her court letters she used an elegant, formal italic hand.[17] A number of women, including Queen Elizabeth I and the calligrapher Esther Inglis, also seem to have been able to write both a secretary and an italic hand.[18] This ability to write a number of hands, a sign of a high level of literacy, also illustrates the palaeographical problems associated with women's letters.

Since it is not possible to establish a female scribe from handwriting alone, it is often useful to look at circumstantial evidence. Sometimes it is possible to rely on internal evidence contained within the letter. For example, a woman might mention whether she had written in her own hand or used a secretary. In particular, it was common for women who wrote their own letters to mention the deficiency of their hand. Alternatively, studying a woman's letters from the perspective of a family collection might help to determine whether she was capable of writing or not, as women were often taught to write by their brothers' tutors. There are also a number of letters that have been established as holograph.[19] From this it is possible to build up a realistic exectation of the types of hand women were able to write. I would further suggest that it is usually fair to assume that if the signature contained in a letter is in a different hand from that of the main body of the letter, it was written by an amanuensis. It is common, for example, to find a letter written in a highly practiced and proficient secretary hand, bearing a signature in a different (and often italic) hand.[20] It would have been highly unusual for a woman to have written such an accomplished and obviously professional hand; therefore, it is most likely that such a letter was written by a amanuensis.[21] Furthermore, for many women, it is possible to examine a number of letters and thus be able to recognize their hand, or hands, with more confidence. However, what is more problematic is either when the same hand is used throughout and the script is less polished, or when there is only one extant letter to study for an individual woman. Equally, where a letter survives only in the form of a secretarial draft or copy, it is not possible to determine whether the version that was sent was holograph or not.

Despite these problems, I have been able to make a judgment about the vast majority of the several thousand letters that I have looked at. I am confident that approximately one quarter of the letters studied were written by an amanuensis, with others showing signs of input by a third party. It is important to note that, in this respect, the writing of women's letters did not differ significantly from men's letters. The concern of this article is the effect this may have had on composition.[22]

Amongst those letters that were not holograph there are a number of categories of people whom women employed to write their letters for them. Most common seems to have been the use of a secretary or amanuensis—that is, a servant or clerk employed, usually by members of the nobility and gentry, specifically for the purpose of writing.[23] Exactly who these secretaries were is often difficult to pin down. Occasionally secretaries are mentioned by name. For example, Mary Throckmorton wrote to her father Thomas Throckmorton, telling him, "I desired Ridley to wryte me a letter to my uncle."[24] Alternatively, it is possible to establish the identity of an amanuensis where a whole collection is studied. In most cases, however, the scribe remains frustratingly anonymous, and even where a name can be traced, there is often little in the way of biographical material to be found.

Significantly, most secretaries were male, which may have had an effect on the way in which women's letters were written. I have found only one example of a woman acting as a secretary: Katherine Ashley, who was governess to Princess Elizabeth and later a woman of the bedchamber when Elizabeth became queen. She was asked by Elizabeth to write a letter to William Cecil on behalf of a Scottish prisoner. It is noticeable that in her letter she felt it necessary to explain why she had been asked to write, where it would have been more normal for the princess's secretary to have done so. She writes, "My ladys graces secretary beyng besy wt my lady about hyr lernyng / hyr grace was lothe to let hym to wrete thes letter / wharefore hyr grace commanded me to wrette hauyng no respecte to the rudenes of my wretyng."[25] This indicates that she felt unease with the situation, not only because she considered herself insufficiently skilled for the task, but also because the role of a secretary was usually performed by a man.

Professional scribes also wrote letters. These were scriveners who were not employed directly by a family, but who operated on a freelance basis, hiring out their writing skills. There is also some evidence that such scribes wrote letters for people lower down the social scale.[26] Additionally, letters were written by family members. For example, there are a number of cases of husbands who penned letters for their wives. Richard Bertie, Katherine Duchess of Suffolk's second husband, wrote a letter to the Earl of Leicester for his wife.[27] Similarly, many of Muriel Tresham's letters survive as drafts in her husband's hand, as do many of those of Anne Bacon, the wife of Nathaniel Bacon of Stiffkey.[28] Alternatively, other relations could be used. William Cavendish wrote to Burghley for his mother Elizabeth Talbot, Countess of Shrewsbury.[29] Similarly, Elizabeth Clinton, Countess of Lincoln, asked her nephew to write for her to Mr. Alderman Marten and his son-in-law, Sir Julius Caesar.[30] Obviously, it is useful to be able to establish precisely who wrote a woman's letters. Where a husband, for example, can be shown to have written letters for his wife, this throws up an interesting question regarding the influence and effect he had over what was written, as well as constraints that might have been imposed on the writing of a letter. This is something that will be dealt with later in the article; the present concern is to outline how letters were actually constructed.

There are a number of ways in which letters were composed, each of which would have affected the degree of control or input a woman could achieve. It is essential to point out here that many women did write their own letters, with no help from others. First, there is evidence to show that some women drafted their own letters. This can be observed in a number of examples where a woman wrote the main body of the letter herself and where subsequent changes to the initial text were also made in her hand. Indeed, this appears to have been the case with many of Anne Newdigate's letters.[31] There is also a holograph draft of a letter, in the British Library, from Lady Conway written to the Privy Council. The letter was written defending her husband in his business dealings. Interestingly, she chose to cross out the phrase 'I ame [a] woman and have smale or no power to determine[32] / of any thing that is my husbands."[33] Second, a number of women wrote in a distinct and individual style, which can be seen throughout their letters and which argues strongly for the fact that they wrote them. These include such relatively well known writers as Lady Anne Bacon, Lady Elizabeth Russell, and Margaret Clifford, Countess of Cumberland. Such examples reveal a high degree of personal control by these women over the texts they wrote.

Having said this, it is clear that one cannot always rely on a letter's holograph status, safe in the belief that it was written by a women unaided or that it represents an unimpaired female voice. Indeed, certain letters that are ostensibly written by women, prove, in fact, to have been more collaborative than one might at first imagine. At the most basic level, there are examples of letters written by someone else that a woman merely copied out in her own hand. Frances, Duchess of Suffolk, asked her then husband, her former equerry, Adrian Stokes, to write a letter for her addressed to the Queen. She wrote to him, asking that he "devise a letter, and rough draw it for me to copy, so that I may write to the Queen's Majesty for her goodwill and consent to the marriage."[34] The letter was to deal with the delicate matter of seeking the sovereign's permission for the marriage of Lady Katherine Grey and Edward Seymour, Earl of Hertford. Clearly, the duchess trusted Stokes to produce a letter that matched her requirements.

In addition, it seems a relatively common practice for women to have written a first draft of a letter, and then to have sought help and advice in correcting and refining it. Frances Lady Burgh, for example, wrote to Thomas Windebank, Clerk of the Signet, regarding a dispute between her and the Lord Justices of Ireland and the Earl of Ormond, arising over the lease of some corn. She sent him a draft of a letter she intended to be sent to Sir Robert Cecil, asking him to "correct or make stronger if [there is] cause."[35] Lady Anne Nevill, who asked that her husband might be reinstated in the post of *Custos Rotulorum* in his locality, also approached Windebank to help in the phrasing of a letter. Lady Nevill asked the Clerk, her "good frende and kinde neighbour," to "polish my rough hewen speach proceading from a minde that never knew how to dissemble."[36]

Men, however, also sought help and advice in the drafting of their letters, which suggests that it was a standard practice regardless of gender. When Robert Bacon sought favor from his aunt, Lady Elizabeth Russell, to use her influence to intervene with Lord Burghley for him in a disputed wardship case, he wrote first to his cousin, Anthony Bacon, sending him a draft copy of the letter for his inspection. The letter was accompanied by the explanation:

> I have herewith sent you a L[ett]re byne written to ye La[dy] Russell w[hi]ch as you shall lyke you may use either in altering the same as you shall think best or in returning it unto me as yt is yt I may wryght it agayn & then send it unto you.[37]

In this instance Anthony Bacon was obviously approached because he was considered to be closer to the situation and therefore possessed of greater expertise in terms of how to word the letter more precisely. In each case discussed, where a third party was involved in the writing of the letter, the language used was not entirely that of the signatory. Indeed, those changes made by a third party may have slightly altered the presentation or effect of certain phrases.

Equally, they may have bolstered the letter with inventions of their own, perhaps advocating a different approach or argument for pleading a case, or the use of a specific rhetorical strategy. In particular, if one is to consider the sense in which letters reveal a woman's rhetorical or persuasive skill, the way in which letters were sometimes collaborative must be kept firmly in mind.

In connection with this there are two letters I would like to look at in greater detail which illustrate a prominent male influence—of a brother, in the first instance, and a servant, in the second—attempting to refashion the self-image of the woman sending the letter. In both cases, the letters were from wives to their husbands during a period of marital dispute. The first example is a letter drafted by Robert Devereux, Earl of Essex for his sister, Dorothy Percy, Countess of Northumberland. In drafting the letter for his sister to send to her estranged husband, Essex hoped to achieve a reconciliation between the couple. He wrote to the countess, saying that "you have written to him [her husband] lres of contrary stiles / some that heale / & others agayne that rankle the wound that you have made in his hart / wch makes him think you unconstant and commanded by your passions."[38] Essex counseled his sister instead to employ a more submissive tone in her letters and drafted an example for her to send, writing, "I do infinitly wisshe that you wold write unto him one lre more to this effect." I quote the drafted letter in full:

> My lo: I haue expected yor resolucion / wch I am willing to hasten out of no ill respect to yor self / And therefore once again will desire that the cawses of these discontentments may not be revived nor disputed / for they are troublesom to me / to think of / & enemyes to a reconcilement wch I offre with a resolved mind to deserve yor love / seconded by hope of better reward / thoughe of late myne ears have receaued terrifyng tales / I will believe [sic] tyll your honor / wisdom & discretion will hold you from wronging both yor self & me / & then I will promise my self a more happye life & approve my desert both to you & the world / wch doth constantly bynd me to be yor faithful wife.[39]

There is no evidence that the Countess of Northumberland followed her brother's advice and sent the letter. What is clear is the importance of not mistaking the letter as an example of her own writing or as representative of the way she felt toward her husband. The letter does not speak with the countess's true voice, but rather with that of her brother; the relative submission and obedience revealed in the letter are not her own. The fact that Essex felt the need to advise her suggests that she was far from submissive. Moreover, it is interesting to note that, although the letter is generally polite and acquiescent, it is not as self-effacing as it might have been. Indeed, there is still a veiled yet firm resolve evident. This must, at least in part, be explained by the fact that if his sister's attempts failed to achieve the desired rapprochement, it was important in Essex's mind "that it might appeare to the worlde it was his fault [the Earl of Northumberland's] & not yours that you live a sunder."[40] On the one hand, there was a need for the countess to be seen publicly to have been a dutiful wife; on the other hand, total submission and personal admission of sole responsibility for the separation were not compatible with the maintenance of Devereux family honor. The letter, therefore, represents a carefully calculated response to these two considerations.

The second example is a letter in the British Library, from Elizabeth Willoughby to her husband, Sir Francis, which provides a useful complement to the letter above.[41] The letter is one of only three original letters of hers that survive, all of which were incidentally written by an amanuensis.[42] The interesting thing about the letter is that it appears to have been dictated and shows signs of modification by a secretary. At the bottom of the letter the secretary writes, "Madame as I haue altred this lre yow may wth good warrant send it to Sr ff [Sir Francis Willoughby, her husband] but in any wise / remember the condicions how they stand wth yow / that yow be not overtaken wth them."[43] The draft is full of crossings out and other amendments in the same hand as this note. In part, the alterations were made to correct grammatical errors; in addition, certain nonessential information seems to have been excluded. The main effect, however, was the toning down of certain passages. While the overall tone of the first draft appears to have been largely conciliatory, there are points in the text where Lady Willoughby's obedient style reverts to extreme submissiveness, revealing an almost desperate desire for reconciliation with her husband whilst at other times her language boils over with the frustration she felt toward him over his maltreatment of her. It is this more emotional side of the letter that the secretary seems to filter out. This can be seen in the following passage:

> I require no one iote of favor at yor handes / ~~So I pray god to dele with me further as wth a most faithles & periured parson both towards him and yow~~ / So againe if yor meaning be to have me acknowleg of my former forgettfullnes of my dutie / ~~many wayes~~ towardes yow for &

concerninge howshold matters only / Then my answere is / that that hath bene donne many times & long synce / both by my lrs / and by my self apon my knees / ~~And for your further & full satisfaction herin / I do here once agayne confesse to yow under my hand & seale that I have behaved my self towardes yow both unadvisedly & undutifully both in worde & deede many wayes & many tymes / for the wch I have bene & am very hartely sory / humbly requiring yow both to forgive me & forgett it.~~[44]

This is a clear example of a secretary helping to construct a female persona, the result of which, as with the last example, is not the censorship or distortion of the writing to conform to inherently male ideas of female behavior. Rather, it seems implicit that Elizabeth Willoughby was fully aware of the effectiveness of presenting a submissive self-image, but that this sometimes went too far, and the secretary was merely colluding with her in the writing of the letter, to develop and shape it. Significantly, his alterations seem to have been designed to moderate this excessive submissiveness and to prevent her from taking the full blame for the rift in relations between her and her husband.[45] What this shows is that where the draft of a letter survives, as in this case, there are a number of levels on which it might be read, each of them revealing. The first draft often reveals more of a woman's initial response to a situation, a response often lost as a result of rewriting. In contrast, the final product can be less spontaneous—instead, showing how a woman wished to project herself. Letter writing as an activity is therefore more self-conscious and more calculated than might at first appear.

One of the problems, where only a holograph final draft of a letter survives, is knowing exactly how much help the female signatory received in writing it. In some ways more straightforward are those letters that have been established as having been written by an amanuensis. Where this is the case, there are a number of different methods by which a letter was composed. For example, letters could have been either dictated orally, or written from notes that a woman provided. Alternatively, secretaries might have used model or form letters and tailored them for a specific situation according to a woman's requirements. Dictation appears to have been one of the principal ways in which women communicated their letters to a secretary in order for him to write them. This possibility is something that has been considered by a number of scholars working on women's writing.[46] Obviously, this method of composition potentially enabled women to maintain a high degree of control over the contents of a letter.

The key issue here is how to tell whether a letter was dictated or not. Unfortunately, the evidence is rather indirect and relies on examining the consistency of style achieved by a particular writer over a range of letters. In this analysis, dictation is thought likely to have occurred if one woman's letters yield a similar style, irrespective of whether they were written in her hand or not. This is a technique that Muriel St. Clare Byrne has used in her work on the letters of Honor Lady Lisle, written during the 1530s. She argues that none of Lady Lisle's surviving letters were actually written in her own hand, but that they had been written by three different secretaries and that this therefore allowed for some degree of comparison of them. Indeed, what she notes is the remarkable consistency in the style of Lady Lisle's letters, regardless of which of the three secretaries she used to write for her. She concludes that this strongly suggests that the letters were dictated.[47]

The type of analysis used by Muriel St. Clare Byrne will work only where a number of conditions apply. Above all, one must be able to detect a unique and personal style for a given epistolary author, in other words, that she wrote in a way that is distinctive enough for one to tell it apart from someone else's writing. In relation to this, the extent to which the phrasing of sixteenth-century letters is merely conventional, or whether letters exhibit an identifiably individual style, have both been questioned. In answer to this, certainly some letters are very stylized, and many writers adopted formulaic phrases with which to open and end their letters.[48] However, it is clear that, beyond this polite observance of convention, many letters have a highly personal element, often employing vivid and emotive language. Indeed, Albrecht Classen has argued that the letters of many female writers "show very surprising directness and uninhibitedly lay bare their innermost feelings."[49] A woman's writing may, for example, have been made distinct by the use of certain common words or phrases, or by the fact that she displayed a particular confidence and self-assurance in her letters, or that she showed a discernible personal intimacy with the person to whom the letter was to be sent.

Additionally, only where there is a sufficient selection of correspondence for analysis will one be able to detect whether a letter has been dictated. It is also essential that there are different types of business and family letters that are both holograph and autograph to enable comparison. Furthermore, to ensure consistency, one must compare only letters of the same type or letters written to the same person. Obviously, the tone of a business letter may differ significantly from a more intimate letter to a family member. This is further complicated by the fact that a woman's style may have changed when dictating a letter rather than when writing herself. There are also a number of formal and stylistic constraints that dictation would have imposed, which I will discuss below. Beyond this, there were variations in the way dictation was carried out. While some letters clearly were dictated verbatim, for others, the majority of the letter was dictated, leaving the secretary merely to add standard endings, beginnings and usually the place and date the letter was written. Clearly then the fact that a particular letter might in some ways be standardized does not mean it was not dictated.

Out of the material I have gathered, there are approximately twenty individual women for whom a sufficient variety of correspondence survives and whose letters I have studied for the possibility of dictation. In the case of most of these women, at least some letters show signs of having been dictated. For Catherine, Duchess of Suffolk, for example, there remain a vast number of letters written to William Cecil. Most of these she wrote herself, and they reveal a considerable degree of intimacy with Cecil. Writing to him, she was open, confident, authoritative, and often playful. On one of the few occasions she used a secretary to write to Cecil, she stated "I write not this wth myne owne hand unto yow." Indeed, the letter bears all the hallmarks of dictation, rather than composition by secretary. "What a weary begger I am," she described herself familiarly to him.[50] The style is at once readily discernible as hers, redolent as it is of her usual determination and frankness of comment. Although an amanuensis had written the letter, it does not differ notably in tone and language from the letters the duchess wrote herself. This indicates that when the duchess used a secretary for her correspondence, he took down her dictation word for word, which further indicates that the end product represents almost exactly what she wished to say.

An alternative method of writing a letter, other than to dictate it, was for an amanuensis to work from notes detailing what a woman wished to have included in the letter. For example, Honor Lady Lisle had notes made for a letter she wished to have written and sent to Madame de Riou, with whom her daughter was lodging at the time.[51] Although I have found no further direct evidence of notes being written for a secretary, there is at least one instance where a woman produced minutes for a letter that she wished another to write. The example is that of Lady Bridget Norris who, wishing to pursue a suit in Ireland, wrote to Lady Elizabeth Ralegh to intervene with her husband Sir Walter. In her letter, Lady Norris enclosed notes for a letter she wished Sir Robert Cecil to write to the Lord Deputy of Ireland. What is also clear from the letter is that, as well as Cecil's help, she also wanted to enrol Sir Walter Ralegh's help in order to compose the letter. She wrote to Lady Ralegh:

> I haue framed the effect of a letter that I desire to Haue derected to the Deputy [of Ireland] from Mr secretarie / I trust yf Sr Walter Raleighe will take the paines to polishe them he shall also preuaile in the subscribing therin[52]

The notes for the suggested letter from Cecil to the Lord Deputy of Ireland that were enclosed for Ralegh read as follows:

> I haue deliuered unto your lo: the Queens pleasure concerning a companie to be leade by the constable of the Lady Noracyes castell desiring yow also ^ at that tyme ^ to signifie unto the president [of Munster] that the same companie should be lodged on her lands the wch shee complaineth not to be obserued by hym but other bands plased their greatlie to Her preiudice by the spoyle the maker of her woods and other comodities I am therfore to desire yor lo: to graunte the La: yor peremtorie warrant to remove anie captaine that lodgeth on her land and to place theire / that in the leadinge of her overseer / But because yt is to be hoped that in shorte tyme the commission maie be lessened yor lo: maie make the warrant so that yf yt be not thought needfull to continewe the whole hundreth and fiftie or that there be more necessarie ocassion for the service to drawe them else wheare that then theire be onely so manie lefte in the castell as to yor lo: shall seem fytt to secure yt from anie sodaine violence being a place of verie great importance in the tyme of warre.[53]

Lady Norris clearly spelt out exactly what she wished to have included in the letter and suggested reasons to support her case. However, the letter's final form, its language and eventual content, would have had more to do with Ralegh and possibly Cecil than it did with her.

In some way related to this is the use of model or standard letters by an amanuensis. That is, a secretary may have written a form letter which could be adapted to the individual circumstances of a woman's particular requirements. The use of such models was already widespread well before 1500, for both men and women.[54] During the sixteenth century itself, a large number of letter-writing manuals were printed, providing a range of sample letters for a variety of occasions.[55] It is also clear that secretaries compiled manuscript formularies for their own personal use.[56] Moreover, in practice, secretaries did sometimes employ model letters when writing on a woman's behalf. This is well illustrated by three letters written by Elizabeth Clinton, Countess of Lincoln, Lady Dorothy Stafford, and Lady Mary Scudamore to Sir Bassingbourne Gawdy at a time when he was rumored to be in the running for the post of Sheriff of Norfolk. These three court women wrote to Gawdy on behalf of Nicholas Fermor, a client of the Earl of Leicester, whom they sought to place as his under-sheriff for the county, if he himself was appointed to the post.[57] What is striking about all three letters is the fact that they are almost identical in what they say. Indeed, Lady Scudamore's and Lady Stafford's letters are almost exactly the same, word for word, including the mode of address, differing only slightly in the last two lines. The similarity of these letters can be explained either by the use of standard forms of letters, or perhaps even by the possibility that Fermor provided copies of the letter he wished to be written. In either case, the role a woman had to play in the actual writing of the letter was minimal. More significant was her position and influence at court and the authority that a letter bearing her signature would have carried.

In each of the various methods of construction I have described, the language used was not entirely that of the women who sent the letters, and the level of influence that a third party may have had will have varied from letter to letter. For example, a letter that was first drafted by a woman will have had a far greater level of female input than one written specifically for her, the actual wording of which would have had very little to do with her. Likewise, a letter dictated verbatim is more likely to represent a woman's wording than those letters that were written from notes, where the secretary had greater freedom to shape the letter according to his own liking. In particular, when a woman drafted or dictated a letter, the greater part of the text can be attributed to her. In relation to the latter, it is important to remember that the basic physical act of putting ink on a page was only one of a range of skills associated with authorship: composition, memory, imagination, legal and business acumen, and attention to detail. Indeed, a woman who dictated a letter would still have used many of these skills, the only difference being that she would not have worked on paper herself. The fact that she did not pen her own words does not mean she was not responsible

Women's Letters and Letter Writing in England, 1540–1603   175

for them; what it does suggest is that we must accept a relatively broad definition of women's writing.

Having said this, it is sometimes hard to gauge exactly how closely a final letter matched a woman's initial intentions, as well as the level of control she had over what went into a letter.[58] The issue of how much influence a secretary might have exerted is one that concerned contemporary writers of the period. In theory, at least, the role of an amanuensis was thought to be to reproduce his master's (or, let us assume, mistress's) words and not to add inventions of their own. For example, Angel Day, in *The English Secretorie*, wrote that a secretary should:

> giue heed to obserue the Order, Method and Forme to him from his Lord or master deliuered: forasmuch as in discharge hereof he is utterly to relinquish any affectation to his owne doings, or leaning herein to any priuat iudgment or fantasie. His pen in this action is not his own, but anothers, and for this cause the matters to him committed, are to depend upon the humor of his commander, and upon none others.[59]

Clearly, the degree of control a woman had over a letter depended entirely upon whether she was able to read it, indeed, whether she did so before it was sent. The fact that it is widely held that more women were able to read than write suggests that those women who themselves could not write were nevertheless able to achieve some control over their correspondence.[60] In this sense, the authorship of letters, in certain circumstances, may have been more a function of a woman's ability to read a letter than her ability to write one.

Moreover, there is widespread evidence to indicate that women did look at and review the letters that were written and amended for them. For example, John Drury, a servant of the Countess of Bath, sent his mistress a copy of a letter that he had written for her and wished her to sign. He wrote:

> [I] umbely desyer your honor to put your hand to a letter that I have sent by this bearer/ wch is acordyng to a copy wch I haue sent also not wth standyng if ther be any thyng not greabell to your plesure & kindnes then to awltar yt as yt shall please you.[61]

What is clear from this is that he expected the countess to read the letter and check whether it was acceptable enough to be sent. Similarly, Elizabeth Bourne, who sometimes sought help in composition from others, thanked Sir John Conway for correcting a draft of a business letter that she had sent to him, writing 'I wyll wryt the leter a newe and I lyke the altering of hit well.'"[62] In this case, Elizabeth Bourne not only read the corrections that had been made for her, but she also implemented them, rewriting the letter herself.

Equally important, where such direct signs of the checking of letters are missing is the fact that almost all the letters bear an autograph signature. A signature is usually understood to connote the ability to read, as well as at least a rudimentary level of writing ability.[63] Furthermore, in order to sign a letter, a woman would have to have seen it before it was sent and presumably would have read it before signing. In addition, many letters contain holograph postscripts, further evidence that women had contact with their letters before they were sent and that they were content with what went out in their name. Clearly, the final draft of a letter would have incorporated suggestions made by a third party, to a greater or lesser extent; but, in the final analysis, it was the woman alone who decided what was to be included and what to be excluded. Where a woman was highly literate, she would have been able to exert a strong degree of control over the writing process, possibly even redrafting the letter herself in light of advice from others. In other cases, undoubtedly, the level of control would depend very much upon the level of a woman's literacy, as well as her personal character.

Somewhat more nebulous is the self-censorship by a woman that might have arisen from the absence of epistolary privacy caused by collaboration in the writing of a letter. Put more simply, there is a sense in which a woman would perhaps have been less inclined either to be as intimate or as personal in a letter written by someone else as she would in a letter written herself.[64] This is apparent in a letter written from Lady Catherine Daubeney to Thomas Cromwell, in which she stated that she preferred to write in her own hand than to "trust any so far as to know my mind."[65] This suggests that there were certain matters some women may have felt uneasy in sharing with a third party. Similarly, there were certain matters that were of too sensitive a nature to be made privy to a secretary. Angel Day, in the section of his book *The English Secretorie* titled "Of the partes, place and office of a Secretorie," wrote of the "Secresie, trust, and assurance, required at the handes of him who serueth in such place."[66] Indeed, when Elizabeth Talbot, Countess of Shrewsbury, was unable to write to Burghley in her own hand, about her guardianship of Lady Arbella Stuart, she asked her son to write for her, rather than a secretary. She wrote to him that:

> I am inforced to use the hand of my sonn Wm Cavendysshe / not beinge able to wryte so much my self for feare of bringing great payne to my hed / he only is pryvy to your lordships letter / and neyther Arbell nor any other lyuinge / nor shalbe[67]

Clearly, there were some things that would be shared with an amanuensis and others for which it would be unsuitable to do so. Therefore, where an amanuensis was used, things may have been either left out or modified. The fact that most secretaries were male may also have made women more self-conscious about what they said to them and therefore what they wished to be put in the letter. However, the extent of this modification would, of course, depend on a number of factors, such as the woman's intimacy with and trust of the amanuensis, her own personal confidence and authority, and perhaps more important the type of letter that was being written, as well as the woman's relationship with the receiver.

Nowhere is the potential effect of a lack of epistolary privacy more significant than in the study of the family, where letters have frequently been used to look at the change over time in the intimacy and emotional content of relationships. In part, differences in sentiment are related to the nature of the sources studied. Those letters written using an amanuensis are less likely to be either as personal or as spontaneous as holograph letters. Just as there were certain matters one might not have shared with a third party, so too were there certain types of emotions or intimacies that one would have been ill at ease in sharing with those outside the family, or even outside a particular relationship. Indeed, Ralph Houlbrooke has argued that correspondence conducted between husband and wife "became a more personal and private matter" in the second half of the sixteenth century. He sees this stemming less from a changing view of a woman's place within society, or a marked shift in spousal affections, than from the increased female literacy of the sixteenth century and the resultant rise in epistolary privacy that this promoted.[68] In this analysis, marital and other family relationships remain relatively constant over the late medieval and early modern periods, marked only by slow and gradual change. Instead, what changes is the nature of the evidence with which the historian and literary scholar is confronted, and it is this to which one must be sensitive.

The effect that the use of an amanuensis may have had upon the style and content of a letter is particularly well illustrated by two letters from Lettice Dudley, Countess of Leicester, to her son, Robert Devereux, Earl of Essex. One of the letters she wrote herself, whereas, for the other, she used a secretary. The majority of the Countess's letters to her son were holograph, and it seems that she valued letters that were personally written. Indeed, she wrote to Essex of her joy in receiving a letter from him in his own hand.[69] What is notable, however, is that the letter to her son for which she employed an amanuensis differs greatly from the letters she sent to him written in her own hand. I have chosen to provide a full transcript of both letters so that the difference between them can be fully observed.

The first letter, dated 11 December 1598, was written in a small neat secretary hand and was only signed by Lettice Dudley. It requests Essex to intervene with the Council of Marches in Wales on behalf of the Dean of Lichfield over a disputed parsonage:

> My good Sonn/ my Cozen Mr docter Bulleyn/ deane of Lichefielde hath bene an earneste suter to mee/ to entreate yow in his behalfe/ to put yor hande to a lre wch I sende yow heareinclosed/ directed to the councell of the marches of Walles and also that yow woulde so mutch fauoure him/ as to procure the Lo: Chamberlayne ^&^ the Lo: Admyrall to joyne wth yow and put theare hands also/ to the same lre/ his requeste to the Councell of the Marches is (as yow ^may^ more at large perceiue by the lre/ directed by yor selfe to them/[70] That wheras theare is now depending a matter in question/ before them/ touching the force of a lease/ graunted by one Charleton/ late parson of the parsonage of Banger in Wales to one Gerrarde for the sum of fortie marks yearely/ being woorthe at the leaste by the yeare (as the Deane Saythe) an Hundreth pounds/ wch parsonage hir matie for his better mayntenance hath lately bestowed on him/ And fynding the beste parte of it so incombred by his predicessor/ feareth unles hee may bee soom what countenanced by his good freends/ by writing to the said Councell to desire them that the matter may haue/(and the rather at yor requests) sutch speedie hearing and determinacon/ as in equitie/ and conscience shalbee thoughte fitt/ ~~Otherwyse~~ hee shalbee longe delayed in his sute to the greate losse/ and hinderance of his present fortune/ I shoulde thearefore bee gladd the (poore Deane) mighte haue what fauoure in this case ~~mi~~[71] coulde conveniently bee afforded him/ and the rather in regarde that hee is our kynesman/ and my good neighboure/ and also keepeth a verie good howse for the releefe of his poore neighboures aboute him/ And so prayinge god to blesse/ and prosper yow in all yor proceedings I ende

From Drayton Bassett this xith of December 1598[72]
your mother that derlye loueth you L Leycester[73]

The second letter is holograph and is undated, probably written sometime after Essex's return from Ireland in September 1599, but before his ill-fated revolt in February 1601. Written in a relatively large italic hand, it is representative of the familiar and flowing style the Countess used when writing to her son. In it, she offers him help and advice:

> Swet Ro[74] / your self hath geuen me such a tast of sume strang matter to be loked for/ as I cannot be quiet tyll I know the trew caus of your abcence anad dyscontentment/ if it be but for Ierland I dought not but you ar wyse and polytyke enufe to counter myne with your enemys whos deuelysh practyces can noe way hurt you but on/ wherfore my dere sonne geue me leue to be a lytle ielious ouer you for your[75] good/ and intret you to haue euer god and your oune honore before your eys so shall you be sure that he will dyspos inded all as you say for the best in dyspyght of all enemyse/ my frend[76] and I cannot but be trobled with thys news and doe wish our selues with you as he[77] would sone be if we thought hys sarues nedfull or that you would haue it so wich let us know and he[78] will leue all other ocasyons what so euer and will presentlye be with you well if it be but mens matters I know you have corage enufe/ if womens/ you haue metlye well paßed the pyks allredy and therein you shuld be skyllfull/ so praynge you not to be to secret from your best frends/ I end beseching the allmyghtye to bles you euer in hys hyghest fauoure whill I am your mother derlyest
> L Leycester[79]

The first letter is notably more formal in tone than the second, which is fluid and expressive in its manner. The former is also appreciably less intimate and affectionate in style. Whereas the secretary very conventionally addresses the letter to 'my good sonn', when writing herself the Countess adopts the more informal, more personal pet name of "swet Ro[bert?]" with which to address her son.[80] More significant are the letters' actual contents, the topics they deal with and their level of candidness. The first is a routine business letter dealing with patronage and giving a rather standard description of circumstances, with very little in the way of a personal flavor to it. The second, on the other hand, concerns a highly sensitive political matter. In it, the Countess shows obvious concern for her son's predicament, expressing herself "to be a lytle ielious ouer you for your good" and is critical of his enemies whom, however, she does not name. She also offers him both her help and that of her husband, Sir Christopher Blount, if needed. Blount was among those executed for their part in the Essex Revolt of 1601, and it may have been his possible involvement in the revolt to which the countess referred. It is thus unlikely that the countess would have entrusted to an amanuensis the writing of a letter of such high political import.

There is an obvious freedom of expression in the countess's holograph letters, which is also found in other letters women wrote themselves. Indeed, letters are commonly cited, along with diaries and autobiographies, as being representative of a female voice and a counterbalance to male voiced prescriptive literature, of which so much survives. What perhaps is harder to get at is the extent to which, within such letters women internalised certain fairly widespread societal values. In this sense, even when the layers of secretarial intervention, the epistolary conventions, the processes of drafting, and the different methods of construction have been peeled away, one is still left frustratingly searching for an elusive female voice, a voice itself shaped and conditioned by society and experience. Unfortunately, this is the nature of the source material with which one must work. What it means, though, is that letters must not be taken at face value.

In conclusion, the period exhibits widely differing degrees of female autonomy in the sphere of epistolary activity. At one end of the spectrum, women merely read what men had written for them, while, at the other, they either wrote their own letters or were able to make more independent use of suggestions made to them. As we have seen, many women were able to exert a high degree of control over the final text. Therefore, any attempt to define women's writing, for both the late medieval and the Renaissance periods, must incorporate letters of a collaborative nature. In short, for a woman to be considered an author, it is not necessary for her to have possessed the ability to write or actually to have written a text herself. What mattered, instead, was that she could communicate orally what she wished to have set down or that she was able to participate in the process of revision. Although such a claim does not square with modern conceptions of authorship or textual production, it still is one that would have been entirely acceptable during the sixteenth century, for both women and men.

Notes

I would like to thank Dr. Ralph Houlbrooke and Dr. Roger Dalrymple for their invaluable comments on an earlier draft of this article. All mistakes however, are undoubtedly my own. I am also grateful to Dr. Houlbrooke and Andrew Stewart for alerting me to examples of female letter writers in the Shakespearean canon.

1. Quotation taken from Stanley Wells and Gary Taylor, eds., *William Shakespeare: The Complete Works* (Oxford: Clarendon Press, 1986).

2. Much of the work in this area has been of a truly interdisciplinary nature. For example, Barbara Lewalski, *Writing Women in Jacobean England* (Cambridge, MA: Harvard University Press, 1993); Esther S. Cope, *Handmaid of the Holy Spirit: Dame Eleanor Davies, Never Soe Mad A Ladie* (Ann Arbor: University of Michigan Press, 1992); Phyllis Mack, *Visionary Women: Ecstatic Prophecy in Seventeenth Century England* (Berkeley: University of California, 1993); Louise Schleiner, *Tudor and Stuart Women Writers* (Bloomington: Indiana University Press, 1994); Susan Frye, *Elizabeth I: The Competition for Representation* (Oxford: Oxford University Press, 1993); and "Women's Household Writing," paper delivered at the Rocky Mountains Medieval and Renaissance Association Conference, Big Sky, Montana, June 1998; Sara Jane Steen, ed. *The Letters of Lady Arbella Stuart* (Oxford: Oxford University Press, 1994), (hereafter cited as Steen, *Letters of Lady Arbella Stuart*) and "Fashioning an Acceptable Self: Arbella Stuart," *English Literary Renaissance* 18 (1988): 78–95 (hereafter cited as Steen, "Fashioning an Acceptable Self"); Victoria Burke, "Women and Early Seventeenth-Century Manuscript Culture: Four Miscellanies," *The Seventeenth Century* 12:2 (Autumn 1997): 135–50; and Susan Dwyer Amussen, "Women's Voices in Seventeenth-Century England," *Journal of British Studies* 35:1 (1996): 114–18.

3. Margaret J. M. Ezell, *The Patriarch's Wife: Literary Evidence and the History of the Family* (Chapel Hill: University of North Carolina Press, 1987), pp. 63–83. Also see Ezell's *Writing Women's Literary History* (London: Johns Hopkins University Press, 1993); and "The Myth of Judith Shakespeare: Creating the Canon of Women's Literature," *New Literary History* 21 (1990): 579–92.

4. Patricia Crawford, "Women's Published Writings, 1600–1700," in *Women in English Society, 1500–1800*, ed. Mary Prior (London: Methuen, 1986; repr. London: Routledge, 1996), pp. 211–82, 214.

5. For examples of work that has attempted to define what is meant by the term *literary* text, see Keith Thomas, "History and Literature," pamphlet (Swansea: University of College Swansea, 1988); and Margreta de Grazia, "What Is a Work? What Is a Document?," in *New Ways of Looking at Old Texts: Papers of the Renaissance English Text Society, 1985–1991*, ed. W. Speed Hill (Binghamton, NY: Center for Medieval and Early Renaissance Texts and Studies, 1993), pp. 199–207.

6. For example, see Margaret W. Ferguson, "Renaissance Concepts of the 'Woman Writer'," in *Women and Literature in Britain, 1500–1700*, ed. Helen Wilcox (Cambridge: Cambridge University Press, 1996), 143–68 (hereafter cited as Ferguson, "Renaissance Concepts of the 'Woman Writer'"); Lynn Staley Johnson, "The Trope of the Scribe and the Question of Literary Authority in the Works of Julian of Norwich and Margery Kempe," *Speculum* 66 (1991): 820–38; and Julia Boffey, "Women Authors and Women's Literacy in Fourteenth and Fifteenth Century England," in *Women and Literature in Britain, 1150–1500*, ed. by Carol M. Meale (Cambridge; Cambridge University Press, 1993), 159–82.

7. For example see Martin Ingram, *Church Courts, Sex and Marriage in England, 1570–1640* (Cambridge: Cambridge University Press, 1987), 20; Natalie Zemon Davis, *Fiction in the Archives: Pardon Tales and Their Tellers in Sixteenth-Century France* (Stanford: Polity Press, 1987), 1–6; and Tim Stretton, "Women and Litigation in the Elizabethan Court of Requests," Ph.D. thesis, Cambridge University 1993, p. 24. In this, women did not differ from male deponents

whose words were similarly buried beneath a layer of protocol and formulaic legal language.

8. I am grateful to Malcolm Parkes, Professor of Palaeography at Oxford University, Laetitia Yeandle, of the Folger Institute, in Washington, and Diane Greenway, at the Institute of Historical Research, for their helpful comments on this subject.

9. Giles E. Dawson and Laetitia Kennedy-Skipton, *Elizabethan Handwriting, 1500–1650: A Guide to the Reading of Documents and Manuscripts* (London: Faber and Faber, 1966), p. 12; hereafter cited as Dawson and Kennedy-Skipton, *Elizabethan Handwriting*.

10. Billingsley, *The Pens Excellencie or the Secretarie Delight* (London, 1618), 37. There are a number of variant editions of this text. The precise copy from which I have quoted is Bodleian Antiq.e.E.1618.2, in which page numbers have been added in pencil; it is these to which I refer.

11. I am grateful to Elizabeth Heale, who informs me that the Devonshire Manuscript contains the italic hands of three women from the 1530s: Lady Margaret Douglas, Mary Shelton, and Mary Howard, Duchess of Richmond. In relation to this, see her article, "Women and the Courtly Love Lyric: The Devonshire MS (BL Additional 17492), *Modern Language Review* 90:2 (April 1995): 296–313; and Helen Baron, "Mary (Howard) Fitzroy's Hand in the Devonshire Manuscript," *Review of English Studies* 65:179 (August 1994): 314–35.

12. Dawson and Kennedy-Skipton, *Elizabethan Handwriting*, pp. 8–9, 12; Alfred Fairbank and Bruce Dickins, *The Italic Hand in Tudor Cambridge* (London: Bowes and Bowes, 1962); Alfred Fairbank and Berthold Wolpe, *Renaissance Handwriting: An Anthology of Italic Scripts* (London: Faber and Faber, 1960), 28–34; Jean F. Preston and Laetitia Yeandle, *English Handwriting, 1400–1650* (Binghamton, NY: Medieval and Renaissance Texts and Studies, 1992), viii; and N. Denholm-Young, *Handwriting in England and Wales* (Cardiff: University of Wales Press, 1954), 73.

13. For a good introduction to the copybooks of this period, see Ambrose Heal, *The English Writing Masters and Their Copy Books, 1570–1800: A Biographical Dictionary and Bibliography* (Hildesheim: Georg Olms Verlagsbuchhandlung, 1962).

14. Jonathan Goldberg, *Desiring Women Writing: English Renaissance Examples* (Stanford: Stanford University Press, 1997), 151.

15. Elizabeth Farber, 'The Letters of Lady Elizabeth Russell, 1540–1609,' Ph.D. diss., Columbia University, 1977, p. 70.

16. John W. Velz, "Giving Voices to the Silent: Editing the Private Writings of Women," in *New Ways of Looking at Old Texts: Papers of the Renaissance English Text Society, 1985–1991*, ed. by W. Speed Hill, Medieval and Renaissance Texts and Studies 107 (Binghamton, NY: Center for Medieval and Early Renaissance Texts and Studies, 1993), 263–72, 272; and Jonathan Goldberg, *Writing Matter: From the Hands of the English Renaissance* (Stanford: Stanford University Press, 1990), 240–41 (hereafter cited as Goldberg, *Writing Matter*); and his *Desiring Women Writing* p. 151.

17. Steen, *Letters of Lady Arbella Stuart*, 107 and 112–13.

18. Paul Johnson, *Elizabeth I: A Study in Power and Intellect* (London: Weidenfeld and Nicolson, 1974), 19–21; and A. H. Scott-Elliot and E. Yeo, "Calligraphic Manuscripts of Esther Inglis (1571–1624): A Catalogue," *The Papers of the Bibliographic Society of America* 84 (1990): 11–63.

19. For example, see *A Select Collection of Interesting Autograph Letters of Celebrated Persons, English and Foreign, From the Sixteenth-Century to the Pres-*

Women's Letters and Letter Writing in England, 1540–1603

ent (Stuttgart, 1849); and Ray Rawlins, *Four Hundred Years of British Autographs: A Collector's Guide* (London: J. M. Dent & Sons Ltd, 1970). It is also not uncommon for manuscript catalogues to mention when a letter is considered to be holograph or not.

20. L. C. Hector, *The Handwriting of English Documents* (London: Edward Arnold, 1958), 59; and Goldberg, *Writing Matter*, pp. 234–35. This is not always the case, since some women, who used a different hand of their own for the body of their letters, seem to have developed highly elaborate, often italic signatures which they used merely for the purposes of signing. Goldberg, *Desiring Women Writing*, p. 145. Professor Goldberg notes that Mary Shelton reserved a neat italic hand for her signature. This also seems to be the case for many of the letters by court women that I have studied.

21. In general terms, the women who used a secretary hand wrote a rather large and bold script easily distinguishable from the hand of a professional writer. For examples of women who wrote in secretary, see Jane Key, ed., "The Letters and Will of Lady Dorothy Bacon, 1597–1629," *The Norfolk Record Society* 56 (1993): 77–112, 81. Interestingly, many female writers within the Norfolk area wrote using similar hands. For an exception to this rule, see John Craig, "Margaret Spitlehouse, Female Scrivener," *Local Population Studies* no. 46 (Spring 1991): 54–57. Dr. Craig details a woman who, as the daughter of a Bury St. Edmunds will writer, took over her father's work upon his death, on a parttime basis to earn extra money. Her hand is described as a "carefully wrought secretary script."

22. Elsewhere I have dealt with the reasons why a woman might have used an amanuensis. See my forthcoming article, "The Conventions of Women's Letters and Letter Writing in England, 1540–1603," in the book arising from the Reading University Conference, 1998, *Privy and Powerful Communications: Women's Letters and Letter Writing in England, 1450–1700*.

23. For the use of secretaries, see Paul E. J. Hammer, "The Use of Scholarship: The Secretariat of Robert Devereux, Second Earl of Essex, c. 1585–1601," *English Historical Review* 109:430 (February 1994): 26–51; and A. G. R. Smith, "The Secretariat of the Cecils, circa 1580–1612," *English Historical Review* (1968): 481–504. For earlier periods, see Muriel St. Clare Byrne, ed., *The Lisle Letters*, 6 vols. (Chicago: University of Chicago Press, 1981) 1: p. 59 (hereafter cited as *Lisle Letters*); and H. S. Bennett, *The Pastons and Their England* (Cambridge: Cambridge University Press, 1922; repr. 1991), pp. 116–17 (hereafter cited as Bennett, *Pastons and Their England*).

24. Warwick Record Office, Throckmorton Papers CR 1998/Box 60 no. 11; Mary Throckmorton to her father Thomas Throckmorton, n.d.

25. British Library Lansd. MS. 1236 f.41. Interestingly, Elizabeth added a postscript of her own in an immaculate italic hand, which reads "I pray you farder this pore mans sute" (hereafter British Library cited as BL).

26. Keith Thomas, "The Meaning of Literacy in Early Modern England," in *The Written Word: Literacy in Transition: Wolfson College Lectures, 1985*, ed. Gerd Bauman (Oxford: Clarendon Press, 1986), 97–131, 106. Thomas claims that during the early modern period, semi-professional letter writers were widespread. See also, David Cressy, *Literacy and the Social Order* (Cambridge: Cambridge University Press, 1980), 16. Cressy, in particular, refers to the letter-writing activities of one Roger Lowe, a provincial shopkeeper who also operated informally as a scrivener during the 1660s (hereafter cited as Cressy, *Literacy and the Social Order*). There is also an example from the late fifteenth century, of a letter written for a woman, in French, by a professional letter writer. See Alison Hanham, ed., *The*

Cely Letters, 1472–1488. The Early English Text Society, No. 273 (Oxford: Oxford University Press, 1975), 49–50, 262.

27. *Historical Manuscript Commission on the Pepys MS Preserved at Magdelene College, Cambridge* (London: His Majesty's Stationery Office, 1911), 71–72. Katherine Bertie, Duchess of Suffolk to Earl of Leicester, 28 December 1565.

28. For examples of Muriel Tresham's letters, see BL Add. MS. 39828 ff. 75, 84, 85, 87, 90, 136, 136v, 137, 147; and BL Add. MS. 39829 f. 35-35v. For Anne Bacon, see Folger Shakespeare Library Ld. ff. 15, 16, 17, 18, 19, 20, 21, 23, 51, 476.

29. BL Lansd. MS. 71 f. 2. Elizabeth Talbot, Countess of Shrewsbury to Lord Burghley, 21 September 1592.

30. BL Add. MS. 12506 f. 81. Elizabeth Clinton to Mr. Alderman Marten and Sir Julius Caesar, 1587.

31. For specific examples, see Warwick Record Office, Newdigate Papers CR 136 B305, B306, B310 and B311a. In each case, the letter appears to have been drafted by Anne Newdigate in her own hand; it also seems to contain corrections or amendments in the same hand. Arbella Stuart also seems to have drafted her own letters. For a discussion, see Steen, "Fashioning an Acceptable Self," pp. 86–87.

32. Lady Conway appears to have written the phrase "to determine" twice here by mistake.

33. BL Add. MS. 23212 f.191; Lady Conway to the Privy Council, n.d.

34. Hester W. Chapman, *Two Tudor Portraits: Henry Howard, Earl of Surrey and Lady Katherine Grey* (Boston: Little, Brown, 1960) 181. The question of who drafted this letter and whether the actual draft survived became a matter of great importance in the interrogations that followed the marriage. See BL Harl. MS. 6286 f. 33.

35. Hatfield House, Cecil MS 64 f. 88. Frances Lady Burgh to Thomas Windebank, 6 October 1598 (hereafter cited as Cecil MS). I would like to thank The Right Honourable The Marquis of Salisbury for his kind permission to quote from this and subsequent documents.

36. PRO SP 12/279/20. Anne Lady Neville to Thomas Windebank, 6 march, 1601.

37. Lambeth Palace Library, Bacon MS. 659 f. 41. Robert Bacon's letter to Lady Elizabeth Russell survives in two drafts written in 1596. See also, Bacon MS. 659 f. 43.

38. Cecil MS 179 f. 157 (2).

39. Cecil MS 179 f. 157 (1). Both surviving letters are themselves copies in the hand of Edward Reynolds, one of Essex's secretaries. See *Historical Manuscript Commission Calendar of the MS of the Most Hon. The Marquis of Salisbury K.G. Preserved at Hatfield House Hertfordshire*, 18 vols. (London: Her Majesty's Stationery Office, 1883–1940) 14: 127–28.

40. Cecil MS. 179 f. 157 (2).

41. The progress of this marriage has been expertly detailed by Alice T. Friedman in her book, *House and Household in Elizabethan England: Wollaton Hall and the Willoughby Family* (Chicago: University of Chicago Press, 1989); and in her article, "'Portrait of a Marriage": The Willoughby Letters of 1585–1586'," *Signs: Journal of Women in Culture and Society* 11:3 (1986): 542–55.

42. The remaining letters survive as copies made by Cassandra Willoughby in the late seventeenth century. A partial transcription of these is printed in *Historical Manuscript Commission Report on the Manuscripts of Lord Middleton Presently at Wollaton Hall* (London: His Majesty's Stationery Office, 1911), 504–610. The actual copies themselves are held at the University of Nottingham Library.

43. BL Lansd. MS. 46 f. 65–66v. Elizabeth Willoughby to Sir Francis Willoughby, c. 1586.

44. Ibid. The crossings out represent the changes made by the secretary.

45. This is made clear by the secretary's note on the bottom of the letter, which I have already quoted.

46. Margaret Ferguson, "Renaissance Concepts of the 'Women Writer'," 151. Indeed, Professor Ferguson proposes the question, "if a woman dictates her words to a male scribe, is she still to be considered a woman writer?"

47. *Lisle Letters*, IV, 229–31.

48. Norman Davies, "The Litera Troili and English Letters," *Review of English Studies* 63 (1965): 233–44; and Keith Thomas, *Literature and History* (Swansea: University College of Swansea, 1988), 9.

49. Quoted in Albrecht Classen, "Female Epistolary Literature from Antiquity to the Present: An Introduction," *Studia Neophilogica* 60 (1988): 3–13, p. 3. Also see his "Footnotes to the Canon: Maria von Wolkenstein and Argula von Grumbach," in *The Politics of Gender in Early Modern Europe: Sixteenth Century Essays and Studies*, 12 (1987): 131–47, 135; and Karen Cherawatuk and Urlike Wiethaus, eds., *Dear Sister: Medieval Women and the Epistolary Genre* (Philadelphia: University of Pennsylvania Press, 1993), 1.

50. BL Lansd. MS. 2 f. 46. Catherine Bertie, Duchess of Suffolk to William Cecil, n.d.

51. *Lisle Letters*, vol. III, p. 155, letter 581a.

52. Cecil MS. 83 f. 28; Bridget Lady Norris to Lady Ralegh, c. 1600.

53. Cecil MS. 83 f. 27; minute for the suggested letter from Cecil to the Lord Deputy.

54. R. A. Griffiths, "Public and Private Bureaucracies in England and Wales in the Fifteenth Century," *Transactions of the Royal Historical Society*, 5th series 30 (1980): 109–30 (pp. 120–21); J. Taylor, "Letters and Letter Collections in England, 1300–1420," *Nottingham Medieval Studies* 24 (19809): 57–70 (pp. 57–61); and W. A. Pantin, "English Monastic Letter Books," in *Historical Essays in Honour of James Tait*, ed. J. G. Edwards, V. H. Galbraith and E. F. Jacob (Manchester, 1933), 201–22 (p. 206).

55. For an introduction to letter-writing manuals, see Jean Robertson, *The Art of Letter Writing: An Essay on the Handbooks Published in England During the Sixteenth and Seventeenth Centuries* (London: Liverpool University Press, 1942); Katherine Gee Hornbeak, *The Complete Letter-Writer in English, 1568–1800* (Northampton, MA, Smith College, 1934); and R. R. Bolgar, 'The Teaching of Letter Writing in the Sixteenth Century," *History of Education* 12: 4 (1983): 245–53.

56. BL Add. MS. 48150. Yelverton MS CLXI (2). Robert Beale's Formulary Book.

57. The letters survive as copies in Sir Bassingbourne Gawdy's letter book. Bodleian Library. Tanner MS. 241 f. 1b-2. The original of Lady Stafford's also survives in the British Library. BL Eg. MS. 2713 f. 54.

58. See Muriel St. Clare Byrne, ed., *The Letters of Henry VIII: A Selection With a Few Other Documents* (London: Cassell, 1936; 2nd 1968), pp. 200–201. The issue of how much influence a person had over something they did not write is not necessarily gender-specific. St. Clare Byrne applies this problem to Henry VIII and his control over policy.

59. Day, *The English Secretorie, or plaine and direct Method, for the enditing of all manner of epistles or letters, aswell Familiar as others: distinguished by their diuersities under their seuerall titles* (London: C. Burbie, 1595), Part II, p. 132; hereafter cited as Day, *English Secretorie*.

60. Given that reading is commonly thought to have been taught before writing, both sexes would have been more likely to have been able to read than to write. For example, see R. S. Schofield, "The Measurement of Literacy in Pre-Industrial England," in Jack Goody, ed., *Literacy in Traditional Societies* (Cambridge: Cambridge University Press, 1968), 311–25 (316); Cressy, *Literacy and the Social Order*, p. 20; and Margaret Spufford, "First Steps in Literacy: The Reading and Writing Experiences of the Humblest Seventeenth Century Spiritual Autobiographers," *Social History* 4:3 (October 1979): 407–35 (410).

61. Cambridge University Library, Hengrave MS. 88 vol. I. f. 130.

62. BL Add. MS. 23212 f. 153. Elizabeth Bourne to Sir John Conway, nd.

63. Cressy, *Literacy and the Social Order*, pp. 53–61.

64. Secretaries also commonly made copies of letters, which would, of course, have made them privy to the letter's contents, and this in turn would have affected their composition.

65. M. A. E. Wood, *Letters of Royal and Illustrious Ladies*, 3 vols. (London: Henry Colburn, 1846), vol. II, pp. 119–24, letter LIII, Lady Catherine Daubeney to Thomas Cromwell, 1534.

66. Day, *English Secretorie*, Part II, p. 102.

67. BL Lansd. MS. 71 f. 2; Elizabeth Talbot, Countess of Shrewsbury to Burghley, 1592.

68. Houlbrooke, *The English Family, 1450–1700* (Harlow: Longman, 1984; eighth impression, 1993), p. 101.

69. Warwick RO. Essex Letter Book. MI 229. The letters are not numbered (hereafter cited as Essex Letter Book). I would like to thank the Warwick County Record Office and more especially The Finch Family for the kind permission to quote from these documents.

70. A closing bracket seems to have been left out here.

71. The amanuensis has almost certainly started to write "might" here, then substituted it for "coulde."

72. A minor point is that the letter written by the secretary is both dated and includes the place where the letter was written from—neither of which are included in the second letter. The Countess is usually remiss with regard to the dating of her letters.

73. The ending and signature are in the countess's own hand.

74. The countess has used a contraction here for her son's name. It is highly likely that it is just a shortening of the name Robert.

75. Word crossed out here and rendered indecipherable.

76. The phrase "my frend" refers to her third husband, Sir Christopher Blount, whom she married in 1589, after the death of her second husband, Robert Dudley, Earl of Leicester, the previous year. This point was made by Simon Adams in a paper, "An Elizabethan Scandal Re-examined: The Earl of Leicester's Second Marriage," delivered at the Oxford University Early Modern Britain Seminar, January/February 1998.

77. Word crossed out here and rendered indecipherable.

78. From this point on, the letter is written along the side on the left hand margin.

79. Essex Letter Book, MI 229.

80. This pet name is commonly used in most of her correspondence to the Earl.

Beauty's Poisonous Properties

Tanya Pollard

In the fourth act of *The Devil's Charter* (1606), Barnabe Barnes portrays Lucretia Borgia entering "richly attired with a Phyal in her hand." In the midst of painting her face, she suddenly cries out in dismay at a burning sensation. The cosmetics contained in her vial have proven treacherous: "rancke poyson / Is ministred to bring me to my death, / I feele the venime boyling in my veines."[1] Reduced through death to an object, a receptacle for paints, Lucretia's body becomes twinned with the cosmetic vial that caused her demise. These poisoned props—paint, vial, and corpse—disrupt material and immaterial boundaries alike, giving physical form to the threat of moral and epistemological contamination associated with both cosmetics and the theater.[2] Spilling out of its rightful space to seep into consumers and spectators, infiltrating and tainting both body and soul, poisonous face-paint offers a disturbingly literal image of the vulnerability of the body to the invasive force of the theater.

A recurring threat in early modern plays, the idea that face-paints could poison offered a particularly vivid focal point for broader cultural fears of cosmetics.[3] Amid intensifying curiosity and concern about chemical technology, testimony from doctors as to the corrosive nature of cosmetic ingredients offered scientifically authorized support, as well as a distinctively material vocabulary, for moral diatribes against artificial beauty.[4] In *A Tracte Containing the Artes of Curious Paintinge Caruinge & buildinge*, Paolo Lomazzo warns women against face-painting by noting that sublimate, the primary cosmetic foundation, is "very offensiue to mans flesh" and "is called *dead fier*; because of his malignant, and biting nature"; in *A Treatise Against Painting and Tincturing of Men and Women*, Thomas Tuke chides that "a vertuouis woman needs no borrowed, no bought complexion, none of these poysons."[5] In a magical conflation of immaterial and material threats, moral, medical, and theatrical writings alike represented the semiotic disorder and sexual impurity associated with cosmetics as "poysonous to the *body*, and pernicious to the *soul*."[6]

As the multiple stagings of this threat suggest, anxieties about the dangers of cosmetics reflect as well on early modern concerns about theatricality.[7] In the light of pervasive and insistent identifications between face-paints and the theater, playwrights who depict cosmetics as fatal poisons can be seen as indicting their own medium, suggesting that fears about the contaminating force of art were not limited to the theater's opponents.[8] Also routinely described as poisonous by its detractors, the theater, like face-paints, is understood as both duplicitous and corrosive, unsettling the relationship between interior and exterior. The link between artistic dissimulation and harmful effects on the body and soul points to magical ideas about the dangerous efficacy of signs. In the case of poison, epistemological havoc—the unreliability of appearances as indicators of reality—can translate directly into bodily vulnerability, and even death. Embodying and fusing together various levels of contamination, anxieties about cosmetics and painted bodies call attention to early modern assumptions about the inseparability of external from internal, of material from immaterial, with implications for the powers and perils of the theater.[9]

Beauty's Poisons

Rarely attended to by readers or critics, *The Devil's Charter* offers an intriguing setting for a vivid depiction of murder by poisonous cosmetics.[10] Although arguably lacking in many literary merits, the play offers an exemplary representative of popular Jacobean revenge tragedy; in its relentless accumulation of vendettas and corpses, it displays its generic conventions so ostentatiously as to verge on parody, forming a virtual catalog of some of the more spectacularly ingenious and morbid forms of murder on the Jacobean stage. Based on a melange of contemporary rumors and historical details from Guicciardini, *The Devil's Charter* dramatizes Roderigo Borgia allegedly making a bargain with the devil in order to become Pope Alexander VI, involving, among multiple other murders, that of his daughter, Lucretia. Corrupt and duplicitous in every possible way—Italian, Catholic, female, adulterous, murderous, from a bad family—Lucretia meets her fitting end through the corrosion of poisoned face-paints.

Beauty's Poisonous Properties

In the scene with which this essay opened, Lucretia is in the midst of having her face made up when she interrupts with a sudden cry:

> I feele a foule stincke in my nostrells,
> Some stinke is vehement and hurts my braine,
> My cheekes both burne and sting; give me my glasse.
> Out out for shame I see the blood it selfe,
> Dispersed and inflamed, give me some water.
> *Motticilla rubbeth her cheekes with a cloth.*
> *Lucretia looketh in the glasse.*
> My braines intoxicate my face is scalded.
> Hence with the glasse: coole coole my face, rancke poyson
> Is ministred to bring me to my death,
> I feele the venime boyling in my veines.
>
> (IV.iii.2247–57)

Cosmetics, in this passage, create a crisis of permeability, penetration, and contagion. Lucretia's paints refuse to sit on the surface of her skin: they invade and pervade her body, entering her nostrils, seeping through her skin, coursing through her veins. Her description of the poisons calls attention to an invasive and corrosive heat: her cheeks "both burne and sting," her face is "scalded," her blood is "inflamed," and she feels "the venim boyling" in her veins. Just after this speech, she similarly cries, "I burne I burne ... / My braines are seard up with some fatall fire" (2265–66), and later reports that "a boyling heat / Suppes up the lively spirit in my lungs" (2276–77). Starting at the surface—cheeks, face—this pervasive fire works its way into progressively more interior sites—into her blood and veins, then her brain, and eventually her "lively spirit" itself. Faced with this corrosive heat, the skin loses its integrity as bodily boundary and barrier: a clear differentiation between external surface and internal substance dissolves. Lucretia's death suggests that cosmetics go beyond the superficial—in fact, by erasing the line that separates the inner and outer, they call into question the category of the superficial, suggesting that artifice can never be only skin deep.

Paints are not only invasive in this model, but uncontainable and irrevocable: their effects can be neither halted nor undone. Motticilla, Lucretia's wonderfully named maid, queries, "Ah me deere Lady; what strange leoprosie? / The more I wash the more spreads on your face" (2258–59). The physician, when called, confirms that "This poyson spreads and is incurable" (2278). His futile offer of "one precious antidote" (2279) has no hope of efficacy; from the first moment of application, the paint's force is irreversible. While other contemporary fears about the transformative effects of external trappings, such as clothing, suggest that changes can be undone by removing the threat, the chemical properties of face-paints evoke an uneasy sense of permanence.[11] Like original sin, or the mark of Cain, to which cosmetics were often compared, their taint was perceived as impossible to cleanse.[12]

As improbable as this scene may seem, the traits it attributes to face-paints closely recall nonfictional depictions of cosmetics at the time. Whereas Barnes portrays Lucretia's face-paints as vehicles for externally imbued poisons, other Renaissance writers asserted that cosmetics themselves were innately poisonous. A glance at their chemical ingredients suggests that these claims were, for the most part, not unfounded. Most cosmetic foundations were made of mercury sublimate and ceruse, or white lead: a typical recipe for face-paint directs the reader to "Incorporate with a wooden pestle & in a wooden mortar with great labour foure ounces of sublimate, and one ounce of crude Mercurie." Giambattista della Porta speaks for many in his claim that there is "nothing better than quick-silver for womens paints, and to cleanse their faces, and make them shine."[13] Not only were these substances known to be toxic, but contemporary medical authorities classified them as hot and dry poisons which operated by burning, in contrast with poisons such as hemlock, nightshade, and henbane, which were understood to kill by coldness, through numbing and dulling of feeling.[14] Describing the effect of sublimate, for example, Ambroise Paré writes that victims will suffer from "the devouring and fierie furie of the poyson, rending or eating into the guts and stomacke, as if they were seared with an hot iron."[15] In context, the corrosive heat of Lucretia's paints in *The Devil's Charter* appears less a result of villainous adulteration of paints than an exaggerated confirmation of their inherent, and medically established, effects. The 1598 arrest of Barnabe Barnes, the play's author, for an attempted poisoning with mercury sublimate he had purchased at a grocer's, suggests that the link may not have been entirely coincidental.[16]

The chemical properties of paint were of considerable interest to writers opposed to cosmetics. "The excellencie of this Mercurie Sublimate," Andreas de Laguna writes,

> is such that the women who often paint themselves with it, though they be very young, they presently turne old with withered and wrin-

keled faces like an Ape, and before age can come upon them, they tremble (poore wretches) as if they were sicke of the staggers, reeling, and full of quick-silver, for so are they.[17]

Extending this line of grotesque imagery, Paolo Lomazzo describes in even more elaborate and morbid detail "the natures and qualities of the ingredients"[18] of face-paints. On mercury sublimate, he writes:

> This the Chirurgions call a *corrosiue*. Because if it bee put vpon mans flesh it burneth it in a short space, mortifying the place, not without great paine to the patient. Wherfore such women as vse it about their face, haue alwaies black teeth, standing far out of their gums like a Spanish mule; an offensiue breath, with a face halfe scorched, and an vncleane complexion. All which proceede from the nature of *Sublimate*. So that simple women thinking to grow more beautifull, become disfigured, hastening olde age before the time, and giving occasion to their husbandes to seeke strangers insteede of their wiues; with diuers other inconveniences.[19]

To Lomazzo, paint is a medium that not only fails, but actively undermines, all of its own goals—it mortifies where it should enliven, blackens where it should whiten, and disfigures where it should beautify—with diverse other inconveniences, left to the reader's imagination. Cosmetics, according to this model, carry in them the seeds of their own destruction: like sirens, their seductive promises of beauty mask an underlying ugliness and death.[20] Lomazzo's portrait of sublimate emphasizes the same dangerous bodily infiltration dramatized in *The Devil's Charter*. Beginning at the skin and moving towards increasingly interior arenas—teeth, breath, marital relations—his catalog of consequences points to a similarly progressive deepening of impact, not only from external to internal, but from physiological to social threats.

As Lomazzo's example suggests, writers opposed to cosmetics argue that the corrosive effects of paints play on, and intensify, the fragility of an already too permeable body.[21] In *Instruction of a Christian Woman*, Juan Vives writes of face painting,

> The tender skynne wyl reuyll the more sone, and all the fauour of the face waxeth olde, and the breth stynketh, and the tethe rusten, and an yuell ayre all the bodye ouer, bothe by the reason of the ceruse, and quick siluer. . . . Wherfore Ouyde called these doynges venomes, and not without a cause.[22]

Echoing Lomazzo's emphasis on bodily corrosion, Vives dwells on the same triplicate blazon of skin, breath, and teeth, liminal zones where external surfaces bear the visible marks of their adjacent interior degeneration.[23] The signs of this erosion offer visible proof of the idea that paints are "venomes," literally as well as figuratively contaminating their wearer. Contemporary scientific accounts of the physiological effects of face-paints offer an authoritative material underpinning to fears about cosmetic corrosion and bodily vulnerability.

The idea of cosmetics as invasive poisons, reinforced by the material properties of their chemical ingredients, offered a forceful way to articulate links between face-paints and less tangible forms of transgression and contamination. Socially and politically, for example, the idea of cosmetic infiltration came to be aligned with concerns about the contamination of national and class identity.[24] More explicitly, cosmetics were associated with moral impurity. The most common complaint against cosmetics was that they sinned against truth: concealing true faces behind false, they undermined the trustworthiness of bodily signs, leading to a general epistemological disarray.[25] Recurrent metaphors of forgery and counterfeiting emphasize the disparity between appealing surfaces and empty or corrupt substances: Tuke likens painted faces to "ill cloth of a good die; or to a *Letter* fairely written, and with good inke, but not without some false *English*, or ill contents."[26] Similarly, cosmetic deception was seen as "a tricke of a wanton";[27] motivated by the desire to seduce, it revealed a lascivious and impure soul. Tuke writes of the face-painting women,

> A good *Bed-friend* shee's commonly, delighting in sheetes more, then in shooes, making long nights, and short daies. All her *infections* are but to gaine affections, for she had rather *die*, then liue & not please. Her lips she laies with so fresh a *red*, as if she sang, *Iohn come kisse me now*.[28]

The wayward sexuality of the face-painting woman was seen as fundamentally linked to the physical impurity of face-painting. Philip Stubbes cites biblical authorities to argue that painting is a form of whoredom:

> S. Ciprian amongst the rest, saith, a woman, through painting and dying of her face, sheweth her selfe to be more then whorish. For (saith he) she hath corrupted and defaced (like a filthie strumpet or brothel) the

workmanship of God in her, what is this els but to turne truth into falshoode, with painting and slibbersauces?[29]

Stubbes's argument almost appears to be tautological—painting is whorish, because to paint is to be like a whore—but his explanation suggests a more complex association. The concealing and remaking of true faces with paint, he argues, suggests an inevitable disregard for purity, which, for a woman, translates directly into a lack of chastity.

The conjunction of sexual impropriety and cosmetic impurity was made most explicit in reference to the threat of adultery. Drawing on the etymological identification between corrupting a substance and a marriage with a foreign and inferior supplement, Downame cites Saint Augustine describing face-painting as "a fault which in some respects matcheth whoredome, for (saith he) *Ibi pudicitia, hic natura adulteratur:* In that chastity, in this nature it self is adulterated."[30] Commonly described as "adulterate beauty," or "adulterate and counterfeit Colours," cosmetic contamination was seen as inherently linked to marital infidelity.[31] Strikingly, face-painting was described as the more serious of the two sins: Vives warns the face-painter, "For though thou be nat an adulterar towarde man yet whan thou corruptest and marrest that whiche is goddis doyng thou art a worse adulterar"[32]; similarly, the anti-cosmetic interlocutor in *A Discourse of Auxiliary Beauty* charges that "all *painting* the face, or adding *to our handsomenesse,* in point of *Complexion,* is directly against *the* 7th *Commandment;* ... [not] to *commit adultery with others,"* because "if all *Adultery* and *adulterating* arts ... are forbidden to us, how much more any such plots and practises, as tend to a *Self adulterating.*"[33] As a dangerous external manifestation of the pollution associated with paints, adultery was understood as both a parallel and an inevitable accompaniment to poison, the most extreme and dangerous form of pollution: during the trial for the murder of Sir Thomas Overbury, Sir Edward Coke commented that adultery was responsible for the vast majority of poisoning cases.[34] In a self-perpetuating cycle, the figurative poison of adultery was seen as both cause and effect of the presence of literal poisons, cosmetic and otherwise.

The moral taint of face-paints was seen as undermining not only marital, but religious fidelity. Tuke writes that "hee loues not God with all his heart, that would haue that affection or commendation, giuen to a picture, or a peece of art, which is due to the worke of God."[35] Lest his Protestant readers miss the implications of this statement, Tuke elsewhere asserts directly that "a painted face is not much vnlike an Idoll."[36] Face-painting women were depicted as actively proselytizing for amorous idolaters; Downame writes that "they inueagle others with carnall loue and fleshly lust, making them adore with their chiefe deuotions, a painted idoll, and a liuing image."[37] They were also, moreover, seen as idolaters themselves: "A good face is her god," Tuke claims of the painted woman, "and her cheeke *well died*, is the *idoll* she doth so much adore."[38] In a curious act of self-division, the woman who paints is subjugated by the independent power of her own face; she is simultaneously altar and worshipper, object and subject.[39] The association between face-paints and idolatry both heightens the idea of paint as spiritually poisonous, and offers a link between idolatry and actual material poisons. Disillusioned to discover that "My glorious idoll, I did so adore, / Is but a vizard newly varnished ore," Dubartas describes Jezebel's face-paints as "poisons one would lothe to kisse"; similarly, he accuses her of bringing "Idol-Sin: / Painting, and Poysning" to the land of Samaria.[40] Borrowing from the vocabulary of paint's chemical properties, references to idolatry reinforce beliefs about the link between material and spiritual contamination.

The perceived correlation between outer impurity (painted faces) and inner impurity (tainted souls) was understood in two ways. Cosmetics were seen simultaneously as symtom and cause of this internal corruption.[41] Philip Stubbes argues that bodily adornment sinks beyond the skin to contaminate the soul, lamenting the use of "certaine oyles, liquors, vnguentes, and waters . . . , whereby they thinke their beautie is greatly decored; but who seeth not that their soules are thereby deformed?"[42] John Downame echoes this idea: "so doe they by this outward decking deforme and defile their owne soules, and bring vpon themselues sinne and condemnation."[43] If the physical corrosion of cosmetics was understood as bringing about a spiritual pollution, that pollution, in turn, was represented as a kind of poison, simultaneously metaphorical and literal, which would spread its contagion to others. Citing Saint Jerome, Downame goes on to write:

> If any wantonly deck themselues, to prouoke others in a wanton manner to gaze vpon them, though no hurt follow vpon it, yet they shall be liable to eternall iudgement, because they prepared a poyson, if there had beene any who would haue tasted of it.[44]

Poisonous Props

The fatal powers of cosmetics are linked not only to the material nature of the paints themselves, but also to the bodies and objects associated with them. Lucretia's death in *The Devil's Charter* is heralded by the uneasy identification between her own elaborately painted body and the array of objects related to her beautification. The fatal "Phyal" that contains her poisoned paints is linked to a catalogue of related props; a stage direction reads: "*Enter two Pages with a Table, two looking glasses, a box with Combes and instruments, a rich bowle*" (IV.iii.2186). The unusual specificity of these directions is echoed by Lucretia's explicit reference to the role of these objects in her preparations: "Giue me some blanching water in this boule, / Wash my face *Motticilla* with this cloth" (2231–32). Another stage direction notes of Lucretia, "*She looketh into two glasses*" (2236), and she announces that she will "correct these arches with this mullet" (2244). The artificial beauty that will poison her is shown to be inseparable from the props that embody and facilitate it.[45]

Associated with vanity and luxury, these objects—particularly the vial and "rich bowle"—evoke an image from the play's prologue. After a brief opening catalogue of the various sins to be dramatized, the prologue concludes with an image of the Whore of Babylon:

> Behold the Strumpet of proud Babylon,
> Her Cup with fornication foaming full
> Of Gods high wrath and vengeance for that evill,
> Which was imposd upon her by the Divill.
>
> (Prologue, 5–8)

Through direct iconographic links, Lucretia's face-painting scene is closely aligned with this moment: already proven a whore by the play, she enters the stage holding a cup filled with seductive poisons.[46] In the context of the close visual and thematic parallels, the fatal cosmetics in Lucretia's vial become a physical transmutation of the sexual and religious fornication associated with her Catholicism: the original image in Revelations describes a woman "arrayd in purple and scarlet colour, and decked with gold, and precious stone & pearls, hauing a golden cup in her hand, full of abominations and filthinesse of her fornication."[47] As the only boundary between these women and the poisons they carry, the cups themselves occupy a crucially liminal position in the transmission of these polluting materials. Perennially open containers, they not only allow, but enforce, the transfer of their contents to any with whom they come into contact. As receptacles of poisons, they embody the contaminating nature of what they contain.

In their inability to keep their cosmetic contents within bounds, these vessels become uneasily interchangeable with the painted female bodies—or, in the case of the stage, male bodies painted as female—which become their new containers and display cases.[48] Under the corrosive force of paint, women are transformed not only into inanimate objects, but into troublingly open and contagious objects. Just as cosmetic vials fail to safeguard their internal pollutions, women are depicted as leaky vessels containing poison.[49]

The idea of the female body as perilously open, both to absorption and to spillage, was rooted in the dominant Renaissance medical tradition, inherited from ancient Greece and associated primarily with Galen, that identified the body's uneasy permeability particularly with women. Through the tenuousness attributed to its boundaries, the female body was viewed as acutely vulnerable to the sort of bodily infiltration represented by cosmetic corrosion.[50] According to a Galenic understanding of the body, "a woman's flesh is more spongelike and softer than a man's," more easily absorbent, just as women's bodies and souls are more susceptible to overthrow in general: "The passive condition of womankind is subject unto more diseases and of other sortes and natures then men are."[51] Medical critiques of cosmetics similarly emphasized women's particular fragility: "those paintings and embellishings which are made with minerals, and corrosiues, are very dangerous," Lomazzo writes, "... especially on the face of a woman, which is very tender & delicate by nature."[52] Because of this delicate nature, the female body was understood to be both more vulnerable to contamination than a man's and, when polluted, more contagious.[53]

Medical accounts of this two-way permeability support literary depictions of women as dangerously open receptacles, whose unboundedness puts men at risk as well.[54] This idea is morbidly literalized in a number of revenge tragedy scenes in which men die from kissing a painted female corpse.[55] In Massinger's *The Duke of Milan*, for example, the female body is explicitly described as a vessel filled with poison. After watching Sforza kiss his dead wife Marcelia, whose face has been painted with poisoned cosmetics, Francisco gloats, "Thou art mark'd for the grave, I've given thee poison / In this cup."[56] Mirroring the cosmetic containers that were used to adorn her, Marcelia becomes a prop, a contaminated and contaminating object used to effect revenge.

The use of the female body—or, more particularly, the female corpse—as a poisonous prop is something of a revenge tragedy convention.[57] In The Revenger's Tragedy, Vindice maintains and cherishes the skull of his former love, Gloriana, for years before putting it to use as a weapon of murder.[58] "This very skull," he vaunts,

> Whose mistress the Duke poisoned, with this drug
> The mortal curse of the earth, shall be reveng'd
> In the like strain, and kiss his lips to death.[59]

Having been poisoned by the Duke, Gloriana's body (or the remnants thereof) becomes a contagious medium, reflecting his own poison back to him. Similarly, if less famously, the aptly named Tyrant in The Second Maiden's Tragedy turns to paint to maintain the illusion of life in the corpse of the women he desires, who has killed herself rather than give in to his lust. "Let but thy art hide death upon her face," he tells the painter he has hired, "That now looks fearfully on us, and but strive / To give our eye delight."[60] But in the hands of the painter—the Lady's actual lover, Govianus, in disguise—her painted corpse becomes a weapon of revenge. After kissing the body in delight, the Tyrant exclaims in dismay:

>   Ha!
> I talk so long to death, I'm sick myself.
> Methinks an evil scent still follows me.
> Govianus. Maybe 'tis nothing but the colour, sir,
>   That I laid on.
> Tyrant.   Is that so strong?
> Govianus.   Yes, faith, sir,
>   'Twas the best poison I could get for money.
> [Throws off his disguise.]
>
>   (V.ii.120–25)

The Tyrant dies poisoned by a double dissimulation. Just as paint conceals the Lady's death (and deadliness); so, too, the painter's robes conceal a vengeful murderer, pointing to an ongoing association between poison and treacherously deceptive appearances.

Although the examples of Marcelia, Gloriana, and the Lady show the poisoned female corpse as an instrument in a competitive battle between men, at times the woman herself is the agent of her own objectification, and revenge.[61] In Kyd's Solyman and Perseda, Perseda dies to avoid Soliman's lust, but first paints her own lips with poison in a canny anticipation of what will follow. Agreeably conceding to his request—"A kisse I graunt thee, though I hate thee deadly"[62]—Perseda just has time to leave a catchy note: "*Tyrant, my lips were sawst with deady poyson, to plague thy hart that is so full of poison*" (V.ii.117–18).

As the neat symmetry of Perseda's note suggests, these vessels of poison—Marcelia, Gloriana, the Lady, and Perseda herself—become the site of a literalization of preexisting spiritual poisons, the poisons of lust and tyranny in the men who pursue them to their deaths and beyond. Even women who originally were pure prove so permeable to contamination that they not only absorb these evils, but instead translate them from abstractions into fatal poisons and transmit them contagiously to other victims. Women may serve as representative models of the body's vulnerability to invasion, but they are not shown as the only, or even the primary, victims of poison. Instead, as vehicles for the materialization and transmission of spiritual and literal poisons, they become destabilizing properties that threaten, by chain reaction, to reduce men to objects as well. These scenes raise the possibility that what is at stake in anxieties about poisoned cosmetics may be not so much the problem of women's vulnerability as the corollary problem that it models: the vulnerability of men.[63] As the tranvestite stage suggests, the permeable body that presents itself as female may, in actuality, be male beneath its paint and costumes; femininity may be more significant as metaphor than as fact.

Properties of the Theater

Disconcertingly for audiences, the painted women dramatized and demonized in plays are often closely affiliated with theatricality itself. As a spectacle of monstrous femininity, Lucretia's demise in *The Devil's Charter* echoes and implicates other devious, duplicitous women of the revenge tragedy tradition. In preparing to murder her husband, she self-consciously and eagerly aligns herself with earlier "heroines": "If womanly thou melt then call to minde, / Impatient Medeas wrathfull furie, / And raging Clitemnestraes hideous fact" (586–88). Lucretia explicitly appeals to a theatrical tradition of women who carry out their revenge against their husbands by means of dissimulation and concealment: Medea and Clytemnestra famously lure their victims into the interior of their house under false pretenses in order to kill them. Her own Machiavellian schemes take on an explicitly theatrical vocabulary; having forced her husband to sign a will and statement clearing her name before she murders him, she muses: "So now that part is playd, what followes now?" (I.v.684). Lucretia's skills at dissimulation unite her face-painting and her theatricality, suggesting an essential link between the two.

Even as suspicions of cosmetics as poison draw on an array of chemical and moral associations, theatrical stagings of cosmetic poisonings point to another area of concerns. The significant role given face-paints and scenes of painting within plays calls attention to the painting, costuming, and self-metamorphosing that constitute theatrical productions. Both metonymically and metaphorically, face-paints come to stand for the theater itself; as crucial theatrical props, they represent the mechanics of the stage, and as a means of deceiving and seducing spectators they embody the spirit of theatrical illusion. Consistently linked by both critics and supporters, plays and face-painting were seen as embodying the same contaminating effect. In the context of these shared associations, representations of death by cosmetic exposure can be understood as taking on a metatheatrical significance. If women such as the dissembling Lucretia, who die from direct contact with face-paint, may be likened to the painted players of stage plays, the men who die from mediated poisons, through exposure to these painted women, seem to stand in for the audience, who absorb the contagious taint of the theater through the player. Due to its mimetic nature, the theater was understood as transmitting its contents into both actors and spectators; "Anglo-phile Eutheo," generally believed to be Anthony Mundy, claims that "al other euils pollute the doers onlie, not the beholders, or the hearers. . . . Onlie the filthines of plaies, and spectacles is such, as maketh both the actors & beholders giltie alike."[64] As passive spectators of painted faces and shows, men may occupy ultimately the most endangererd place in the equation, becoming invaded, effeminized, and objectified by the poisons on which they gaze.

As standard stage props, face-paints were a deeply entrenched part of theatrical production: early theater company records include accounts such as "Payd to the paynter for payntyng the players facys, lllj d," and "Item, paid to the paynter ffor peyntyng of ther fasses Viij d."[65] Renaissance folk-etymologists played on the association: In his *An Apology for Actors*, Thomas Heywood offers a derivation of the word tragedy from "τρυξ, a kinde of painting, which the Tragedians of the old time vsed to stayne their faces with" suggested that make-up was seen as the root of theater, both philologically and practically.[66] The two arts were understood as mutually reinforcing: Webster writes of the actor, "Hee is much affected to painting, and tis a question whether that make him an excellent Plaier, or his playing an exquisite painter."[67]

Critics of theater and face-painting—often the same in both cases and, for the most part, Puritans—saw the two as linked in their shared epistemological and ontological confusion: both are associated with disguise, duplicity, and chameleon-like fluidity of identity.[68] Likening painted women to the standard figure for the theater, Stubbes writes: "Proteus, that monster, could neuer change himselfe into so many formes and shapes as these women doe."[69] John Earle asserts that "A Player" is "like our painting gentlewomen, seldom in his own face,"[70] and Thomas Draiton writes of the face-painting woman, "shee'le please men in all places: / For she's a Mimique, and can make good faces."[71] The false faces common to both cosmetics and the theater threaten semiotic stability: William Prynne condemns "this common *accursed hellish art of face-painting*" because it, like stage players, perverts God's works "*in putting a false glosse upon his creatures.*"[72] John Greene curtly summarizes the accusations of dishonesty:

> A Comedy is not like vnto truth, because it is wholly composed of Fables and Vanities: and Fables and Vanities, are lyes and deceipts: and lyes and deceipts are cleane contrarie to truth, and altogether vnlike it, euen as vertue is vnlike to vice.[73]

Along with their shared associations with dangerous dissembling, the theater is also linked to face-painting by ideas of lascivious, excessive self-adornment and display: Bulwer says of face-painting that "in adorning and setting forth the Body [it] differs nothing from the ostentation of Stage-plaies, and is no lesse indecent then fiction in manners."[74] Prynne castigates face-painters who "adorne themselves like comicall women, as if they were entring into a Play-house to act a part."[75] William Cave writes that "Christians should be "leaving *fucus's* and *paintings*, and *living pictures*, and fading beauty to those that belong to Playes and Theatres."[76]

As was the case with cosmetics, concerns about ostentation and seduction in complaints leveled at the theater merged with fears of infiltration and penetration. To moralist critics, theatergoing was inexorably associated with sexual vulnerability. Regardless of the play and its contents (although these generally were seen as adding to, rather than alleviating, the problem), exposure to spectacles and spectators in a public space was seen as in itself a threat to chastity, particularly for women. In an address "To the Gentlewomen Citizens of London," Stephen Gosson warns:

> We walke in the Sun many times for pleasure, but our faces are taned before we returne: though you go to theaters to see sport, Cupid may catche you ere you departe. The litle God houereth aboute you, & fanneth you with his wings to kindle fire: when you are set as fixed whites, Desire draweth his arrow to the head, & sticketh it vppe to the fethers, and Fancy bestirreth him to shed his poyson through euery vaine. If you doe but listen to the voyce of the Fouler, or ioyne lookes with an amorous Gazer, you haue already made your selues assaultable, & yelded your Cities to be sacked.[77]

Gosson's vocabulary identifies the theater with a violently invasive sexuality, threatening the tenuous boundaries of the female body: women exposed to it become "assaultable," and yield their "Cities to be sacked," suggesting that the penetrating force of Cupid's arrow is in itself a sort of rape. His opening metaphor, of the effect of the sun on the faces of those who let themselves be publically exposed, links the dangerously invasive effects of the theater to both the "poyson" of desire and the perils of artificial color burnt into the faces.

As the metaphors of sunbeams, arrows, and poison suggest, attacks against the theater, like critiques of face-painting, understand its sexual and semiotic transgressions as taking the form of an invasive contamination. Like the force of cosmetics, this pollution was envisioned, in a magical conflation of the material and immaterial, as seeping physically through the body in order to enter the soul. In *Playes Confuted in Five Actions*, Gosson warns,

> yf we be carefull that no polution of idoles enter by the mouth into our bodies, how diligent, how circumspect, how wary ought we to be, that no corruption of idols, enter by the passage of our eyes & eares into the soule? We know that whatsoeuer goeth into the mouth defileth not but passeth away by course of nature; but that which entreth into us by the eyes and eares, muste be digested by the spirite, which is chiefly reserued to honor God.[78]

The theater, like cosmetics, problematizes the relationship between surface and substance. Not only are its external trappings misleading signs of what lies within, but its exterior show penetrates the boundaries of the audience's body through ears, eyes, and all senses, to take control of what is inside, the mind and soul.

In a further analogy with face-painting that takes us back to the starting point of this essay, this strange synesthetic contamination was routinely understood in terms of poison by its detractors: Gosson refers to plays as "ranke poyson" and "venemous arrows to the mind," and Greene claims they are "as bad Poyson to the Minde, as the byting of a Viper to the Flesh."[79] Downame similarly argues that plays "poyson the mind with effeminate lust."[80] Although in the case of face-paints the association was clearly catalyzed and reinforced by the fact of their chemical ingredients, the parallel example of theater seems to absorb the principle by analogy, transcending the need for a material explanation. The perceived power of theater to infiltrate and corrupt the spectator lent itself naturally to the literalizing rhetoric of poison, even in the absence of literal poisons.

While accusations of art as poison may be unsurprising in the context of antitheatricalist condemnations of the stage, for plays themselves to stage scenes that contribute to arguments condemning their effects and existence is more striking.[81] Literary representations of the invasive poisons of paint suggest that, despite ordinarily opposing perspectives, both critics of the theater and voices from within it shared foundational assumptions about the power of immaterial images to exert a material effect—and vice versa—on both players and spectators. Although this synesthetic power can be perceived as operating for better as well as for worse,[82] the invasive and transformative powers it attributes to art have threatening implications for the vulnerability of both body and mind. Aligned with, and authorized by, fears about the invasive nature of paint's chemical properties, anti-cosmetic and antitheatrical rhetoric draws on concerns about the reliability of boundaries at large, pointing to corollaries in the distinct but intertwining discourses of medical, moral, and theatrical authors. As overdetermined symbols for this contaminating force, poisonous cosmetics and painted bodies point to vivid magical beliefs about the power of surfaces to seep into substances, of appearances to alter and endanger bodies and souls.

Notes

I would like to thank Jesse Gale, Matthew Greenfield, Sarah Knott, David Quint, Eric Wilson, and Susan Zimmerman for their advice at the various stages of writing this essay.

1. Barnes, *The Devil's Charter*, ed. Jim C. Pogue, IV:iii (New York and London: Garland, 1980): 2255–57; further citations will be in the text.

2. Any work on anxieties about contamination and the transgression of boundaries is necessarily indebted to Mary Douglas; see her *Purity and Danger: An Analysis of Concepts of Pollution and Taboo* (London: Routledge & Kegan Paul, 1966). Much intelligent work on contamination has taken ancient Greece as its model; see Louis Moulinier, *Le pur et l'impur dans la pensee et la sensibilité des Grecs* (Paris: Université de Paris, 1950); Robert Parker, *Miasma: Pollution and Purification in Early Greek Religion* (Oxford, Clarendon Press, 1983); and Jean-Pierre Vernant, "The Pure and the Impure," in *Myth and Society in Ancient Greece* (New York, Zone Books, 1988).

3. Plays featuring poisonous cosmetics include *Soliman and Perseda* (1592), *Jack Drum's Entertainment* (1600), *The History of the Tryall of Cheualry* (1601, *The Gentleman Usher* (1602), *The Devil's Charter* (1606), *The Revenger's Tragedy* (1607), *The Second Maiden's Tragedy* (1611), and *The Duke of Milan* (1622); relatedly, cosmetics are closely juxtaposed with poisons in *Sejanus* (1603) and numerous other plays. Thoughtful studies of early modern discomfort with face-paint include Frances Dolan, "Taking the Pencil Out of God's Hand: Art, Nature, and the Face-Painting Debate in Early Modern England," *PMLA* 108 (1993), 224–39; Annette Drew-Bear, *Painted Faces on the Renaissance Stage: The Moral Significance of Face-Painting Conventions* (Lewisburg: Bucknell University Press, 1994); Laurie Finke, "Painting Women: Images of Femininity in Jacobean Tragedy," *Theatre Journal* 36 (1984), 357–70; and Jacqueline Lichtenstein, "Making Up Representation: The Risks of Femininity," *Representations* 20 (1987): 77–87. For useful accounts of these concerns in neighboring periods, see R. Howard Bloch, "Medieval Misogyny," *Representations* 20 (1987): 1–24; and Tassie Gwilliam, "Cosmetic Poetics: Coloring Faces in the Eighteenth Century," in *Body and Text in the Eighteenth Century*, ed. Veronica Kelly and Dorothea Von Mucke (Stanford: Stanford University Press, 1994), 144–59. Taking a transhistorical perspective, Katherine Stern sees hostility to cosmetics as a manifestation of discomfort toward femininity; see her "What Is Femme? The Phenomenology of the Powder Room," *Women: A cultural Review* 8:2 (1997): 183–96. While building on arguments from these essays regarding the identification between cosmetics, femininity, and art, this essay departs from prior scholarship in situating anti-cosmetic attitudes in the context of early modern fears about chemical technology, bodily security, and magical effects attributed to the theater.

4. On the changing place of chemicals in English society, see, for example, Allen Debus, *The Chemical Dream of the Renaissance* (Cambridge: Heffer, 1968). The most crucial figure in chemical innovation was Paracelsus: see esp. Walter Pagel, *Paracelsus* (Basel, 1958); Charles Webster, *From Paracelsus to Newton: Magic and the making of modern science* (Cambridge: Cambridge University Press, 1982); and Henry Pachter, *Paracelsus: Magic into Science* (New York: Henry Schuman, 1951). On the impact of Paracelsus in England, see Allen Debus, *The English Paracelsans* (London: Oldbourne, 1965); and Paul Kocher, "Paracelsan Medicine in England," *Journal of the History of Medicine* 2 (1947): 451–80.

5. Paolo Lomazzo, *A Tracte Containing the Artes of Curious Paintinge Caruinge & buildinge*, trans. Richard Haydocke (London, 1598), 130; and Thomas Tuke, *A Treatise Against Painting and Tincturing of Men and Women: Against Murther and Poysoning: Pride and Ambition: Adulterie and Witchcraft. And the Roote of all these, Disobedience to the Ministery of the Word* (London, 1616), 21.

6. John Downame, cited in *A Discourse of Auxiliary Beauty* (London, 1656), 106. On the conflation of signs with things characteristic of magical thinking,

see Keith Thomas, *Religion and the Decline of Magic* (London: Weidenfeld and Nicolson, 1971); Thomas Greene, "Language, Signs and Magic," in *Envisioning Magic*, ed. Peter Schäfer and Hans. G. Kippenberg (Brill: Leiden, 1997), 255–72; and Brian Vickers, "Analogy vs. Identity: The Rejection of Occult Symbolism, 1580–1680," in Brian Vickers, ed., *Occult and Scientific Mentalities in the Renaissance* (Cambridge: Cambridge University Press, 1984), 95–163.

7. On Renaissance uneasiness toward the theater, see esp. Jonas Barish, *The Antitheatrical Prejudice* (Berkeley, University of California Press, 1981); Laura Levine, *Men in Women's Clothing: Anti-theatricality and Effeminization, 1579–1642* (Cambridge: Cambridge University Press, 1994); and Ramie Targoff, "The Performance of Prayer: Sincerity and Theatricality in Early Modern England," *Representations* 60 (Fall 1997): 49–69.

8. Asking "why a playwright would rehearse and even heighten or embody the arguments of his attackers," Levine argues that early modern playwrights "are both contaminated by the anxieties of the attacks they defend against and obsessively bent on coming to terms with them"; *Men in Women's Clothing*, 3.

9. In emphasizing the pervasiveness and significance of these beliefs, this essay confirms Targoff's account of "the commitment among certain early modern thinkers to the direct correspondence between outward behavior and inward thought," in contrast to some current critical emphases on the gap between outer show and interiority; Targoff, "Performance of Prayer," 50.

10. The appearance of the first critical text edition of *The Devil's Charter*, in the Globe Quartos series, ed. Nick Somagyi (London: Nick Hern Books, 1999) may both indicate and facilitate a growth of interest in the play.

11. On fears about the power of garments to alter the body's gender, see Levine, *Men in Women's Clothing*.

12. Andreas de Laguna, for example, writes that "this infamy is like to original sinne, and goes from generation to generation, when as the child borne of them, before it be able to goe, doth shed his teeth one after another, as being corrupted and rotten, not through his fault, but by reason of the vitiousnesse and taint of the mother that painted her selfe"; *The Invective of Doctor Andreas de Laguna, a Spaniard and Physition to Pope Iulius the third, against the painting of women*, trans. Elizabeth Arnold, printed in Tuke, *Treatise*, B4.

13. See Sir Hugh Platt, *Delights for Ladies* (London, 1609; repr. ed. G. E. Fussell and Kathleen Rosemary Fussell [London: Crosby Lockwood & Son Ltd, 1948]), 92; and *Natural Magick by John Baptista Porta, a Neapolitane* (London, 1658), 242. Other examples of popular Renaissance cosmetic recipes and ingredients can be found in *The Secretes of the Reverende Maister Alexis of Piemount* (London, 1558) and John Jeans Wecker, *Cosmeticks Or, The Beautifying Part of Physick*, trans. Nicholas Culpeper (London, 1660). For discussions of toxic ingredients in cosmetics, see, for example, Maggie Angeloglou, *A History of Make-up* (London: Macmillan, 1970), 48; Elizabeth Burton, *The Pageant of Stuart England* (New York: Charles Scribner's Sons, 1962), 335–337; and Drew-Bear, *Painted Faces*, 22–23.

14. See, for example, Petrus Abbonus, *De Venenis*, trans. Horance M. Brown, *Annals of Medical History* 6 (1924), 40; also Ambroise Paré, "Of Poysons," *The Workes of that famous Chirurgion Ambroise Parey*, trans. Thomas Johnson (London, 1634), 775–815. Despite being a medieval text, *De Venenis* was regularly reprinted throughout the Renaissance and remained the primary toxicological authority.

15. Paré, "Of Poysons," 810.

16. See Mark Eccles, "Barnabe Barnes," in *Thomas Lodge and other Elizabethans*, ed. Charles J. Sisson (Cambridge, MA: Harvard University Press, 1933), esp. 175–92.

17. de Laguna, *Invective*, B3.
18. Lomazzo, *Tracte*, 129.
19. Ibid., 130.
20. Like many feminist critics, Finke echoes these arguments, identifying the "life-denying tendencies" of cosmetics with patriarchal poetic ideals of female beauty: "by attempting to kill herself into art, to realize in her own flesh the idealizations of the lyricists, [the] painted woman literally kills herself" ("Painting Women," 358 and 364). Though acknowledging the literal dangers of early modern chemical make-up, I align myself with Stern's argument that feminist support for attacks on cosmetics suggests complicity with an entrenched antagonism towards the seductive adornment and proteanism often associated with both art and "femininity"; "What Is Femme?"
21. Also alert to the problem of the body's fragility, beauty-marketers argue that cosmetics can cure rather than exacerbate the problem: "The Body, that weak and moving mansion of mortality, is exposed to the treacherous underminings of so many Sicknesses and Distempers, that its own frailty seems petitioner for some artificial Enamel, which might be a fixation to Natures inconstancy, and a help to its variating infirmities"; *Artificial Embellishments* (Oxford: 1665), 5.
22. Vives, *Instruction of a Christian Woman*, trans. Richard Hyrde (London, 1541), G3.
23. Teeth were widely identified as a protective barrier to the body's interior; a beauty writer notes: "Least the Microcosme might by supprized by any treacherous *invader*, the teeth are set as ivory *Portcullis's* to guard its entrance" (*Artificiall Embellishments*, 142). These guards, however, were notoriously vulnerable to the effects of mercury: della Porta complains of women's "rugged, rusty, and spotted Teeth", noting that "they all almost, by using Mercury sublimate, have their Teeth black or yellow" (*Natural Magick*, 250).
24. The relationship between cosmetics, expanded trade, and English attitudes toward foreign nations is a large and separate topic which cannot adequately be developed in the context of this essay. Briefly, fears of paint's corrosive power to penetrate the skin were paralleled by the threat of exotic and morally suspect foreign imports infiltrating English markets and identity: Bulwer complained that "Our English Ladies . . . seeme to have borrowed some of their Cosmeticall conceits from Barbarous Nations"; and Westfield writes of painted women, "Complexion speaks you Mungrels, and your Blood / Part Europe, part America, mixtbrood; / From *Britains* and from *Negroes* sprung, your cheeks / Display both colours, each their own there seeks" (John Bulwer, *Anthropometamorphosis: Man Transform'd: or, The Artificial Changling* [London, 1653], 260–61; and E. Westfield, printed in Misophilus, *A Wonder of Words: or, A Metamorphosis of Fair Faces voluntarily transformed into foul visages* [London, 1662], A2iii). On the impact of foreign trade on cosmetic practices, see Neville Williams, *Powder and Paint: A History of the Englishwoman's Toilet, Elizabeth I—Elizabeth II* (London: Longmans, 1957), 17–18; and Angeloglou, *History of Make-up*, 42–44. On the representations of foreigners as poisonous threats to the English body, see Jonathan Gil Harris, *Foreign Bodies and the Body Politic* (Cambridge: Cambridge University Press, 1998).
25. To early modern thinkers, the skin was understood as the sign through which one could read the body; see, for example, Margaret Pelling, "Medicine and Sanitation," in *William Shakespeare: His World, His Work, His Influence*, ed. John F. Andrews (New York: Scribner's, 1985), 1:79; and Carroll Camden, "The Mind's Construction in the Face," in *Renaissance Studies in Honor of Hardin Craig*, ed. Baldwin Maxwell, W. D. Briggs, Francis R. Johnson, E. N. S. Thompson (Stanford: Stanford University Press, 1941). On the desire to find epistemological

proof in the body, see especially Stanley Cavell, *Disowning Knowledge in Six Plays of Shakespeare* (Cambridge: Cambridge University Press, 1979); also, David Hillman, "Visceral Knowledge: Shakespeare, Skepticism, and the Interior of the Early Modern Body," in *The Body in Parts: Fantasies of Corporeality in Early Modern Europe* (London: Routledge, 1997), ed. David Hillman and Carla Mazzio, 81–105.

26. Tuke, *Treatise*, 14.
27. Ibid., 12.
28. Ibid., 58.
29. Philip Stubbes, *Anatomy of Abuses*, (London, 1583), 57–58.
30. John Downame, Foure Treatises, Tending to Disswade all Christians From Foure no less hainous than common sinnes; namely, the abuses of Swearing, Drunkennesse, Whoredome, and Bribery (London, 1613), 203.
31. Downame, *Foure Treatises*, 165; and Misospilus, *Wonder of Words*, 1. Painted women were routinely described as "*polluted with counterfeit colours*"; Tuke, *Treatise*, 5.
32. Vives, *Instruction*, I2$_v$–3.
33. *Discourse*, 33, 34.
34. See *State Trials*, ed. Howell, II, 911; cited in Fredson Bowers, "The Audience and the Poisoners of Elizabethan Tragedy," *Journal of English and Germanic Philology* 36 (1937), 491–504.
35. Tuke, *Treatise*, 41.
36. Ibid., 2. Anxiety about idols and icons was a central aspect of English Reformation thought; see, for example, "Against Perill of Idolatrie," in *Certain Sermons or Homilies* (London, 1623). Critical writings on literary preoccupations with the topic include Ernest Gilman, *Iconoclasm and Poetry in the English Reformation* (Chicago: University of Chicago Press, 1986); Kenneth Gross, *The Dream of the Moving Statue* (Ithaca: Cornell University Press, 1992); and James Siemon, *Shakespearean Iconoclasm* (Berkeley: University of California Press, 1985).
37. Downame, *Foure Treatises*, 203. He may not have been wrong, either; rather than refuting the charge, beauty guides appropriate the same rhetoric in making their appeal to cosmetic consumers: "Your Alabaster Armes and Hands Ladies, are the fleshie *altars* whereon your *superstitious* Inamorato's offer to you, as female Deities the *first fruits* of their devotion in zealous kisses. Your care should be to keep them in such a soul-inchanting symmetrie, that might confirm your Idolizing lovers in the opinion they have conceived, that you are more then mortal"; *Artificiall Embellishments*, 160.
38. Tuke, *Treatise*, 57. He similarly queries an imagined self-painter, "dost thou loue thy selfe artificiall, and like an Idoll . . . ?"; ibid., 8.
39. On idolatry and the precarious boundaries between subjects and their potential objectification, see "Introduction," *Subject and Object in Renaissance Culture*, ed. Margareta de Grazia, Maureen Quilligan, and Peter Stallybrass (Cambridge: Cambridge University Press, 1996), 1–13, esp. 3. On early modern beliefs about the autonomy of body parts, see David Hillman and Carla Mazzio, "Introduction: Individual Parts," in *The Body in Parts*, xi–xxix.
40. Guillaume Dubartas, *Divine Weeks and Works*, trans. Josuah Sylvester (London: 1608); "The Decay," 4th book of 4th day of 2nd week, ll. 153–54 and 173–75.
41. Intriguingly, some cosmetics recipes similarly assume spiritual effects from physical interventions, albeit in a more positive direction: a recipe from 1660 offers "*A Lye to make the hair yellow, bright, and long; and to help the Memory*"; Wecker, *Cosmeticks*, 45.
42. Stubbes, *Anatomy of Abuses*, 55–56.

43. Downame, *Foure Treatises*, 203.

44. Ibid., 203. Similarly, Downame describes harlots as "sweet, but poysonous potions, which delight in the taste, but kill in the digestion"; ibid., 166–67.

45. An edict from Elizabeth's reign explicitly describes the use of objects associated with artificial beauty as witchcraft: "Any woman who through the use of false hair, Spanish hair-pads, make-up, false hips, steel busks, panniers, high-heeled shoes or other devices, leads a subject of her majesty into marriage, shall be punished with the penalty of witchcraft"; cited in Angeloglou, *History of Makeup*, 45.

46. Anonymous libels warn of Lucretia's whoredom: "For neuer was the shameless *Fuluia*, / Nor *Lais* noted for so many wooers, / Nor that vncast profuse *Sempronia*, / A common dealer with so many doers, / So proud, so faithlesse, and so voyd of shame, / As is new brodel bride *Lucretia*"; I.iii.296–301. Noting the link between these scenes, Drew-Bear comments that the whore of Babylon's "branded forehead provides the biblical source for using a marked face to symbolize lust and other sins"; *Painted Faces*, 51.

47. See Revelations 17:4. The image became a popular one for the sensual and spiritual temptations of Catholicism. John Downame writes with alarm of "that cup of carnall fornications, wherewith the great whore of Babylon allureth the Kings and inhabitants of the earth to drinke also of the cup of her spirituall whoredome, and as it were the great drag-net, whereby she catcheth and captiueth more in her idolatries and superstitions, then by almost any other meanes whatsoeuer"; *Foure Treatises*, 134.

48. A beauty marketer explicitly identifies both painted and unpainted women with vessels of differing qualities, promising the purchaser of his merchandise that "Other ladies in your company shall look like brown-bread sippets in a dish of snowie cream, or if you will, like blubberd juggs in a cupboard of Venice glasses, or earthen Chamberpots in a Goldsmiths shop"; *Artificiall Embellishments*, A5.

49. On women as a model of the troublingly unbounded body in the Renaissance, see Gail Kern Paster, *The Body Embarassed: Drama and the Disciplines of Shame in the Renaissance* (Ithaca: Cornell University Press, 1994), and "Leaky Vessels: The Incontinent Women of City Comedy," *Renaissance Drama*, New Series XVIII, ed. Mary Beth Rose (1987), 43–65; also, Peter Stallybrass, "Patriarchal Territories: The Body Enclosed," in *Rewriting the Renaissance: The Discourse of Sexual Difference in Early Modern Europe*, ed. Margaret Ferguson, Maureen Quilligan, and Nancy Vickers (Chicago: University of Chicago Press, 1986), 123–42.

50. Ruth Padel explicates classical Greek beliefs about women's greater physical and spiritual susceptibility to invasion, in "Women: Model for Possession by Greek Daemons," *Images of Women in Antiquity*, ed. A. Cameron and A. Kuhrt (Worcester: Billings & Son, 1983).

51. Hippocrates, "Diseases of Women 1," trans. Anne Hanson, *Signs* 1 (1975), 572; and Edward Jorden, *A Briefe Discourse of a Disease Called the Suffocation of the Mother* (London, 1603), B1. On general medical beliefs about the female body in the early modern period, see Ian Maclean, *The Renaissance Notion of Woman* (Cambridge: Cambridge University Press, 1980).

52. Lomazzo, *Tracte*, 132–33.

53. Heinrich von Staden notes in early Greek culture "a recurrent, well-known tradition according to which women are exceptionally susceptible to impurity and dirt"; "Women and Dirt," *Helios* 19 (1992), 13. See also, Robert Parker, *Miasma*, 101–3.

54. Padel, similarly, finds in Greek medicine and literature a "general notion that women endanger men by being enterable"; "Women: Model for Possession," 11.

55. Similarly, but less directly, when Lucretia dies from exposure to her own paints, she is not their only victim; the duplicity and infidelity which her paints embody have already led her to kill her husband.

56. Massinger, *The Duke of Milan*, in *The Plays and Poems of Philip Massinger*, ed. Philip Edwards and Colin Gibson, vol. 1 (Oxford: Clarendon Press, 1976): V.ii.239–40.

57. This striking topos can be seen as a gendered subset of a broader generic fascination with using bodies and body parts as props; Robert Watson comments on this macabre revenge tragedy motif in "Tragedy," in *The Cambridge Companion to Renaissance Drama* (Cambridge: Cambridge University Press, 1990), 319–34, esp. 319.

58. A recent London production of the play used an actual complete skeleton, to brilliant effect. Unfortunately, the producer was investigated by police after a worried subway passenger noticed and reported his unusual parcel; apparently the Jacobean fondness for displays in corpses has not been inherited by contemporary Londoners.

59. *The Revenger's Tragedy*, ed. R. A. Foakes (Manchester: Manchester University Press [The Revels Plays], 1966): III.v.101. The play's attribution has long been controversial. Foakes's edition, like many, attributes the play to Tourneur, but current critical consensus suggests that the author is Middleton; see, for example, Roger Holdsworth, "The Revenger's Tragedy as a Middleton Play." The play will appear, edited by Macdonald P. Jackson, in *The Collected Works of Thomas Middleton*, gen. ed. Gary Taylor (Oxford: Oxford University Press, forthcoming).

60. *The Second Maiden's Tragedy*, ed. Anne Lancashire (Manchester: Manchester University Press, 1978), V.ii.81–83. As with *The Revenger's Tragedy*, attribution has been debated, but critical consensus favors Middleton. See Lancashire's introduction, and the forthcoming edition (titled *The Lady's Tragedy*) by Julia Briggs, in *The Collected Works of Thomas Middleton*.

61. On these triangulated structures and their homoerotic overtones, see René Girard, *Desire, Deceit, and the Novel*, trans. Yvonne Freccero (Baltimore: Johns Hopkins University Press, 1966).

62. Thomas Kyd, *The Tragedye of Solyman and Perseda*, ed. John J. Murray (Garland Publishing: New York and London, 1991): V.ii.67.

63. While women tend to be at the center of discussions of the dangers of face-paints, ample evidence indicates that men were significant consumers of cosmetic products as well. Tuke, for example, refers in his title to *Painting and Tincturing of Men and Women*; and Platt, among others, offers recipes on "How to colour the head or beard" (*Delights for Ladies*, 102). Similarly, Bulwer writes of "the like prodigious affectation in the Faces of effeminate Gallants, a bare-headed Sect of amorous Idolaters, who of late have begun to vye patches and beauty-spots, nay, painting, with the most tender and phantasticall Ladies, and to returne by Art their queasie paine upon women, to the great reproach of Nature, and high dishonour and abasement of the glory of man's perfection. Painting is bad both in a foule and faire woman, but worst of all in a man" (*Anthropometamorphosis*, 263). For further examples and analysis, see Drew-Bear, *Painted Faces*, 28–31, 73–78, and 82–84. Scenes satirizing male face painting occur in comedies such as Marston's *Antonio and Mellida*, Glapthorne's *The Lady Mother*, Massinger's *The Bashful Lover*, and Ford's *The Fancies Chaste and Noble*.

64. Anglo-phile Eutheo, *A second and third blast of retrait from plaies and Theaters* (London, 1580; reprinted in *The English Drama and Stage Under the Tudor and Stuart princes, 1543–1664*, ed. W. C. Hazlitt [London, 1869]), 104.

65. From 1548 and 1499; see Coventry, in *Records of Early English Drama*, ed. R. W. Ingram (Toronto: University of Toronto Press, 1981), 181, 193; also, Drew-Bear, for other references and discussion, *Painted Faces*, 32–33. On the use of blackface in productions of *Othello*, see Dympna Callaghan, "Othello Was a White Man," in *Alternative Shakespeares II*, ed. John Drakakis (London: Routledge, 1996), 192–215.

66. See Thomas Heywood, *An Apology for Actors* (London, 1612), ed. Richard H. Perkinson (New York: Scholars' Facsimiles & Reprints, 1941), D1v. Curiously, Heywood's adversary, John Greene, offers the same theory about "the Wine leese with which they besmeared their faces, (before that Aeschilus deuised vizors for them) called in Greek τρυγας (I. G. [John Greene], *A Refvtation of the Apology for Actors* [London, 1615; printed in Perkinson's edition of Heywood], C3).

67. John Webster, "An excellent Actor", in *New and Choise Characters, of seuerall Authors* (London, 1615), reprinted in *The Complete Works of John Webster*, ed. J. H. Lucas 4 (London: Chatto and Windus, 1966): 43.

68. Moralists who attacked both face-painting and the stage include Philip Stubbes, William Prynne, and Stephen Gosson. Gosson is a notable exception to the tendency to Puritanism; see William Ringler, *Stephen Gosson: A Biographical and Critical Study* (Princeton Studies in English, 25 [Princeton, 1942]), and Arthur F. Kinney, ed., *Markets of Bawdrie: The Dramatic Criticism of Stephen Gosson* (Salzburg: Salzburg Studies in English Literature, 1974).

69. Stubbes, *Anatomy of Abuses*, 67.

70. John Earle, *Microcosmography* (London, 1628), 57.

71. Draiton, "Of tincturing the face," printed in Tuke, *Treatise*, B2.

72. William Prynne, *Histriomastix, or the Players Scourge* (London, 1633), 159–60.

73. Greene, *A Refvtation of the Apology for Actors* (London, 1615; reprinted in Thomas Heywood, *An Apology for Actors*, ed. Richard H. Perkinson [New York: Scholars' Facsimiles & Reprints, 1941]),F1.

74. Bulwer, *Anthropometamorphosis*, B2v.

75. "Cut therefore from thee all this counterfeiting"; he continues: "circumcise from thee all this demeanour of the Stage and Players: for God is not mocked. These things are to be left to Players and Dancers, and to those who are conversant in the Play-house: no such thing is suitable to a chaste and sober woman"; *Histriomastix*, 219–20.

76. William Cave, *Primitive Christianity* (London, 1673), 66.

77. Gosson, *The Schoole of Abuse*, in *Markets of Bawdrie: The Dramatic Criticism of Stephen Gosson*, ed. Arthur F. Kinney (Salzburg: Salzburg Studies in English Literature, 1974), F2v.

78. Gosson, *Playes Confuted*, in *Markets of Bawdrie*, B8v. Gosson's comparison with the "pollution of idoles' entering by the mouth suggests a parallel between theater and the Catholic eucharist.

79. Stephen Gosson, *Apologie for Schoole of Abuse*, in *Markets of Bawdrie*, L8v; Greene, *Refutation*, A3v.

80. Downame, *Foure Treatises*, 197. The term was invoked so regularly that defenders of the theater seem to have felt compelled to offer specific refutations of it: Richard Baker writes, "Indeed, it is not so much the Player, that makes the Obscenity, as the Spectatour himself: as it is not so much the Juyce of the Herb, that makes the Honey, or Poyson, as the Bee, or Spider, that sucks the Juyce. Let

this man therefore bring a modest heart to a Play, and he shall never take hurt by immodest Speeches: but, if he come as a Spider to it, what marvel, if he suck Poyson, though the Herbs be never so sovereign" (Richard Baker, *Theatrum Redivivum, or the Theatre Vindicated. In Answer to M. Pryns Histriomastix* [London, 1662], 30). Heywood's *Apology for Actors* opens with a verse from Richard Perkins expressing the same idea: "Giue me a play; that no distaste can breed, / Proue thou a Spider, and from flowers sucke gall, / Il'e like a Bee, take hony from a weed: / For I was neuer Puritannicall" (*Apology for Actors*, A3).

81. Again, Laura Levine addresses this topic insightfully in *Men in Women's Clothing*.

82. See, for example, Sidney on poetry's ability to model, and hence create, people and things "better than nature bringeth forth" (Philip Sidney, *A Defence of Poetry*, ed. J. A. Van Dorsten [Oxford: Oxford University Press, 1966], 23).

REVIEWS

Between Nations: Shakespeare, Spenser, Marvell, and the Question of Britain.
By David J. Baker.
Stanford: Stanford University Press, 1997.

Shakespeare, Spenser, and the Crisis in Ireland.
By Christopher Highley.
Cambridge and New York: Cambridge University Press, 1997.

Reviewer: *Dympna C. Callaghan*

The image of Rodney King lying on the roadside while Los Angeles policemen rain blows down upon him is now vividly etched in the national consciousness. When the case went to court however, deconstructing the videotape frame by frame, lawyers for the defense endeavored to convince the jury not only that the brutality of this incident had been necessary because of the alleged threat represented by the lone, African-American motorist, but also that at every stage of the beating, the tables could have turned, and King might have overpowered the officers who so far outnumbered him. I mention this incident because I believe it encapsulates the problems of reading and interpreting instances of brutal, racist oppression which currently face cultural historians.

Brutality, because it is blunt and unidirectional, runs contrary to the received principles and procedures of reading and interpretation—that is, of scholarship—which aim to be careful, nuanced, and multivalent. Literary scholarship, in particular, whose practices are themselves the historical product of a certain species of political hegemony, works to complicate rather than simplify, to weigh evidence slowly and carefully rather than jump to hasty judgment. The danger is that, in so doing, such studies may become the critical equivalent of the police defense in the Rodney King case. What may seem to be simple and straightforward brutality, so such thinking goes, is, when one examines the text itself with sufficiently objective and scrupulous scholarly attention, actually enormously complex, precarious even to the point of vulnerability; a dispersal of power from a deeply conflicted and already fragmented locus of authority. What makes matters even more difficult is that those who articulate such views are, by the standards of Ph.D. programs everywhere, sophisticated readers and, no doubt, sensitive souls who would vehemently deny any allegiance with the brutality they are at such pains to mitigate.

Well-intentioned efforts to excise the brutal unidirectionality of colonialism and racism run rampant in revisionist Irish historiography, but they also represent a clear and present danger in the work of cultural scholars in general. In the current academic climate, where the impassioned anti-racist readings of the 1980s are now too often dismissed as a passing phase, it has become increasingly difficult to argue the validity of reading from the perspective of the oppressed, let alone offer that what is needed is to deconstruct the equation whereby recognition of brutality is equated with unscholarly simplemindedness. "Oppression" is, of course, now itself a dirty, outdated word onto which the evils of the colonial enterprise are regularly displaced, a word believed not only to deprive subject people of agency but also to render them abject victims. This is not to deny that long-term subjugation is a complex affair involving many cross-cultural influences and negotiations; instead, it is to deny—categorically—the much vaunted notion that power is reversible.

It is into this highly charged terrain of (post)colonial cultural studies that two excellent books, David J. Baker's *Between Nations* and Christopher Highley's *Shakespeare, Spenser, and the Crisis in Ireland*, intervene, both refusing either to simplify the complexity of early modern Anglo-Irish relations or to deny the English attempt to annihilate Gaelic culture. Baker explains:

> In Britain, the conquerors who left behind the texts by which our sense of the period has been shaped were English. And it occurred to me, as by now it will have occurred to the reader, that one of the prime repositories of this triumphal "consciousness" was the archive that we call the literature of the English Renaissance" (5).

In this literature, Baker argues, national and other identities are ceaselessly under negotiation, but:

> the communities that were caught up in the uneven and often bloody writing of the nation of England were not all of them English, and that in those communities there were many for whom "being English" was not always possible or desirable, or was so only ambiguously. These people wrote the English nation too, even sometimes, as they were being written out of it. (16)

The path taken by these books through current debates is perhaps best illustrated in relation to the grounding text (at least for literary scholars) of early modern Anglo-Irish relations, Spenser's *View of the Present State of Ireland*. The *View*, which, if it were written today about Jews, women, or people of African heritage would swiftly be rounded upon, has been, instead, in what is now the almost de rigeur apology for Spenserian fascism, painstakingly rationalized as an ambivalent and self-subversive utterance. Baker, although he goes through the obligatory rhetorical contortions that align Spenser with the Irish whom he would happily have seen removed from the face of the earth, in the end, offers a refreshing and decisive retreat from such special pleading:

> Like other English officials, Spenser can speak the language of official terror. And he does—copiously, implacably. He too insists on difference and patrols the boundaries. However, I argue that Spenser's *View* also manages to blur, if not erase, those boundaries, and that in his treatise he implies affinities with the very folk he disparages. . . . It may be that Spenser seems to exclude any recognition of Gaelic interests or values, but is this exclusion perhaps designed to 'shield' an affinity that Spenser could find no way to articulate directly? The answer to this question is of course, nowhere in the text of the *View* . . . (78–79).

But what, it might be asked, is the cultural critic to say once she or he has denounced the text? The problem with political criticism, which Christopher Highley's reading of Spenser's tract implicitly addresses, is that outright condemnation of the *View* (hitherto, the only alternative to the paralyzing ambivalence of postcolonial theory) leaves no path open for reading or discussing it. Highley argues:

> Critics have long accepted Irenius' harsh conclusion [that all bards should be executed for treason] as Spenser's final word on the bards,

but in so doing they have overlooked the nuances of Irenius's full analysis. Only superficially does Spenser's attitude to bardic culture resemble that of either Gainsford or Perrot (21).

Of course, nuance and ambivalence are everywhere to be found if one looks hard enough. But who would bother to do this, for, say, *Mein Kampf*, where undoubtedly these characteristics could also be dredged up? For Highley, however, nuance is not to be had by making out that Spenser actually is more humanitarian than he might first appear (he isn't), but in the difference between Spenser, Gainsford, and Perrot—that is, in terms of the divisions within the ruling group itself. Spenser's engagement with bardic culture is thus characterized by the familiar colonial strategy of appropriation, where the colonizer robs from a subjugated culture all those elements of it which the dominant group finds most useful. Appropriation is thus quite distinct from, and diametrically opposed to, arguments for cultural eradication. Appropriation, naturally, means that the subjugated culture then comes to have some influence on the dominant and even perhaps some sympathy with it: "[A]mong the available perspectives on Ireland were indeed angles that could foster, however tentatively, an imaginative empathy with the Irish victims of English power, and could also destabilize prejudicial constructions of Ireland and its 'wild' inhabitants" (Highley 9). Appropriation does not, however, mean that the Irish suddenly acquire as much or more power than the English any more than in our own time, for instance, the African influence on contemporary music is likely to bring about black supremacy any time soon. What concerns Highley, then, is the difference within the ruling group. For what *is* always unstable in Anglo-Irish relations is not the power relation between the occluded, subjugated Gaels and the English, but the way that power is brokered amid the ruling factions, both in England and across the Irish Sea. Herein lies the considerable contribution represented in different ways by these books to early modern (post)colonial studies.

David Baker's book, which deals not only with Ireland but also addresses itself to the other nations that comprise Britain, opens with a useful summary of the debates on English versus British national identity. The remainder of the book is divided into three sections: the first on *Henry V*, the second on the *View*, and the last on Marvell's "An Horation Ode upon Cromwell's Return from Ireland" and "The Loyal Scot." The first chapter examines "the international relations that pertained *within* the British Isles, and that were registered within *Henry V.* If ... an English audience could be brought together in xenophobic solidarity by such dramatic exhortations as *Henry V,* could this same concord be achieved when they confronted the sometimes tacit, sometimes violently overt divisions within Britain[?]" (20). By way of answering this question, Baker takes up the more famous interrogative posed by Captain MacMorris, "What ish my nation?" in relation to a real historical subject, Captain Christopher St. Lawrence. In a brilliant juxtaposition, Baker argues that the latter was, like Shakespeare's character, not indigenous Irish, but Old English, that is, part of the pre-Reformation wave of settlers who found themselves no longer sharing a religious identity with their monarch and increasingly understood to be dangerously alien rather than fellow subjects of the Crown. In fact, the play is fraught by the disparate identities that are woven into the fabric of the powerful fiction that constitutes Henry's sovereignty.

Baker's chapter on Spenser takes up the issue of why the *View* was not published when it was entered in the Stationer's register in 1598. The argument here is tricky: "[I]t was not only *what* the *View* (did not) 'reveal'—the incoherence of the common law in Ireland—but *how* Spenser chose (not) to 'reveal' it" (73). Spenser's tract, it would seem, represents too radical a solution to the Irish problem for divided policymakers. When it was finally published in 1633, conditions had changed as Irish rebels were seen to present a greater and ever more Catholic threat. Thus, the text's position "which Elizabeth's government could not countenance, was in retrospect granted full authorization" (122).

In the final chapter of the book, on Marvell, Baker introduces a new and vital dimension to his study, namely that of sexuality. Marvell was repeatedly, especially in his later years, accused of sodomy. Baker offers intriguing juxtapositions of sexual, national, and religious identities here and argues that the "Ode" is not a polemic for British union. In contrast, the intensely homoerotic "Loyal Scot" does make the case for union and takes the form of a paean to Archibald Douglas who had burned to death on his ship in England's war against the Dutch in 1667:

> Fortunate boy, if e'er my verse may claim
> That matchless grace to propagate thy fame,
> When Oeta and Alcides are forgot
> Our English youth shall sing the valiant Scot.

The homoeroticism of the poem's patriotism, Baker argues in a beautiful reading, figures precisely relations "between" that are the matter of the entity, "Britain."

Baker's title, *Between Nations*, suggests his reluctance to "take sides"; but his rigorous insistence on the multiplicities of a history which has too long presented itself as a single, unified entity is immensely valuable. My only quibble is that the national multiplicity of "Britain" did not represent multiculturalism *avant la lettre*, as Baker is sometimes in danger of implying but, rather, constituted a profoundly hegemonic, not to mention imperialist, concept.

Highley's *Shakespeare, Spenser, and the Crisis in Ireland*—although its focus, as the title indicates, is on Ireland, like Baker's book—also addresses wider "British" concerns, especially the issue of a pan-Celtic identity. The texts he addresses are *2 Henry VI, 1 Henry IV, Henry V*, and *The Faerie Queen* Book V, and the inclusion of three chapters on plays which are not primarily—or even very obviously—concerned with Ireland goes a long way toward addressing the conundrum about the precise nature of representing Ireland in the drama of the period and in the culture more generally.

> Public discussion about Ireland was, if not officially prohibited, extremely sensitive; the subject of Ireland represented a marginal, "grey," area included under the rubric of "matters of later yeeres that concern the State," and which writers in the public domain approached with extreme caution. (5)

Surprisingly, Highley argues, there was more leeway for addressing the problems of Ireland on stage than there was in print, even though dramatists (with rare exceptions) utilized strategies for disguising their subject. Thus, for example, Highley reads Prince Hal as a displaced treatment of both Essex and the notoriously rebellious Earl of Tyrone, and the effete French become the English who are incapable of engaging with the political realities of Ireland. These enormously powerful and sophisticated readings suggest a new way of analyzing historical and colonial "context" that are no longer dependent on the positivist representation of Ireland as a "theme" in a given work of literature.

Also impressive is how, throughout the book, Highley never loses sight of issues of gender. For example, his argument about *The Faerie Queene* is that, "As a reaction to the deepening crisis of the 1590's, Spenser's agenda increasingly conflicts with the queen's as he comes to imagine Ireland as a female-free zone, the site of a New

English homosocial community" (5). Indeed, Highley represents policy in Ireland as a battle between the sexes with the cult of militant masculinity set against the cult of what Essex sourly referred to as the goddess who would not listen to prayers. But the achievement here is not just one of the general argument; there also are wonderful insights into the details of the text, as when Highley identifies Sir Richard Bingham, the brutal governor of Connaught, as the hypermasculine war machine, Talus.

Highley also sheds some light on the nonpublication of the *View*. The tract was not, he argues, suppressed. Rather, registering the book without intent to publish served to stake Spenser's claim to his ideas and prevent anyone else from publishing them; but it also allowed for the controlled, semi-public manuscript circulation Spenser actively sought.

Taken together, these outstanding books offer a wealth of new information and fine literary readings. Most important, however, they open up debate about the intractable problems of reading cultural history from the perspective of the ignominious victor in the long-waged colonial contest with Ireland.

Big Time Shakespeare.
By Michael D. Bristol.
London and New York: Routledge, 1996.

Reviewer: Scott Cutler Shershow

The central question of Michael Bristol's *Big Time Shakespeare* is embodied in the near-pun of its title. Bristol considers how and why Shakespeare continues to "make it" in "the big time" (contemporary popular and commercial culture, especially the movies) even as he remains a central figure in what Bristol calls, using a phrase of Bakhtin's, "the great time," the *"longue durée"* of Western civilization (10). Has Shakespeare attained his current prominence in literary culture despite, or because of, his success in "popular" culture, both in the Renaissance and today? In particular, given that "Shakespeare" has always been, and obviously remains, a commodity with tangible value in the cultural marketplace, how are we to assess his Value in some more absolute or transcendent sense? Bristol signals at the beginning the answer to this question, which he will gradually develop as the book proceeds. He argues that "the striking adaptability of Shakespeare within the market for cultural goods and services, tends to confirm the vernacular intuition that his works have some real social worth and importance above and beyond their contingent market value" (xi).

In the first of two sections, however, Bristol pursues this argument by considering the historical construction of the latter: that is, Shakespeare's "marginal utility," his value in a hard-edged commercial sense. Here, Bristol offers a wide variety of intriguing observations about what he calls the "supply-side of culture," adapting this term (with no apparent irony) from Reaganomics to denote the shaping role of cultural producers (not only writers but also printers, performers, editors, and even critics) in determining both commercial and cultural preeminence. In an introductory chapter, he engages with various poststructuralist and "cultural materialist" critiques of Shakespearean authority, while attempting to steer a middle course between them and a "conservative culture criticism." On the one hand, Bristol clearly wants to argue, as above, for the immanent value of the Shakespearean text; on the other, he will, in the rest of the book's first section, position Shakespeare as more or less entirely a product or function of the economic marketplace. Successive chapters consider the theater business of early modern London, the development of publishing and entertainment as industries in the eighteenth century, and, finally, contemporary "mass" culture. Although Bristol treads somewhat familiar ground in much of this, he also maintains a focus on his tendentious argument about Shakespearean value. Thus, he finally reasserts that, even in the most "trivial" appropriation of Shakespeare's text (again citing Bakhtin), "the semantic potential of Shakespeare's works can 'break through' to a 'more intense and fuller life'"—which means, of course, that Shakespeare is still "essential" (117).

Accordingly, Bristol then interrupts the book with a "Reintroduction" on this "essential Shakespeare," which restates in stronger terms Bristol's own mediate position in the theoretical debate about culture. This time, more broadly and more explicitly, he expresses his desire "to bridge the gap between the conservative demand for unreflective affirmation of the ideals and achievements of Western civilization and the equally unhelpful oppositional programs of compulsive resistance and critique" (146). Next, in three final chapters, he offers complex and multifaceted readings of three Shakespeare plays. These three plays, he claims, "represent the pathos of tradition with extraordinary force and clarity" (145); and thus manage to achieve what he now bluntly calls a "literary value" (144). These plays, in other words, are "gifts" (in the famous sense of Marcel Mauss)—values that transcend the commodity marketplace in which they nevertheless continue to function.

In the remainder of the book, Bristol first interprets *The Winter's Tale* in fairly traditional thematic terms as a play that "articulates the complexity of social time and the hope of compensation and reconciled wholeness" (175). By contrast, Bristol's reading of *Othello*—which was, for me, a highlight of the book—reads the play against the grain as a kind of hideous blackface farce. If one ignores the apparent subjective depth and interiority of its characters, Bristol suggests, the play reveals itself as enacting a kind of "charivari," a carnivalesque exorcism of a marriage which the play invites us to see in racist terms as grotesque and degrading. This powerful and unusual reading seems to exemplify the critical approach Bristol had earlier described as an "honest reflection not only about the aspirations of our civilization, but equally about its costs, betrayals and its failures" (146). The last chapter discusses *Hamlet*, Mark Twain's *Huckleberry Finn*, even the comic strip *Calvin and Hobbes* in the context of a lengthy meditation on "democracy" that is difficult to summarize briefly. In effect, Bristol suggests that *Hamlet*, like Shakespeare more generally, remains an "essential" text of democratic citizenship, an expression of "communal solidarity with the past" (233)—both of which, however, are now threatened by the pervasive influence of the mass culture industry.

In the end, one can perhaps effectively summarize the question asked in *Big Time Shakespeare* as the book's publisher does on its back cover. "Is Shakespeare great? Or is it all just hype?" Perhaps it will not surprise anyone that, in Bristol's account, Shakespeare is not only "big" and not only "*longue*," but also really great. Bristol repeatedly claims, as we have seen, to be taking a middle position between an "essentialist humanism" and a kind of deconstructive or postmodern stance of resistance and critique. Despite this reiterated moderation, however, and despite even the studied hipness of its examples, the book's real agenda is, as I hope I've made clear, a reaffirmation of Shakespeare as a transcendent literary value. Similarly, for all his emphasis on the market, Bristol repeatedly asserts his belief in "the power of strong narrative forms to assert their pre-eminence over the supply side of culture" (123). Bristol envisions a "Shakespeare" who is infinitely adaptable and susceptible to appropriation at every level of cultural practice; yet who also, precisely as such, has an immanent or intrinsic worth, a "durable . . . value and authority" (xii). This, indeed, is, for me, a fundamental contradiction in the book's argument. Bristol demonstrates in detail how "Shakespeare" is merely constructed, and thus literally exists only in the process of interpretation and appropriation; but then he takes issue with the conclusion to which his own evidence inexorably leads and relocates the source of Shakespeare's "cultural stamina" (3) in the Author himself.

Bristol even seems to think that his reaffirmation of Shakespeare's "substantive value" is somehow "controversial" (xii), and that ours is "a time when the practice of reading and careful study of [Shakespeare's] works appears to be in decline" (4). I confess myself to be baffled by both claims. Is any writer today studied and celebrated, both inside and outside the academy, even remotely as much as Shakespeare? And again, isn't such a claim contradicted by Bristol's own observations about the cultural "supply side," his insistence that "the brisk circulation of Shakespeare's works in the cultural market" (xii) is what powers their success in the *longue durée*? Finally, and most importantly, does anyone truly believe that resistance to the imprisoning illusions of "literature" and "culture" is today so widespread that a reassertion of traditional values has now become the radical position? It seems to me, conversely, that both the field of "Shakespeare" and literary studies in general today are in the midst of a broad conservative retrenchment, marked by a nostalgic return to canonicity and, especially, by the adamant reassertion of "literary value." *Big Time Shakespeare*, despite its many strengths, must unfortunately be seen as contributing its voice to this retrenchment.

"Household Business": Domestic Plays of Early Modern England.
By Viviana Comensoli.
Toronto: University of Toronto Press, 1996.

Reviewer: Marion Wynne-Davies

Just as we in the late twentieth century have our television soaps, so it seems the early modern public became hooked on domestic plays. Even the themes of these Renaissance dramas appear familiar to us—"adultery, and fornication, bigamy, scolding, desertion, and violence" (p. 20)—except that, where we watch Dr. Ross in ER, they went to see Frankford in *A Woman Killed With Kindness*. This recognition of comparability is, however, by no means meant to suggest that Viviana Comensoli takes a timeless view in *"Household Business,"* although, in her Epilogue, she concludes: "there is much to recommend the earlier domestic play to the age in which we live" (151). Indeed, the text is fully grounded in a detailed and thorough historicism coupled with solid sections of close textual analysis. Thus, Comensoli traces the development of the family as "the foundation of the orderly Christian state" (18), but simultaneously acknowledges that "the domestic play brings into relief the instability of the early modern household, together with the passions, rivalries and ambivalence attending early modern theories of order" (16).

In her initial excavations, Comensoli demonstrates that the early modern domestic play was anticipated by local medieval drama, rather than the classical tradition, and draws particularly upon cycle plays and Tudor moralities in her argument. As a demonstration of this indebtedness, she focuses on the Patient Griselda narrative, especially *Patient Grissil*. In the process of this analysis, it becomes clear that her use of historicism is matched by her indebtedness to feminist theory. In this sense, perhaps the most interesting chapters of the book are those which look specifically at the way in which certain plays questioned, or indeed radically challenged, the dominant patriarchal order of the early modern family and its echo in the structure of the state. Here, Comensoli discusses *A Woman Killed With Kindness*, *Arden of Faversham*, *A Warning*

For Fair Women, *A Yorkshire Tragedy*, and *Two Lamentable Tragedies*, relating these works to shifts in economic prosperity during the period. Subsequently, in a surprising but not unreasonable shift, she turns to the witchcraft plays, *The Witch of Edmonton* and *The Late Lancashire Witches*, arguing:

> on the English Renaissance stage, the witch is a signifier of female insubordination, and witchcraft a powerful threat to patriarchal hierarchy and authority, [thus] the construction of the witch is the inversion of the ideal Protestant wife, whose insubordination overturns the orderly household and, by extension, the social order. (113)

After dealing with the marginal woman, Comensoli turns her attention from wife to husband and looks at the "Prodigal son . . . [and] profligate husband" (132) in *How A Man May Choose A Good Wife From A Bad*, *The Fair Maid of Bristow*, *The London Prodigal*, and *The Honest Whore*—although she points out that the harmony brought about at the conclusion of these plays remains fragile in comparison with the forces of disruption that precede it.

"*Household Business*" thus is an ambitious, comprehensive work covering a wide range of plays, some of which often are regarded as marginal or minor. Comensoli proves conclusively that their "patterns of resistance" deserve "critical synthesis" (26). As such, the individual sections of the book that focus on various plays will provide a much needed resource for undergraduate teaching. Finally, however, this important text offers a welcome contribution to the small, but expanding field of research on domestic literature of the early modern period.

A New History of Early English Drama.
Edited by John D. Cox and David Scott Kastan.
New York: Columbia University Press, 1997.

Reviewer: Phyllis Rackin

One of the things that make this history new is that there are no essays about individual authors and plays. Designed to displace playwrights and plays from their traditionally central position in dramatic history, *A New History of Early English Drama* focuses instead on "the social and material circumstances" in which the plays "were written, produced, performed, sold, published, patronized, read, censored, ... exploited ... and watched and listened to" (5). It is also designed to displace Shakespeare from his traditional status as "the implicit goal toward which drama before him is seen to move" instead of "a working playwright functioning within the enabling (and inhibiting) circumstances of the playhouse and printing shop" (2). It is a history of "early" rather than "Renaissance" English drama because it rejects the traditional period boundary that separates the drama of Shakespeare and his contemporaries from that of their medieval predecessors. "Renaissance," the editors argue, is an artifact of the "humanist bias against the prehistory of the Renaissance itself." The more recently favored term "early modern" is also rejected because it implies "that the essence of 'the period' is to be found primarily in its relation to a modernity of which of course it could know nothing" (3). This critique of modernity is elaborated in the first essay, "World Pictures, Modern Periods, and the Early Stage," in which Margreta de Grazia situates the book in the history of historical periodization as a postmodern "attempt to offset the modern privileging of time over space" (20–21). Perhaps, she speculates, the reason why 1576, the date of the building of the first public theater in London, is not seen as an epochal moment in history is that a "modern temporal schema tend[s] to subordinate or bar spatial transformations" (15). "To pursue them beyond their documentary value in the annals of stagecraft is to begin to break out of the limitations of modern epochality and the subjectivity it upholds" (20).

The remaining twenty-four essays are divided into three groups. The first of these, "Early English Drama and Physical Space," consists of seven essays, of which only John Orrell's focuses on purpose-built theaters. The other six deal with performances in churches, households, universities, streets and markets, and with printed drama in early libraries. The second section, "Early English Drama and Social Space," describes a variety of social contexts for theatrical production: religious, civic, domestic, royal, literary, and popular. The third section, "Early English Drama and Conditions of Performance and Publication," includes essays on touring, costumes and properties, censorship, audiences, acting styles, personnel and professionalization, authorship and collaboration, the publication of playbooks, patronage and the economics of theater, the revision of scripts, the repertory, and plays in manuscript. The divisions between the three sections and among the individual essays are somewhat amorphous, resulting in a certain amount of overlap, repetition, and sometimes contradiction. This is probably inevitable, given the fact that the editors have rejected the old maps which charted the territory by the traditional divisions of playwright or dramatic genre, and that many of the essays cover new terrain. Nonetheless, a more extensive index would have been helpful, and perhaps a timeline as well. The dates of the establishment of various companies and theaters, for instance, are given in a number of places, but only a few can be found by consulting the index.

Playwrights and plays appear only incidentally in the book, which often focuses on theatrical performances that are not ordinarily called to mind by the term *drama*. Suzanne Westfall, for instance, emphasizes that "household theater frequently foregrounded the arts of various entertainers that have never been considered in the mainstream of theater history," such as fools, animal managers, acrobats, jugglers, mimes, and minstrels, whose performances are not text-based. She cites records of a land grant awarded to one Roland le Fartere in 1331, for "making a leap, a whistle and a fart" and of "an entertainment performed in 1297 for King Edward I by Matilda Makejoy, a female acrobat and dancer" (45). Anne Higgins provides a richly detailed account of civic processions in fifteenth-century York, and Gordon Kipling describes pageants that celebrated royal entries into cities.

Historical precedents for the deemphasis of plays are provided in a number of the essays. For instance, John Orrell notes that when the first English theater with a perspective set was built in 1605, King James rejected the initial placement of his throne "in the center of the audience where the theatrical illusion would be most nearly perfect" because the other spectators would be unable to view him head-on (65). John R. Elliott, Jr. cites a spectator's account of plays staged for Queen Elizabeth's August 1566 visit to Oxford, which describes the scenery on stage, the decoration of the hall, and the seating of the playgoers but fails to mention either the titles or the authors of the plays. As Elliott concludes, the writer of the account "seems to have considered the playtexts themselves the least important part of the occasion" (71). Similarly, Jean MacIntyre and Garrett P. J. Epp point out that, because costumes were the most expensive investment made by a theatrical company, decisions to revive an old play or commission a new one may very well have been dictated by the company's ownership of the appropriate costumes (278–79).

Some of the essays are self-consciously engaged in retheorizing their subjects; most, however, simply go about the traditional business of history. Informed by the dogged empiricism of patient archival research, they make for slow reading, but they constitute a treasure-trove of information, and they offer well-documented and convincing challenges to a number of traditional assumptions. For instance, John M. Wasson argues that more than half of all vernacular plays of the English Middle Ages and Renaissance were performed not, as is usually assumed, outdoors, but inside churches (25). These included performances by professional actors as well as by choirboys and amateur players from the parishes. Wasson also argues that, contrary to the standard view, drama did not "develop in any chronological order from clergy to folk to professional actors," all of which "existed together throughout the time period under consideration. The last professional performance in a church seems to have been in 1625–26" (35). Peter H. Greenfield refutes the notion that touring the provinces was "a desperate measure taken only in times of plague in London or declining company fortunes." Previous scholarship, he notes, has emphasized the cases when towns expelled players or paid them not to perform, but these "records make up less than 5 percent of the more than three thousand records concerning performance during Shakespeare's lifetime. The "remaining 95 percent . . . indicate that entertainers were allowed to play, were rewarded, or were otherwise successful." Players, he concludes, were actually "expected to tour as a normal requirement of their occupation, not as an act of desperation" (251–52). Touring, in fact, "did not begin to decline noticeably until the second decade of the seventeenth century" (253). Kathleen E. McLuskie and Felicity Dunsworth demonstrate that the movement from a system of patronage to one of commerce was much more complicated than we have assumed, and Roslyn L. Knutson shows that the traditional practice of relating plays by dramatist and company obscures important relationships between the offerings in competing repertories.

Traditional notions of authorship are challenged by Jeffrey Masten, who argues that "early modern playwrights were far less interested in keeping their hands, pages and conversation separate than are the twentieth-century critics who have studied them" (361). As a result, the plays resist the "categories of singular authorship, intellectual property, and the individual that are central to later Anglo-American cultural, literary, and legal history" (361–62). Similarly, Eric Rasmussen challenges the traditional editorial practice of attempting to distinguish between revisions made by the authors of plays and those made by others. "The question of authorship," he demonstrates, "can never be satisfactorily resolved" (442); and Paul Werstine decisively refutes W. W. Greg's influential theory of "fowle papers," which posited a "linear model of playtext transmission from author to players" (489).

Standard assumptions about the printed plays are also challenged. Heidi Brayman Hackel points out that, despite Thomas Bodley's often-cited decision to exclude English playbooks from the new public library at Oxford, these books frequently were included in large numbers in private book collections. Barbara A. Mowat, citing examples of printed playtexts annotated for performance that were later reproduced as manuscript playbooks, refutes the standard assumption that manuscript and performance inevitably preceded print (215–16). In what will surely be the definitive study of the publication of playbooks, Peter Blayney demonstrates that there is no evidence for "the supposed reluctance of acting companies to allow their plays to be printed" (386) and the supposed eagerness of stationers "to wrest—honestly or otherwise—a play or two from the supposedly protective clutch of an acting company." "No more than one play in five would have returned the publisher's initial investment inside five years. Not one in twenty would have paid for itself during the first year" (389). In fact, Blayney concludes, the publication of plays was most likely instigated by the players as a form of advertisement to attract paying customers to their playhouses (386). Similarly, Roslyn L. Knutson points out that, despite the "canard of old theater histories . . . that players guarded their playbooks from printing in order to keep other companies from acquiring their properties and presenting them on rival stages," the companies actually "left one another's repertory holdings alone" and instead commissioned their own scripts on subjects that had proved popular in competing repertories (469).

Other essays complicate our assumptions about the social hierarchy. Michael D. Bristol argues, "Although it could not accurately be characterized as a dominant culture, the customary practices and forms of expression of the base, common, and popular element of early modern society nevertheless constituted a majority culture" (in Bristol's view, this included the "middling sort"—that is, "wealthy yeoman farmers and successful merchants," and "masters within the various craft guilds or livery companies" as well as the humbler people that the phrase "base, common, and popular" is more likely to call to the mind of a modern reader [232]). Thus, "Contrary to what earlier historical scholarship has always maintained, notions of hierarchy, subordination, and a 'great chain of being' were not the only recognized tenets of social rationality at the time" (234). Regarding the place of women, Diana E. Henderson reminds us that there were aristocratic women who "managed to avoid being confined to any of their numerous homes, much less 'the' home," while women "at the other end of the social scale might have no home at all, and they could hardly afford to create gendered space." She also points out that in Southwerk, the district where many theaters were located, "at least 16 percent of households were headed by women" (192).

Strictly speaking, this is not really a new history of early drama, but rather a collection of new historical essays planned by an editorial board consisting of David Bevington's former doctoral students at the University of Chicago as a tribute to his scholarly achievements and in gratitude for his continuing support of their work. As is the case with any anthology, some essays will interest individual readers more than others. Some, such as Peter Thomson's demonstration that modern notions of acting and character are inapplicable to early plays, should be required reading for students, but all will be required reading for scholars in the fields they cover. Most of the writers have already proved themselves as leading authorities on the subjects of their essays, and the younger contributors stand up well in this distinguished company. This is an important book.

The Homoerotics of Early Modern Drama. By Mario DiGangi. Cambridge and New York: Cambridge University Press, 1997.

Reviewer: Denise Albanese

DiGangi's book, an account of same-sex affective relations in early modern drama in England, questions the centrality that "sodomy" has assumed as a discursive category in previous studies of such relationships. Like Jonathan Goldberg, Valerie Traub, and other scholars, DiGangi notes the different taxonomic systems that anatomize Renaissance desire and that have foregrounded sodomy as a proscribed, because sensational, practice. He expands on this work by arguing, in effect, that the pressure of a Foucauldian historicism deforms recognition of a multitude of orderly same-sex relations, against which the spectacular disorder of sodomy plays itself out. In Elizabethan and Jacobean England, what throws sodomy into relief is not necessarily licit marital congress, but affective ties between men, as variously exemplified by friendship, favoritism, and the bonds between servants and masters, all of which are focal points of his study.

In interpretive practice, however, it is sodomy that throws them into possible relief. The difficulty of the task DiGangi has undertaken can be seen by way of an illustrative example early in the book. In discussing an apparently suggestive poem about Apollo's "friendship" for Hyacinth by Lewes Machin, DiGangi tellingly indicates how little we really know about what counts as "sex" for the period. But the word is part of the problem. Although DiGangi properly puts "sexual" in scare quotes, the fact is, he must invoke it normatively in order to make the case that normative and uncontroversial same-sex relations, however inscrutable, do exist in the period. One might make a similar point with respect to sodomy itself: while indubitably a category of transgression—famously, "utterly confused"—it paradoxically becomes in DiGangi's study the stable marker in relation to which a homoerotic substrate may be excavated.

As a strategic counter to the evidentiary problems a discourse of orderly homoeroticism implies, DiGangi offers a wealth of closely read passages from both little-known texts and of comparatively better-known, sometimes even centrally canonical, drama. These readings are the book's principal strength. For instance, DiGangi's analysis of the circuits of desire informing *As You Like It* is supple and informative. And he is always attentive to the deconstructive potential implicit in the contemporary texts he cites: time and again, DiGangi nicely turns around an admonitory passage, one that seems simply to inveigh against disorderly congress, to argue for the covert stability of bonds between men it presumes, and to turn the tables on the putative defenders of orthodoxy. As an instance of this latter facility, DiGangi's deft accounts of both *Edward II* and *Richard II* focus attention not on their monarchs' involvement with favorites (indeed, given other instances of male "friendship," Edward's relationship with Gaveston reads as rather lyrical), but on the men who name that involvement as sodomy—and who, in so doing, open themselves up to the charge of bringing disorder on the realm. DiGangi convincingly associates Mortimer and Bolingbroke with the transgressive effects of sodomy, which renders them all too like the monarchs they dethrone. Having thus inverted the trajectory of discourse, from accused back to accuser, DiGangi examines Chapman's tragedies of the French court to undergird his claim that homoerotic desire and sodomy need not always coincide.

At times, however, DiGangi's study would benefit from supplementation by a different kind of argument. In considering favoritism in tragedy in light of Jacobean scandal and practices, DiGangi focuses almost entirely on the image and reputation of King James, whose personal infirmities, he argues, contributed to throw the monarch's otherwise normatively homoerotic conduct into scandalous, and therefore sodomitical, relief. Given the burgeoning conditions that contributed to the revolution—and regicide—that occurred not very long after James's reign, DiGangi misses an opportunity to amplify, and render concrete, the broader conditions under which sodomy is deployed as a sign of disorder. Here, criticism of James seems symptomatic of emergent shifts in the public discourse of monarchy, undergirded of course by the material causes and agents of civil unrest. This particularly symptomatic invocation of sodomy could then enable a tweaking of the often noted link between sodomy and treason as categories of transgression.

Augmenting his readings with other types of evidence would also complicate the claims of discursive materialism with which DiGangi aligns his study. Although language is, of course, productive of cultural differentiation and the archive for early modern research is overwhelmingly linguistic, texts benefit from being read both as events and as representations, and from being placed in relation to nondiscursive formations. For instance, in chapter 3, DiGangi calls attention to research that the words *ganymede*, *ingle*, and *catamite* first appeared in English at the beginning of the 1590s, yet he does not engage with what might subtend this linguistic novelty. That new terms are available certainly might precipitate an increase in their use, and hence in representations of male-male relations, both orderly and disorderly; however, confining analysis to those representations implicitly ascribes too much unspecified agency to literary texts for the production of cultural change. More ample historical analysis would not detract focus from the aesthetic documents that otherwise occupy the chapter and, indeed, other chapters in the book. Rather, it would enable DiGangi to suggest how drama functions dialectically in relation to actually existing structures themselves in flux, and under pressure from a variety of sources. (In fact, DiGangi moves in that direction in chapter 5, where he juxtaposes evidence of a decline in traditional military service among the aristocracy with plays that represent courtiership as ceremonial and "effeminate.")

These criticisms aside, DiGangi's book nicely complements the work that has already opened up the field of early modern queer studies, via its analyses and via the wealth of new texts it introduces into the discussion; it is a useful and illuminating contribution to an important, and ongoing, project.

The Project of Prose in Early Modern Europe and the New World.
Edited by Elizabeth Fowler and Roland Greene. Cambridge and New York: Cambridge University Press, 1997.

Reviewer: Bruce Avery

Claiming that "prose remains one of the last undefined, untheorized bodies of writing in the early modern European languages" (1), in this collection editors Roland Greene and Elizabeth Fowler assemble essays that venture "outside their disciplinary confines to appraise more clearly the textual production of a period before those confines were in place" (1). The editors make no attempt to offer a comprehensive survey, however—admitting the absence of such canonical prose writers as Castiglione, Elyot, and Machiavelli—insisting, rather, that the essays printed here were selected for their focus on moments wherein the poetics and structurings of prose are on display.

By this means they hope to subject prose to the kind of surveillance heretofore reserved for the gaudy contours of verse and drama. This would put pressure on the early modern writers who ran the con that prose was transparent and conveyed the unvarnished truth, unlike the poems and plays tarted up with fancy writing that Montaigne complains of: "Fie on that eloquence, which leaves us with a desire of it, and not of things" (3). Bluntly put, this citation claims that prose is a medium invisible, so it also expresses a desire to deny that all writing—not just eloquent, literary writing—mediates experience. In response, the authors in this volume have set themselves the task of examining prose as a mediating structure, a "signifying practice" (3) whose codes enact a representation of the world far more complex than any glass could reveal.

It's a rich topic. The rise of the bureaucratic state, the emergence of print technology, proliferation of lawyers and laws, religious dispute, and the public appetite for geographic knowledge and colonial narratives are just a few of the forces shaping the pliant structures and soft textures of early modern prose. For the most part, the authors in this collection concentrate on the relationship between those forces and the formal strategies writers used to respond to them.

Stephanie Jed, for example, casts her discerning eye on the diplomatic prose of Milan, the economic and cultural transactions between Hispanola and Venice, and the marginalia of an Este military servant to show that the chivalric romance held not only a power over the imagination of kings and soldiers, but also formed a "system of particular social relations ... constructed, organized, and maintained in particular prose contexts on a daily basis" (49). Jed emphasizes that the great imaginative construct we know as chivalry was not then confined to literary discourses, but instead formed a way of knowing running through prose accounts in many different aspects of life. She shows how this discourse functioned in Venice to attract readers to newly published accounts of the New World, and to organize the facts and exotic details of the periphery in a form recognizable to the clients and investors of the metropole. Although the insight that the home authority demands representations of the exotic that fit its preconceptions is not particularly new, Jed shows this dynamic operating in a far more pervasive fashion than had been acknowledged before now.

Perhaps the most accurate aim taken at the target of this collection is by Paula Blank, in her essay "'niu reiting': The prose of language reform in the English Renaissance." Blank links the eruption of language reform tracts in the seventeenth century to an increasing anxiety over crime and social decay, showing how "inkhorn terms," or neologisms, were associated with the cant of the cutpurse classes. Prose reform, therefore, was akin to social reform. Yet, Blank concludes that for all their social zeal, many reformist schemes were also intensely personal, that "for all their ... interest in social reform," these reformers intended "to write themselves directly onto the culture" (44). The most ostensibly public writing, that is, was still structured in part by the most personal of yearnings.

Ann Rosalind Jones looks in a different realm of public prose with her study of the Swetnam controversy and the pamphlets it provoked. Swetnam's 1615 *The araignment of Lewde, idel, froward, and unconstant women*—a breathtakingly misogynistic piece, even for the seventeenth century—found itself answered by three pamphlets published under women's names. Jones ably demonstrates an important premise of this collection, that it was through prose that most of the social work of early modern culture was done. In this case, public pamphleteers brought the ancient debate over women out of the scholar's study and "into the streets and the market" (122).

In the concluding essay of the volume, co-editor Roland Greene identifies in Sidney's *Apology* and Puttenham's *Arte of English Poesie* two distinct theories of early modern fiction. Sidney's work describes fiction as "embassy," wherein "a reader enacts a diplomatic role as a visitor and mediator" between the fictional world and the actual one. Puttenham's "immanence," by contrast, "presents an alternative view of fiction as located not parallel and adjacent to actuality but deep within it, and the poet and the reader as adepts or magi rather than ambassadors" (177). Ultimately, Greene argues, "while the poetics of embassy and immanence respond to the same worldly pressures, their construals of the world are different enough to force them into what we can see only as opposed views on sixteenth century cultural politics" (191). So deft is Greene's move from the small world of Puttenham's dialog with Sidney over poetics into the large world of cultural politics, this reviewer found little to argue with and much to learn from.

That observation stands for the collection as a whole. If some of the grander claims in the introduction are overstated—whatever one's views of early modern studies over the past two decades, one cannot accuse it of neglecting prose—the individual studies collected here represent useful approaches to diverse areas of culture in the early modern period. Whether the writers studied in this collection were conning their readers or themselves when they claimed prose was transparent, these essays show the important cultural work their medium performed while eyes were turned the other way.

Shakespeare Among the Moderns.
By Richard Halpern.
Ithaca and London: Cornell University Press, 1997.

Reviewer: Kiernan Ryan

The impasse at which most criticism finds itself today is by now a familiar one. Whatever one's theoretical assumptions and political objectives may be, there seems to be no way to avoid choosing between two equally unsatisfactory procedures when tackling a text from the past. On one hand lies the option of some form of historicism, which seeks to anchor the meaning of the work in a reconstruction of the world that once cradled it, but which thereby runs the risk of rendering it irrelevant to the preoccupations of the present. On the other lies the option of releasing the work from its thraldom to its origins, treating its author as our contemporary and mining its language for modern meanings, undeterred by considerations of cultural context and historical constraint. There have, of course, been valiant efforts to dissolve this bind. New historicism and cultural materialism in particular have striven to do justice both to the strangeness and remoteness of the texts they address and to their own entrenchment in the late-twentieth-century assumptions that govern their aims and methods. But the readings produced by these approaches turn out time and again to be intractably retrospective or stubbornly narcissistic nonetheless. If the work is not reduced to a symptom of a vanished reality at the mercy of critical hindsight, it is doomed to serve solely as a mirror of the modern mind that gazes into it. This impasse is aggravated by the cognate quandary it habitually entails: how to write historically grounded, theoretically acute accounts of texts without neglecting the specifically literary qualities of their language and form, as so much of what passes for criticism these days is notoriously prone to do. What is clearly needed is a criticism that can develop a genuine dialogue between past and present; a criticism that can place the text in history and trace history itself in the letter of the text; a criticism that can reconcile aesthetic analysis and theoretical critique, that refuses to sacrifice the poetry to the politics of the work. But, although the holy grail of hermeneutics is not hard to imagine, it remains as elusive as ever.

If Richard Halpern is right, the reason why it remains elusive, the reason why criticism has proved unable to break the deadlock in which it languishes, is that the economic and cultural conditions that produced the deadlock have not disappeared. The central contention of his book is that we are still the prisoners of the contradictions faced by modernism at the start of the century, and that nothing shows this more plainly to be the case than the history of modern Shakespeare criticism. It may have appeared that the advent of theory had put paid to the dispensation founded by Eliot and sustained by the likes of Leavis, Frye, and Cleanth Brooks, leaving us to wrestle with the quite different problems posed by a postmodern universe. But, in Halpern's view, as far as criticism is concerned, modernism never ended and the postmodern condition should be seen simply as a mutation, not the nemesis, of the modernist paradigm. In the exemplary case of Shakespeare criticism, Halpern maintains, "High modernism not only dominated the cultural and critical reception of Shakespeare during the first half of our century, but continues to exert a powerful influence that is often unacknowledged or disavowed" (2). The glaring idiosyncrasies of idiom and approach that divide critics as diverse as Wilson Knight, C. L. Barber, Jan Kott, René Girard, and Stephen Greenblatt pale to insignificance beside their shared commitment to the practice of what Halpern calls "historical allegory." By this, he means basically what Eliot means in "Tradition and the Individual Talent," when he commends the special "historical sense" that allows the critic to perceive in a work both the pastness and the presence of the past. It is also what Walter Benjamin sought to achieve in his study of the baroque *Trauerspiel* in *The Origin of German Tragic Drama*: a way of mapping the profile of the present onto the contours of the past without losing respect for the text's resistance to our retroactive impositions. In short "Historical allegory," as Halpern neatly puts it, "is anachronism raised to the level of policy" (4). The crucial qualification is that "While anachronism naively collapses two historical periods by absorbing one into the other, historical allegory willfully violates distinctions without obliterating them" (4).

The rejection of the antiquarian, positivist historicism that characterized so much of nineteenth-century thought left modern criticism no alternative but to read history through literature as an allegory of modernity. At their worst, these readings have indeed succumbed to pure anachronism in their suppression of historical difference; at their best, they have at least locked horns with the impossibility of retrieving an extinct reality. Either way, this chronic loss of purchase on the pastness of the past through a lopsided absorption in the present is not a predicament, Halpern believes, that we should waste time lamenting, because the allegorising urge that accounts for it is pervasive and inescapable. It is pervasive and inescapable, he argues, because it is a cultural consequence of our subjection to the sway of commodity capitalism in its late imperialist or monopoly phase. "Under mature capitalism," Halpern claims, "allegory is no longer simply a literary technique but is rather the phenomenology of the entire social world" (13). For the rule of the commodity breeds a climate in which the meanings of objects are condemned to lie not within them but beyond them, in a parallel universe of ulterior abstraction. Everything means something else, and thus the ostensibly arcane art of the literary critic, who cracks codes for a living, is transformed into a paradigm of this ubiquitous modernist mentality.

For Halpern, historical allegory is the only critical game in town, so one might as well deal oneself in and play to win, especially when the stake is nothing less than the significance of Shakespeare. With this prize in view, he embarks on a series of allegorical interpretations of four plays—*Julius Caesar, Pericles, The Merchant of Venice,* and *Hamlet*—in each case taking a key concern of high modernism as his point of departure. Thus, the chapter on *Julius Caesar* locks onto the modernist anxiety about mass society, reading the play as an allegory of the shift from the active bourgeois public sphere described by Habermas to the passive mass culture of consumer capitalism and the welfare state. The chapter that pivots on *Pericles* builds on this by showing how the critical system of Northrop Frye, the chief champion of Shakespearean romance, "reproduces the dynamic of consumer capitalism in its most pacifying aspect" (139) and might itself be seen as "simply another romance fiction which, like *Pericles* itself, both mimics and devises a utopian response to the totalizing movement of capital" (153). Chapter 4, "The Jewish Question: Shakespeare and Anti-Semitism," begins with an illuminating comparison of the representation of the Jew in Shakespeare and in Joyce, and proceeds from there to argue, through a critique of Girard's account of *The Merchant*, that Shylock is a compound allegory of finance capital, Karl Marx, literary theory, and the author of chapter 4 himself. The final chapter trumps this argument by proposing that *Hamlet* should be read as an allegory of allegory, because Hamlet's repetition-compulsion makes him an allegorical image of the machine, the epitome of the modern capitalist economy, whose commodity fetishism turns everyone into a compulsive allegorist of one kind or another.

Shakespeare Among the Moderns is a bold, forcefully argued book, bulging with original ideas and bristling with astute observations. At its most exhilarating, it affords ample proof that reports of the death of Marxist criticism have been grossly exaggerated, and that our understanding of Shakespeare in his time and our own would be much the poorer without the insights that only Marxist methods of analysis, explanation, and critique can deliver. All the virtues of Halpern's study are on parade in the first chapter, "Shakespeare in the Tropics," which tracks the hermeneutic bind of historical allegory back to its source in the modernist cult of the primitive and the cultural crisis of imperialism. En route, Halpern restages the bizarre Victorian debate about the Bard's ethnic origins and traces its distorted echoes not only in Eliot but also in Wyndham Lewis's *The Lion and the Fox* and Orson Welles's legendary "Voodoo" version of *Macbeth*. And he winds up with a convincing genealogy for New Historicism, using Greenblatt's seminal essay, "Invisible Bullets," to demonstrate that the central role of ethnography in this allegedly postmodern school of criticism is the direct descendant of the modernists' obsession with anthropology. The crucial difference, as the punch line of the chapter makes plain, is that New Historicism "reverses the polarities of its precursors. In Eliot's criticism, methodological problems pointed to an embedded colonial content. In the New Historicism, by contrast, colonialism becomes largely an allegory of method; that is to say, narratives of colonial encounters come to signify both the interpretive dilemmas and the interpretive possibilities of Renaissance historicism" (50). A gift for elegant, tightly plotted arguments, theoretical sophistication lightly worn and lucidly deployed, a flair for exposing unsuspected affinities, and a sharp cultural historian's eye for the quirkily apt anecdote: these enviable strengths are displayed in abundance throughout *Shakespeare Among the Moderns*.

The book's tragic flaw is that its prowess is purchased at the cost of gross injustice to the plays themselves, which merely provide the hooks on which the author hangs his absorbing exercise in cultural historiography. Halpern's allegorical accounts of the plays are striking as stages in a grand theoretical argument, but they prove intolerably abstract and reductive, and thus ultimately implausible, when confronted with the complexity of the plays' poetic language and dramatic form, which have no place in his discourse. If that seems an unreasonable or uncharitable charge to level at an otherwise admirable study, it is one to which Halpern himself pleads guilty in several preemptive attempts to inoculate his thesis against critique. "It might well be objected," he observes at one point, "that my analysis of *The Merchant of Venice* bypasses its aesthetic dimension, and that my theoretical apparatus hangs heavy chains about Shakespeare's comedy. Do I not treat as a demystifying tract what is, after all, a *play*?" (210). You do, indeed, one is obliged to reply, but such a shrewd anticipation of the reader's objections does not dispose of them. Nor does Halpern's appeal to the fact that the problem with his approach is one "which haunts contemporary criticism more generally: the seemingly irreconcilable tension between literary experience and literary theory" (212). For this only confirms the suspicion that a close engagement with the verbal detail, narrative structure and theatrical techniques of Shakespeare's texts would have made it impossible to reduce them to manipulated muppets of the mode of production.

Towards the end of *Shakespeare Among the Moderns*, Halpern makes one final attempt to forestall dissent by openly conceding the reductive, mechanical nature of his method and defiantly citing Hegel's biting indictment of allegory: "It is therefore rightly said of allegory that it is frosty and cold and that, owing to the intellectual abstractness of its meanings, it is even in its invention rather an affair of the intellect than of concrete intuition and the heartfelt depth of imagination" (quoted 236). Once again, however, far from disarming the reader's qualms, this only reinforces them and brings them into sharper focus. Earlier on, by a nice stroke of irony, Halpern reproduces the cover illustration of a popular primer published by the New Home Sewing Machine Company of Chicago in 1890. The cover portrays the Bard submerged to the shoulders and simmering away in a cannibals' pot, across which is stamped the legend *Shakespeare Boiled Down*. Halpern naturally seizes the opportunity to wax witty at the pamphlet's expense. But insofar as he is just as guilty of "boiling Shakespeare's works down to their narrative bones," avoiding "the sheer labor of reading entire plays," and thereby "eliminating the difficulties as well as the beauties of Shakespearean language," *Shakespeare Boiled Down* might well have served as the subtitle of his own book.

Reading the Renaissance: Culture, Poetics, and Drama.
Edited by Jonathan Hart.
New York and London: Garland Publishing, 1996.

Reviewer: Elizabeth Fowler

These days, collections of essays have a difficult life. Festschrifts are out of fashion with presses and have to be smuggled in under cover of some unity other than the "genealogical." No one, I suppose, gets credit for writing that flaunts its derivation as a debt to someone of a senior generation rather than, say, some newly discovered theorist preferably dead, foreign, and in another field. Still, one regrets the loss of such a motive for contributors' writing—if it sometimes produces embarrassing anecdotes, the awareness of an esteemed audience with a personal interest in one's achievement can inspire an accountable excellence. For when volumes are spawned by the momentary excitement of conferences or other collaborative brainstorming, the thrill is gone by the time the finished essays have been collected. Contributors often put their own future projects ahead of a line of credit that has already bought its space on their vitas. Early finishers threaten to pull their essays as they grow cold, later finishers forestall their editors from editing by means of pinched time and relief. Under pressure of a difficult sell, introductions appear after having been shopped around as advertisements to editors, and they may resemble the urgent if threadbare manifestos of moderate compromise political parties more than they resemble the contents of the volumes. Once the volume is out, purchasing it can cost five times as much as a photocopy. Perhaps more journals should be open to special-issue proposals by guest teams of contributors; the potential coherence such an undertaking can bring about—somewhere between the unified topicality of collaborative writing and the miscellany of a journal—seems worth promoting. There is still a substantial brief to be argued for the festschrift as it makes visible how teaching influences the vicissitudes of literary history.

Meantime, a reviewer can take up the job of explaining what a volume has done. In the case of Jonathan Hart's *Reading the Renais-*

sance: Culture, Poetics, and Drama, the individual works have no apparent relation to or interaction with each other (why must they?) except the good will they must represent to the dedicatee, elder statesman G. Blakemore Evans, and the editor. The title is a less strenuous echo of Rewriting the Renaissance, now ten years old and still much cited. This volume has nothing particular to do with reading, except insofar as it collects work by literary critics. The echo conveys the fact that Hart brings together work on literatures in different languages, though not too different: English, French, Italian, and Spanish and the writers covered are the usual suspects. The lack of surprise no doubt makes the work more useful. On the criterion of usefulness, I must register a complaint that French, Italian, Spanish, and Latin are not translated into the language of the essays. As there are relatively few quotations throughout, taste, rather than space, must have been the obstacle. More than merely assisting ignorant readers, translation can provide expert direction on texts for the classroom. Hart does append a bibliography and index, both welcome and increasingly rare.

It is unremarked in the introduction, but with the exception of three otherwise useful essays, the volume is all about genre. Perhaps some of the contributors would balk at this description (does it seem a little old hat?), but nearly all of the premises and most of the conclusions drawn by the authors produce their meaning in terms of genre theory. Further, seven of the eleven essays treat Shakespeare at length; the index competently refers us to individual plays as well as to mentions of the playwright. Unlike Rewriting the Renaissance, this volume isn't cheap, exciting, or topically focused enough to order for graduate seminars. However, reading about Shakespeare in the context of thought about genre and of writings in the languages of the Western European high Renaissance is virtuous, and there are a few important essays here that should not be neglected. Genre is one of our means of talking about large-scale events in language across time and culture, as well as in texts as brief as a few lines. It has always been central to comparative literature. If genre theory is to sustain its power as a methodology, we must be able to collocate genre with other large-scale events as they are registered in language—events such as those that we call subjectivity, the disciplines, gender, and ideology.

The most important piece here, in my view, is Paul Morrison's. In an essay on *Hamlet* and *Phèdre*, he adds a crucial qualification to the (overly) received wisdom that *Hamlet* is about a newly interior, modern subjectivity. In the face of Harold Bloom's grand pronouncements that Hamlet sets an epistemological horizon around an "us" originated by Shakespearean characterization ("we cannot judge a mode of representation that has overdetermined our ideas of representation," says Bloom), Morrison reminds us that there is more to *Hamlet* than characterization. He does this partly by making a distinction (one the play undoes) between Hamlets: the play, the son, the father. (Here, I wanted an engagement with Peter Stallybrass and David Aers, who, among others, have powerfully qualified the thesis that the Renaissance originates individual subjectivity.) What more than characterization is there? Morrison calls upon Aristotle, whose notion of tragedy requires the precedence of action (praxis) over character (ethos). The whole of the play, represented here by genre, confounds the notion of interiority it attributes to the Prince Hamlet of the early scenes. It reveals that notion to be an effect of Hamlet's passion and standpoint. There are many fine points and passages in the course of Morrison's argument. He manages to work not only according to notions of tragedy and characterization, but also, ambitiously, in terms of genre history and ontology.

It is important, and not always easy, to discriminate between the formal and the historical evidentiary force of one's arguments. I disagree with Morrison's assumptions that drama is the central cultural form of the Renaissance and that it is displaced in this status by the modern novel (181); even among literary forms, one need only recall the sermon to see that his view is a projection of the curriculum of departments of English upon the past. A greater involvement with Shakespeare's English contemporaries—especially Marlowe—would also have readjusted his sense of what about his analysis admits of chronology. I wish he had opposed Bloom more directly, which his argument allows, and had conceded that Stanley Cavell's observation is about Hamlet's *perception* of the human condition, his "sense of debarment." This is very different from Morrison's representation of Cavell as declaring that Hamlet is debarred (185). I wish that Morrison hadn't shifted his (and Aristotle's) terms in order to bring Racine together with Shakespeare: whereas the relation between *praxis* and *ethos* is constitutive in the first (Hamlet) half of Morrison's essay, suddenly, at page 198, we find: ". . . for Aristotle 'role,' be it construed in social or dramatic terms, enjoys priority over 'character,' and for Racine, the role of Princess, the status of Princess, is itself a full explanation of motives." It's a long way from "praxis" and dramatic action to "status," and that distance makes, for me, a very creaky hinge between the two plays. The comparison between them is helpful perhaps mainly because it allows us to consider Barthes on Racine.

The essay subordinates the propositional content of Hamlet's soliloquies to the dramatic action: this is important because it allows us to see Hamlet's pride of place in the history of subjectivity as an effect of individualism. Over time, Hamlet's subjectivity has been excerpted from its context just as the soliloquies have become set pieces isolated from the plot. In Morrison's treatment, we can glimpse how even the play's recalcitrantly secret or interior subjectivity is projected out of the investments of character in devotional practices, the duties of genealogy, plot, dramaturgy—all the machinery of the dramatic text and the theater. This throws a powerful light on the status of genre. When Morrison writes, "The unwittingly oxymoronic declarations of the earlier Hamlet—the public insistence on a secret singularity, the self-dramatizing refusal of the dramatic—become the fully conscious paradox of a willed abandonment of the volitional" (191), we must remember that he's talking about a revenge tragedy. Together with the (perhaps more disastrous) willed *embrace* of the volitional, the "willed abandonment of the volitional," makes an apt description of the plot of revenge tragedy. Its propositions about subjectivity are always subordinate to the action of the plot. The model of subjectivity that grows out of the revenge tragedy has an event-horizon in history. Once we see that genre is a means of producing the experience of subjectivity as well as representing it, we'll be able to take our genre theory with us, as Paul Morrison has done, in order to chart that history of subjectivity more precisely.

The method of another contributor again raises the question of the proper relation of plot to character, but in a less satisfying way. Katy Emck's essay on transvestism in *As You Like It* and *La vida es sueño* places gender at the center of identity (not unlike Shakespeare) in a comparison of the two plays that relies almost entirely on plot summary, quoting only a couplet from Shakespeare and two brief passages from Lope de Vega near the end. Her thesis is that "the heroes emerge into masculine authority through the maturing and civilising processes which the heroines enable in them" (82). The "pleasurable incommensurability" that she traces in Rosalind is inextricably tied to an implicit ideal of the independent woman, a tricky (and individualist) ideal to import into comedy, with its closure by marriage for all genders.

Jonathan Hart's own contribution, twice the length of most of the others, takes up the topic of closure in comedy (including *As You*

Like It and *Twelfth Night*) and draws our attention to its "loose ends." Certainly he is correct in emphasizing the ways in which the strong, resolving moves of comedy are accompanied, in the many plays he treats in four languages, by significant exceptions. (The familiar demurring note is best suggested by the figure of Malvolio.) Yet the significance and effects of such mixed endings are not yet digested here. Hart, too, relies heavily on plot summary, which perhaps is useful for teachers thinking of adding to a syllabus a play they do not know, but is not the most powerful mode of argumentation. Since the loose ends of comedy turn out, in this essay, to have to do with gender ideology and audience response to strong vice characters, and since Hart's emphasis is on emotional tone, I felt the lack of historical research into reception.

The essay by Richard A. Young shuttles between *Fuenteovejuna* and *El beso de la mujer araña* in order to struggle with the extent to which genre is mutable, mixable, and prone to figuring its opposites within itself. The topic is rich, and so is the comparison, but it seems to dissolve in Young's hands to the point where he states flatly on the last page that the works are "not comparable." The migrations that genre makes across time and texts also inspire the essay by Keir Elam, who offers a tight argument with wonderfully clear evidence and occasional moments of giddiness. His example treats *As You Like It* and its prose source in Thomas Lodge, showing that the richest use of source study is as a laboratory for literary issues and that it can avoid entirely the object of discovering Shakespeare's attitude to Lodge or to the pastoral. Elam's intensely formalist genre history not only opens up to theoretical propositions, but also returns to the play, constantly testing its observations against the details of the play's effects. The essay is chock-full of specific and well-expressed observation; it convinces me that there is still much to learn about genre history in action. Among fine readings of plays, Harry Levin's account of *Richard III* succeeds in a rich style without the aid of an argument. It's a pleasurable way to get a fair amount of digestible information and, though its focus is on Act V, would serve nicely as an introduction to an edition of the play.

Among the other essays, three brief calls for (or heralds of) future work appear. Steven Rendall takes paradigms that have grown up in recent histories of reading and looks for representations of the social situation of reading in Marguerite de Navarre's *Heptaméron* and elsewhere, making provocative comments about the pacing of writing and reading (and the experience and theoretical force of boredom) in a culture which is temporally much different from our own. This attention to reading as a practice that has a sociological dimension is a nice complement to Thomas Greene's sweeping essay on ritual. Both employ philological sketches (Greene of "ceremony," Rendall of "reading") that help to keep them from the kind of associative surfing that plagues or enlivens—depending on your taste—Robert Rawdon Wilson and Edward Milowicki's essay on *Troilus and Cressida*. Greene floats a hypothesis that ceremonial and ritual acts play a central role in earlier societies and an impoverished role in our contemporary life. The Renaissance is a moment where we might be able to trace profitably the effects of this shift, which entails secularization, changing theories of language and semiotics, evolving political ideologies, and, of course, developments in art. After a series of episodic treatments of crises that "confronted the communal, performative sign" (20) and are conveyed rather in the style of an extremely brilliant answer to an orals examination question, Greene proposes a new subdiscipline to be called "historical semiotics" that might include an academic program and a scholarly journal. Such a manifesto is particularly welcome at a time when Yale's own interdisciplinary Ph.D. program in Renaissance Studies, to which Tom Greene has been a pillar, has been undergoing generational changes of the guard. The ritual magic that creates objects of study and academic degrees wanes and waxes in its practices and efficacy, too, and deserves such sound argument. The emphasis on ritual that this essay provides has much to recommend it: Greene directs our attention to the effects of art, even though most of his adduced examples lead us to ideas *about* such effects: the essence of ritual is that it is performative rather than propositional. Surely the history of ideas, if it is to survive at all, must reconceive the status of ideas themselves in similar ways. There is much work on the ritual capacities of language and their relation to art (including important work in the Renaissance such as Roland Greene's, which draws on the anthropologist Tambiah); I would have liked to see this essay benefit from a more complex notion of ritual itself.

The third essay that prepares for future work is Carla Freccero's brief manifesto on women writers in Italy and France. In a characteristically heavy style charged with political urgency, it surveys the now canonical women writers of the Renaissance and considers their situations in the light of patronage systems and gender ideologies. It would make a good starting point for scholars about to take up these authors, although it is bibliographically thin and contributes nothing in the way of primary research to the questions it takes up. Reading recent work on women writers in the Renaissance, I am struck by the fogginess of our sense of their interests and motives. When we evaluate patronage systems according to the criterion of gender, a task Freccero admirably and rightly takes up, what kinds of things are good for women? What do they choose or wish for or benefit from when they write? How can we characterize their ambitions? Now that work such as that of the trio of Lisa Jardine, Anthony Grafton, and William Sherman suggests that poetry is often written in order to advertise one's talents for other kinds of occupations, we much consider our attribution of interests to women afresh and look for evidence outside of the poetry— in the institution of patronage as well as elsewhere—in order to understand more about how gender ideology works for and against women in the act of writing.

Finally, an essay by Lisa Neal on the topos of *ultima verba* in Montaigne is clearly a foretaste of work she will be doing on the topos in other authors. The central perception of this essay, in my view, is the recognition of the crucial relational quality of theories of meaning. Friendship as a model for reading and meaning is rich (her sense of it might be deepened by the work of Wayne Koestenbaum and Jeffrey Masten), and the role of the friend in death is a nice way into this problem in Montaigne. Neal is quick to cause particular passages to stand for propositions and ideas, a kind of crunching that takes skill; but she is not as clear about the consequences of her observations. In fact, ideas as they appear in the essays may not always sort out logically, but they are bound to be up to other things besides the ideational proposition. The dramatic context she traces in the deathbed scene of *ultima verba* is a promising setting for pursuing such other activities.

The Body in Parts: Fantasies of Corporeality in Early Modern Europe.
Edited by David Hillman and Carla Mazzio.
New York and London: Routledge, 1997.

Reviewer: Graham Hammill

The anthology *The Body in Parts* presents itself as a kind of critical blazon of the early modern body, each essay focusing on some body part which, in its negotiations with the whole, frustrates and suspends attempts towards a corporate unity. The net effect is to produce "a new aesthetic of the part" which does not "rely upon the reintegration of the part into the whole" (xiv), as David Hillman and Carla Mazzio put it in their introduction. This is, I think, what is least interesting about the anthology. Rather, to my mind, the critical value of *The Body in Parts* lies in the attempts of a number of its quite intelligent and probing essays to confront the problem of how a cultural studies of the sixteenth and seventeenth centuries might address historical change and its embodiment. That the body and various corporeal parts serve as an archive which sustains layered cultural memories is an argument so familiar as not to need any rehearsal here. But, insofar as this argument focuses solely on corporeality as an archive of cultural tradition—no matter how quirky or interesting that tradition, and no matter how critical one might be of that tradition—it affords no place for change: how history might impinge on culture, fracture it, render it incoherent; how culture might capture, display, and embody historical change as such.

Confronting these questions through an analysis of the joint, Marjorie Garber considers how a gesture that purports to enact, secure, and embody continuity turns against itself to posit discontinuity as a mode of being. Beginning with the political gesture of kneeling, Garber discusses how the bending of the knee is a physical act whose ritual significance can be "bent" to mean something other than what it is supposed to mean: "the knee as body part does not always connote homage or prayer. Although it is *metaphorically* a sign of linkage and thus obeisance, *metonymically* the knee rebels" (27). The cultural trope for this bending of meaning, she proposes through references to Shakespeare, is the bending of the joint. This relationship between gesture and trope allows Garber to imply that the phrase "out of joint" abstracts the failure of the knee's metaphorical capacity to express fealty and historical continuity. With reference both to *Hamlet* and to Slavoj Zizek's reading of F. W. J. Schelling, Garber argues that "out of joint," a philosophical statement about being in a time of discontinuity, is itself an abstraction of the failure of the gesture of kneeling to secure homage, obeisance, and thus continuity. Finally, Garber concludes by positing dismemberment as a particularly theatrical aesthetic phenomenon which she pits against the fascist aesthetic of the body without joints—a body whose main emblem is, for Garber, the Nazi goose step and salute. Throughout, Garber refuses to limit her analysis to the "writing" of culture on the body. Instead, she sustains an analysis of subjectivity and embodiment exactly at the place where culture as the expression of tradition falters, that is, exactly at the place where culture as the social mechanism for expressing historical continuity productively turns against itself.

One of the best features of this collection is that some of the essays in it address the problem of corporeality and historical change by focusing on relations between medical and religious discourses and practices. Beginning with an analysis of Francis Bacon's *Sylva Sylarum*, but mainly discussing Helkiah Crooke's *Microcosmographia*, Gail Kern Paster focuses on medical representations of arteries, veins, and nerve fibers as the networks of a particularly explosive spirit which keeps things alive and in motion in order to propose that these networks comprise an early modern imaginary physiology of the self which replicates, naturalizes, and displaces the constitutive violence of what Norbert Elias calls the civilizing process. Persuasively arguing for a dogged literalism when interpreting this body, Paster is able to avoid a simple treatment of the imaginary physiological body as social allegory, and instead begins to develop—quite eloquently, I think—a poetics of force in which the figuration of a physiological, explosive spirit is an historically specific crystallization of the civilizing process's aggressivity. This crystallization, Paster suggests, tends to rationalize contrasting ethical tropes "like impulsiveness versus self-containment, spontaneity versus calculation or strategic thinking" (121) that one might find emplotted in Shakespeare's plays. Paster's argument could serve as the chiasmic "other half" of Katherine Rowe's intelligent analysis of Crooke's *Microcosmographia* and of the anatomist's hand. Rowe argues that the cut of the anatomist is organized and contained by configurations of the hand, both as mechanistic instrument and as an emblem for the expression of intention and unity. Rather than develop her argument simply through the familiar interpretation of dissection as a form of violence on some chaotic maw of corporeality complicit with other forms of violence such as the execution of prisoners, Rowe begins suggestively to tease out the ways in which the anatomist's touch is a creative gesture for "integrating sacred mystery and corporeal mechanism" (287) precisely as a tactic for suspending a clear alignment between interiority and intention one finds in developing notions of privacy. While Rowe's analysis makes a strong attempt to extend the arguments of Jonathan Goldberg's *Writing Matter* (Stanford, 1990) implicitly against Jonathan Sawday's *Body Emblazoned* (Routledge, 1995), Paster's argument, especially concerning Elias, could allow for a stronger articulation of exactly how she is reconfiguring violence through strategies of dispossession. Moreover, Rowe's focus on the cut as a methodological way for conceiving of relations between medical and religious discourses and practices outside a simply linear narrative of the paradigm shift could quite productively extend Paster's analysis of spirit as force. What these two essays together begin to posit is a way of thinking about the embodiment of a historical change that modes of cultural expression cannot, per se, grasp.

In order to raise corporeality in terms of temporality rather than cultural memory, Stephen Greenblatt focuses on mutilation as a mark which is distinguished from the "local accounts" (222) that have characterized a great deal of his own obviously extremely influential historicist work. Beginning with a discussion of Jewish circumcision as a Christianity myth of origins that serves to validate Christianity's insistence on the centrality of the mutilated body of Christ as an allegory referent for its own assertions of universalism, Greenblatt goes on to argue that, in its encounters with non-Europeans, Christian Europe developed an ethnography that translates the Pauline historical and hermeneutic opposition of Christian spirit and Jewish flesh into an "early modern heterology" that reads the peoples of the "New World" with attention to "particular, distinctive bodily customs" and to "the universal meanings that are disclosed in those same customs" (229). Instead of thinking of history as a secularizing supercession of religious modes of thought, Greenblatt mobilizes the cut in order to propose that sixteenth- and seventeenth-century ethnography reconfigures Pauline tropes of sacred and demonic as natural and unnatural, figured both in exploration narratives and in the culture of dissection. Greenblatt's analysis could, I think, be productively paired with Kathryn Schwarz's essay on the Amazonian breast. Schwarz begins with the assertion that the breast is both a physical referent for the domestic categories to which women are relegated and also, in its instrumentality, the body part which imposes the supposedly self-evident cause of women's subjection to those categories. It is the Amazon, Schwarz continues, and specifically her displayed cut—("Everyone knows that the Amazon is missing a breast" [148])—that threatens to derail the iconicity and instrumentality of the breast such that its formal, metonymic figuration is exposed as such. Schwarz concludes with a discussion of exploration narratives and their preoccupation with the inability of European explorers to find Amazon who displays the cut of the missing breast. Not only would Schwarz's analysis compel a rethinking of Greenblatt's understanding of Paul (which follows the formative essays of Jonathan and Daniel Boyarin) to include at an integral level sexual difference, but also the two essays together would allow for a more extensive analysis of the cathexis and remnants that result from the use of the cut as historical trope.

Hillman and Mazzio divide the essays collected in *The Body in Parts* into three sections. Part One, "Subjecting the Part," includes essays by Garber, Hillman, Mazzio, Paster, and Nancy Vickers. According to Hillman and Mazzio, these essays all focus on how the part "becomes a *subject*, both in the sense of being subjected—of being isolated and disempowered—and of being 'subjected'—imagined to be endowed with the qualities of intention and subjectivity" (xix). For example, Vickers compares French anatomical blazons and the woodcuts that accompanied them with contemporary anatomical dissections in order to argue that, whereas anatomical treatise relied upon a projected reintegration of the dissected body through medical knowledge, in the blazons, especially in their printed form, the part takes on the capacity to "[undermine] any integrity the poems themselves might have made" (8). In her essay on rhetoric and treatise on language, Mazzio argues that the tongue, imagined as separate from its corporeal habitation, comes to embody worries over "the powers and the vulnerabilities" of language and social codes, resulting in the fantasy of an aggressive sense of orality that dominates a "heavily textualized culture" (69). And, in his essay on *Troilus and Cressida, Hamlet,* and *The Winter's Tale,* Hillman argues that the question of skepticism, understood and developed mostly via Stanley Cavell, infuses Shakespeare's references to human entrails such that skepticism turns into a desire for "absolute knowledge of the body's interior" (84). But, Hillman adds, following Cavell, skepticism is at root a refusal to acknowledge the otherness of the other—a refusal portrayed in "stiffening" of the skeptic's body, "more or less physically steeling the interior of his body against the coming of an unbearable thought" (94).

Part Two, which includes essays by Sergei Lobanov-Rostovsky, Jeffrey Masten, Katharine Park, and Schwartz, is entitled "Sexing the Part." Perhaps it is to be expected that the essays in this section show how "logics of sex, gender, and sexuality are to be located in quite specific bodily sites" (xx). Perhaps also to be expected, these "sites" tend to turn into loci of power and/or cultural anxiety. Park focuses on the clitoris, the *tribade*, and the "problematicization" of enlarged female genitalia in early modern French medical literature in order to map out changes in mid-sixteenth-century French medical thinking on sex and sexual difference and to suggest the "discovery" of the clitoris figured "the perversity of women" (187) usually figured in the *tribade* as French medical writers' primary worry. Lobanov-Rostovsky focuses on the eye in order to argue that its capacity to transcend its status as flesh in its assertions as the organ of epistemic domination—evidence of which he finds in both literary and medical texts of the period—produces a "privileged male subjectivity threatened by anatomy's reduction of the eye to the flesh" (197), a subjectivity he locates (quite predictably, I think) in the development of the sonnet. And, Masten, seeking to expand the work of Jonathan Goldberg and Patricia Parker among others, argues that critical attention to a "discourse of fundament" (138), a word used in sixteenth- and seventeenth-century England to mean variously "foundation," "buttocks," and "anus," might allow for the assertion of the sodomitical as something other than "preposterous." Masten poses this philological insight alongside worries over the psychoanalytically engaged discussions of male homosexuality of Leo Bersani, Lee Edelman, and Guy Hocquenghem.

Part Three, "Divining the Part," includes essays by Greenblatt, Rowe, Michael Schoenfeldt, and Scott Manning Stevens. According to the editors, the essays in this section "reveal ways in which not only the condition of embodiment but even the very vulnerability of the body can empower the believer, linking him or her to the central image of corporeal suffering in Christianity, the body of Christ" (xxii). For example, Schoenfeldt locates the stomach as "a particularly intense focus of inwardness" in its capacities for accomplishing digestion (243), mainly in an effort to consider how "early modern individual inhabited and experienced their [Galenic] bodies" (244), and developed through that habitation an ethical relation to the self as en route to the Divine. Stevens's essay, too, focuses on relations between the sacred and the medical bodies. Why is it, he asks, that a Counter-Reformation liturgical practice "locates Christ's self in the image of the heart" at the same time that "medical science is coming to recognize the brain as the center of the human self"? (264). His answer is that the Counter-Reformation church developed an iconography of the medically accurate heart precisely because it was so overdetermined by religious traditions. The medically accurate heart could thereby make a frontal assault on science and its privileging of the brain. Christ's sacred heart—even anatomically accurate in its portrayal—seems iconographically effective for the production of religious sentiments, whereas Christ's anatomically accurate brain is iconographically unthinkable, so Stevens argues.

The volume concludes with an essay by Peter Stallybras on feet.

Engendering a Nation: A Feminist Account of Shakespeare's English Histories. By Jean E. Howard and Phyllis Rackin. London and New York: Routledge, 1997.

Reviewer: Susan Frye

When Jean Howard and Phyllis Rackin, two of the field's most eminent and lively scholars, collaborate to produce *A Feminist Account of Shakespeare's English Histories*, it is an intellectual occasion of note. Shakespeare's histories, as the authors point out, have been a neglected area for feminist scholars until just recently. This readable and timely new book participates in filling the gap with insights into theatrical history and the history plays that make it a must read for anyone interested in English drama. As the authors demonstrate, how we interpret the histories is central to our conception of Shakespeare, since characters like Richard III and Hal anticipate his male tragic figures and since the tragedies themselves frequently are rooted in history. The histories are equally crucial to enlarging and "re-viewing" the connections drawn between early modern plays and the society that produced and consumed them.

In *Engendering a Nation*, Howard and Rackin combine their complementary but different perspectives—and selections from their earlier research and writing (xviii)—into a single work that argues that the study of gender in the history plays provides new insight into the development of nationhood. In this argument, carried across all the history plays except *Henry VIII*, nationhood is an imagined community that the theater helps to create and explore. Gender is inseparable from these processes, because gender "is constructed in and through the entire fabric of society" (40).

The book is divided into three parts, each with several short chapters. This organization is ideal for the graduate and undergraduate reader, as well as for the scholar and the more general reader. Part I, "Making Gender Visible: A Re-viewing of Shakespeare's History Plays," functions as an introduction to the issues taken up within the volume. In "Thoroughly Modern Henry," the authors demonstrate how plays may be situated historically by considering the very different contexts that produced the *Henry V* films of Laurence Olivier and Kenneth Branagh and the different ways in which they treat Katherine of France. The second chapter, "The History Play in Shakespeare's Time," situates the theater in the growing commerce of England. Because the theater was based in London, the fast-growing economic hub of an emergent nation, it became a site for the development of an imagined community (in Benedict Anderson's phrase) of subjects and nationhood.

The third chapter, "Feminism, Women, and the Shakespearian Play," gets down to the fact that not one of the protagonists in Shakespeare's histories is female. Here, Howard and Rackin demonstrate the importance of studying not only individual female characters but also gender difference, marriage, and the distinction between "public" and "private" actions and spaces. This chapter also puts forward a driving argument of the book glimpsed in Rackin's earlier work, that between the two groupings of Shakespeare's history plays known as the "tetralogies" a profound shift occurs in how gender is staged. Chapter four, "The Theater as Institution," builds on and recontextualizes Howard's research on the women in Shakespeare's audience to explore the contrast between the public milieu of the theater and the increasing injunction for women to stay at home as part of a larger argument about how the history plays present new structures of performed monarchial authority.

Part II, "Weak Kings, Warrior Women, and the Assault on Dynastic Authority: The First Tetralogy and *King John*," contains four chapters demonstrating the transition the authors identify between the *Henry VI* plays and *Richard III*. Because the more episodic *Henry VI* plays focus on heredity rather than nationhood, the figures of women are far more significant than in the later plays of *Richard III*, *Henry IV, Parts I & II*, and *Henry V*, which are concerned more with representing the problems of unifying a nation under a single male figure. The powerful female figures of the *Henry VI* plays, however, are represented as demonic and violent, whether associated with marriage and offspring or not. In *Henry VI, Part I*, Joan La Pucelle's cross dressing on the field of battle and charges of promiscuity associate her with the "disreputable feminized world of the playhouse" (51). In *Henry VI, Part II*, the demonized, ambitious female figures of Margaret and Eleanor threaten the masculine order, while the class issues associated with Joan are picked up in the rebel, Jack Cade. In *Henry VI, Part III*, Margaret charges into the gap left by failed masculine authority figures, most notably her husband, Henry VI.

Much of the chapter on *Richard III* makes available Rackin's earlier pathbreaking argument that Richard is a demonic tragic hero on whom fall the theatrical power and agency of Joan, Margaret, and Eleanor. The demonic male and the powerless, complaining females in turn produce the opportunity for Richmond to appear at the play's conclusion, while the entire idea of a wife is so tainted that Richmond's intended, Elizabeth, does not even appear. The fifth chapter in this second part, "*King John*," provides a provocative reading of this frequently overlooked play to argue that Shakespeare rewrites his sources to expose the extent to which patriarchal succession and the marginalization of women are central to the historical enterprise associated with masculinity. As such, *King John* may well constitute a reaction to the masculinist control of *Richard III* and so might be dated between the two tetralogies. I can only hope that this analysis of *King John* may increase interest in staging this play.

Part III, "Gender and Nation: Anticipations of Modernity in the Second Tetralogy," engages the most familiar of Shakespeare's history plays, *Richard II*, the *Henry IV*, plays and *Henry V*. As in

Richard III, in *Richard II* the women come from the upper classes and subsist in the world of contemporary England, where the division of labor and placement of women in private spaces is strictly enforced. *Richard II* destabilizes the relation between male and female, between the authority of history evident in the *Henry VI* plays and the authority of theater in ways partly dramatized in Deborah Warner's 1995 production in which Fiona Shaw played Richard. The chapter on the *Henry IV* plays emphasizes their displacement of the chronicle by "chorography," or construction of readers as inhabitants of England as a geographical space (49). Acted at the tavern, the court, Gadshill, battlefields, and a London street, the spaces of these plays themselves argue for a definition of an English person not as a subject but as the native of a place called England.

This chapter in particular highlights the authors' abilities to use their earlier scholarship as foundational. Howard's previous work on the tavern as contemporary London space and Rackin's on the play's chorography create an even richer argument about the relationship between the tavern and the theater, as well as brilliant analysis of the instability of the figure of Mistress Quickly. The final chapter, on *Henry V,* returns to the discussion at the beginning of the book about Branagh's juxtaposition of Katherine of France with the threatened rape of the women of Harfleur. After the entrepreneurial energy of Mistress Quickly in the proceeding two plays, the women of *Henry V* are lodged in private spaces and vulnerable to rape and possession. As a result, the second tetralogy concludes with the ultimate equation between masculinist political order and confinement of women within the domestic.

The book's interrelated arguments are exciting: the construction of female characters shifts radically in the history plays. This shift is the result of the development of new economic modes of gendered interaction central to the developing ideology of a nation-state. The very complexity of these arguments calls for more historical development than the authors are able to provide, but this lucid book encourages its readers to continue the ongoing work of examining connections among economics, gender, and the nation in Shakespeare's history plays and beyond.

Roman Shakespeare: Warriors, Wounds, Women. By Coppélia Kahn. London and New York: Routledge, 1997.

Reviewer: Lynn Enterline

Coppélia Kahn's study of Shakespearean masculinity opens by situating Shakespeare's career-long preoccupation with valorous Roman warriors in the twin contexts of the public theater and the curriculum of the early modern grammar school. Kahn begins with an analysis of the institutional forms that shaped early modern ideas of Rome because her readings of Shakespeare's Roman works propose that they "articulate a critique of the ideology of gender on which the Renaissance understanding of Rome was based" (1). Designating as "Roman" those plays "whose plots and characters are based on Roman history and legend" and which are "set in Rome" (11), Kahn examines a host of Latin subtexts to demonstrate how profoundly the complex, and often inconsistent, demands of Roman "manly virtue" *(virtus)* inflect the way Shakespeare represents gender difference in these plays. With chapters on *The Rape of Lucrece, Titus Andronicus, Julius Caesar, Antony and Cleopatra, Coriolanus,* and a postscript on *Cymbeline,* the book spans Shakespeare's career. In the process, it offers a rich semiological and historical account of masculinity and its vicissitudes as inflected by the ideology of Roman *virtus.*

Roman Shakespeare pays close attention to the intersection between masculine subjectivity and "the social dimensions of *virtus*" (2). By this, Kahn means the way ideologies of the state and the family (Roman and early modern) inflect the code of manly honor and, more generally, the discursive construction of *virtus* in the Latin narratives that provide the material for Shakespeare's wounded warriors. One of the book's great strengths, therefore, is its extensive engagement with the numerous representations of valor in the Latin authors available to Shakespeare. Kahn has a keen eye for the incongruities to which those representations could give rise—incongruities either internal to the Latin texts themselves (for example, the vacillation between rivalry and identification that defines Roman "emulation" but undermines conventional, heteronormative notions of masculinity) or resulting from their later reception by a culture with different institutions, political ideologies, and codes of conduct. In one of the most illuminating discussions in the book, for instance, Kahn observes that modern critical consensus about Antony's attempted suicide in *Antony and Cleopatra*—that it is a "botched" affair—arises from insufficient attention to the fact that "suicide has a history." Proposing that we read Antony's death in light of "the codes that gave meaning to Roman suicides," Kahn compares Antony's failure to kill himself with dispatch to Cato's prolonged, agonized end as related in Plutarch's *Life*. Recalling Cato's suicide, the logical extreme of Roman emulation ("cheating the enemy of the triumph he seeks") and therefore a death that even Cato's enemy, Caesar, claimed to "envy," Kahn reminds us that Cato's misdirected sword finally reduced him to tearing out "his bowels with his own hands." She therefore argues that "smoothness of execution was not—for the Romans or for the Renaissance—a criterion of suicide's dignity or moral value" (122–27). What matters, rather, is that both Cato's and Antony's suicides betray the strain of rivalrous, homosocial emulation that defined the deeply contradictory structures of *virtus* (that is, "Thou strik'st not me, 'tis Caesar thou defeat'st," 4.14.68). Kahn develops a similarly compelling account of masculinity in *Julius Caesar* by tracing the inconsistencies Shakespeare inherited in the tradition of Roman republicanism. In her view, Shakespeare allows us to see that, when Cassius and Brutus appeal to masculine republican virtue, their attempts at self-definition are "ideological" in the Althusserian sense of the term, revealing their speakers' "imaginary" relation to their "real conditions of existence." Arguing that the tradition of republican *virtus*, with its internal contradictions, both "constitutes the fractures its male subjects," Kahn also demonstrates that, although republicanism is at work in the play to distinguish *polis* from *oikos* along gendered lines, it simultaneously unsettles such distinctions. The gesture that performs this internally critical function is Portia's "voluntary," and very Roman, "wound . . . in the thigh" (2.1.300–301).

These examples bring us to the overlapping concerns that Kahn raises in her subtitle: "warriors, wounds, women." Drawing on the tripartite anaphora dear to Roman poets, Kahn concisely summarizes the three areas of investigation that define her study of Shakespearean masculinity. By putting "wounds" between "warriors" and "women," the subtitle designates the vexed and unresolved relationship between the latter two terms: it suggests, among other things, that the wound cuts both ways. Her sense of gender's instability derives from feminists like Joan Scott who stress the ongoing "processes of differentiation and distinction" necessary to the cultural production of difference—processes that make gender, like *virtus*, "at odds with itself" (15). Taken as a whole, *Roman Shakespeare* shows that, in Shakespeare's representations of Roman valor, masculinity becomes the "wound of *virtus*." It therefore asks for further critical reflection on a striking pattern of images across the plays—the wounded bodies of Lucrece, Lavinia, Julius Caesar, Portia, Antony, Coriolanus, to name a few—and argues that these figures of corporeal violation and pain put the stability of gender difference into question. The position of "wounds" in the subtitle, a kind of unhappy bridge that implicates "warriors" in "women," and vice versa, epitomizes its author's sense that masculinity, while discursively inflected by the Roman ethos of manly *virtus*, is a paradoxical cultural production. As such, the "wound that signifies *virtus*" is not, Kahn writes, a fixed set of masculine character traits. It is, rather, always implicated in the discursive construction of femininity: Roman masculinity in Shakespeare's plays remains "an open wound" and thus "an open question, still" (169).

The figure of the open wound draws its critical force from the concept of the fetish as elaborated in recent feminist psychoanalytic theory. That is, the fetish is a resonant sign of the many ways in which culture's binary machine of difference fails in its mission; it attests to the "masculine" subject's contradictory, "double epistemology" when it comes to the unresolved *question* of difference.[1] Kahn therefore calls the wound in Shakespeare's Roman works a "fetish of masculinity," arguing that these wounds of *virtus* function as signs of fracture, of an "ideology of gender difference in process" (17). Both the role of fetishism in her argument and her more general interest in sexual difference as an unresolved process will suggest Kahn's affinity with those feminist theorists who turn to psychoanalysis to analyze the discursive production of sexuality and subjectivity. Because of such affinity, however, the sharp methodological division with which she opens the book—between what she calls a "psychoanalytic" account (masculinity as "an intrapsychic phenomenon") and a historical account (masculinity as "an ideology discursively maintained through an appropriation of the Latin heritage for the early modern stage," 2)—seemed to put unnecessary constraints on the scope and direction of her readings. As both a thing and a sign—a conjunction of "words and wounds" that, as Kahn astutely points out, unsettles the very claims to masculinity that Shakespeare's vexed Roman heroes make—the fetish might mark the place where we begin to analyze how the "intrapsychic" and the "discursive" (and thus social and historical) determinations of Shakespearean subjectivity intersect.

By situating the wound of *virtus* in its richly inconsistent Roman and early modern literary and social contexts, *Roman Shakespeare* asks us to think further about the deep ideological contradictions within which Shakespeare's Roman warriors lay claim to a sense of their own manhood. The editors have advertised the book as "accessible" to "scholars and students" alike. A model of lucidity, the book is true to its billing. It offers a thorough and accessible account of what Shakespeare's extensive, institutionally inflected, engagement with classical texts means for his representation of male and female experience. Kahn's book will therefore be extremely useful to teachers of Shakespeare eager to open up the question of gender difference in the Latin heritage for their students and to introduce them to historically sensitive feminist modes of analysis.

Notes

1. I borrow this useful phrase from David Rodowick, *The Difficulty of Difference: Psychoanalysis, Sexual Difference, and Film Theory* (New York and London: Routledge, 1991).

Unspeakable Subjects: The Genealogy of the Event in Early Modern Europe.
By Jacques Lezra.
Stanford: Stanford University Press, 1997.

Reviewer: Jonathan Crewe

Jacques Lezra would never perpetrate the gaffe of saying outright, "We are all Lucretians." Yet that, in effect, is the proposition advanced by *Unspeakable Subjects*. Who, then, are "we?" And what might be implied by our assent to, or dissent from, that proposition? How free are we to choose?

If we assent to the proposition, we will recognize ourselves as heirs to the particular form of Greek materialist enlightenment propounded by the atomists and decisively realized, according to Lezra, by Lucretius' Latin "translation" of Epicurus in the poem *De rerum natura*. That heritage of enlightenment will necessarily have been mediated—or indeed successively reconstituted—by Renaissance humanism, by the European Enlightenment and Nietzschean anti-Enlightenment, by Freud, by modernism and postmodernity, and much besides. Those who recognize themselves in this book will thus be heirs who retroactively constitute themselves as heirs; in so doing, they at once constitute the lineage from which they derive and the heritage they accept. Yet to put it this way is still to risk situating such readers only at the end of a disembodied history of ideas.

Before we proceed, it will simplify matters if we agree, for the sake of argument, to call these readers "us." Lezra will then additionally want us to recognize ourselves as bearers of a shared political consciousness (one in which "May 1968" requires no historical gloss) and of a shared institutional history, that of the professionalized academy in the Age of Theory. Accordingly, we will inhabit a shared universe of meaning constellated by Descartes-Kant-Hegel-Burke-Nietsche-Marx-Freud-Heidegger-Wittgenstein-Foucault-Lacan-Derrida. (The lesser lights need hardly be named, but none, as they successively come into view throughout the book, will be unfamiliar to inhabitants of this cosmos, or disrupt its configuration.) Partly because of Lezra's historical focus on the early modern period, Shakespeare and Cervantes are included among the luminaries; even those who do not share Lezra's historical focus will hardly question their presence.

Lezra's book avowedly tells three complicated stories concurrently. It need hardly be said that none of them is simply linear, and none is posed as a master narrative. Granted that the book tells no single Lucretius story, I shall nevertheless briefly abstract a story it tells about Lucretius—and us. Lezra begins with the aspect of *De rerum natura* that is most familiar to us, namely the one summarized in standard reference works. Here is how the *Encyclopaedia Britannica* puts it:

> No thing is either created out of or reducible to nothing. The universe has an infinite extent of empty space (or void) and an infinite number

of irreducible particles of matter (or atoms) ... all atoms would have moved everlastingly downward in infinite space and never have collided to form *atomic* systems had they not swerved at times to a minimal degree. To these indeterminate swerves is due the creation of an infinite plurality of worlds; they also interrupt the causal chain and so make room for free will.

It is with exactly this standard account, supported by quotation from *De rerum natura*, that Lezra begins. Such is the Lucretian doctrine, versified in Latin and translated from Epicurus, with which we may (or should?) be familiar.

Lezra's implicit point, of course, is that even the familiar Lucretius may not be so familiar to us after all, especially if familiarity means having read Lucretius carefully in Latin and having really comprehended the philosophical, cultural, and literary-historical force of his poem. If we lack that degree of familiarity, it would seem that we hardly know Lucretius, and can thus hardly claim to know ourselves either.

What is crucial for Lezra's purposes is Lucretius's positing of an uncaused "swerve" *(declinatio, clinamen)* from which everything eventuates, and which institutes *eventuation* as such in an otherwise eventless cosmic void. If Epicurus can be said to have conceived of this event, Lucretius does more than merely paraphrase the Greek atomist's argument; he articulates the *poetics* of the event, or, in other words, articulates what tends to follow, in the field of representation and cultural construction, from its positing. More than versified natural philosophy, *De rerum natura* situates the event in the realm of discourse, and thus of poetics both narrowly and broadly construed. In Lezra's account, the ramifications are practically endless.

In the story I am still abstracting from Lezra's book, Lucretius produces a powerful impact ("blow" is another Lucretian term) on Renaissance humanism, particularly Ficino's. (Here, Lezra picks up on earlier work by Michel Serres.) The force of the impact can be gauged positively from Ficinio's known interest in Lucretius and negatively from Ficino's resigned decision to burn his Lucretian manuscripts in the end. Ficino's decision attests to the radical heterodoxy of Lucretianism with respect to both Platonism and Aristotelianism, as well to inherited medieval theology, to all of which Ficino finally capitulates, along with many of his humanist contemporaries. Far from impeding the cultural dissemination of Lucretianism, however, Ficino's book-burning was, in symbolic and actual terms, only a momentary interruption in the emergence of an increasingly hegemonic Lucretianism, of which the scientific dimensions would become apparent in the pre-Newtonian era. In other words, the renunciation of a deeply assimilated Lucrectianism by Ficino and other Renaissance humanists wasn't enough to prevent their humanism from serving as the crucial relay in Lucretian transmission to the Enlightenment and beyond.

According to Lezra, this early modern reconstitution and relaying of Lucretian poetics is the key event that makes us all Lucretians. Or, as Lezra puts it (possibly rephrasing Thomas Greene), "we still read by the light of that fire." The Lucretian story told in Lezra's book is thus a neo-Burckhardtian story as well. As plotted by Lezra, the originary (or reoriginating) dynamism of the Renaissance / early modern era, reflexively thematized by scholars working in the field, still animates our political and cultural existence and determines its tendencies. Lezra thus rehearses the traditional grand narrative of the Renaissance as "origin." Yet his retelling has to be pursued in the full rigor of its conscious *Nachträglichkeit*, and subject to obligatory problematization of all its terms and assumptions. (Lucretian "eventuality" is not merely the object but the premise and medium of Lezra's hermeneutic, a fact that imposes a stringent discipline of problematization.) What Lezra additionally has to factor in is the micro-history of recent Renaissance studies: the emergence of the new historicism, the conceptualization of "cultural poetics," field-specific impasses regarding the nature of history and agency, critical Burckhardtian revisionism, and much besides, in all of which *Nachträgliche* reading of the Renaissance is being pursued, wittingly or not. Lezra's undertaking thus seems exceedingly ambitious: little less that everything in our constellation of significance has to be accounted for, at least putatively. (It must be added that Lezra sets tough admission requirements for us, he being extremely well versed in high theory, intellectual history, Renaissance studies, and European languages.) Since not everything can be "covered," however, Lezra's necessary *assumption* of a shared universe of significance allows him to confine his demonstration to some accepted key indices in cultural history: canonical texts by Freud; Descartes' First and Second Meditations; *Don Quixote, Measure for Measure*.

Before trying to assess the outcome, let me add that Lezra's exegesis of the Lucretian event is theoretically subtle, resourceful, and far-reaching. In his view, the heterogeneity of Lucretius's uncaused swerve with respect to Platonic ontology and Aristotelian causality, as well as to scholastic distinctions between essence and accident, matter and form, etc., makes Lucretianism a permanent scandal. According to Lezra, Lucretius's atomistic "thinking" of the eventuation of the subject possessed of free will is culturally, philosophically and scientifically irrepressible, yet always unthinkable (or "unspeakable"). Both individual agency and history are simultaneously instituted and forestalled by the primacy of the unpredictable, uncaused event. It follows that any naturalistic continuum labeled "life," whether it be an individual life story or what used to be called life itself, will be permanently disaligned from the domain and logic of eventuation. If this Lucretian story must be called a fable, as Lezra calls it on occasion, it is at certainly at home among other great, mind-blowing humanist fables. (Even the most cursory acquaintance with Lucretius's broader field of reference is enough to indicate, for example, the thoroughgoing Lucretianism of Shakespeare's *King Lear*.)

What are we to make of all this, and hence of ourselves? Obviously, the Lucretian event is being glossed retroactively in *Unspeakable Subjects*, very much in light of our current preoccupations as well as of the Lucretian fire (they aren't quite the same). Lezra's entire project is labelled an essay in Foucauldian genealogy, and the broadly poststructuralist reframing of the Lucretian event will be obvious to any remotely qualified reader. Reciprocally, however, we are being invited to recognize the entire constellation in which we find ourselves as Lucretian, thereby recognizing who and where we are.

Granting—seriously granting—both the challenge and the accomplishment of Lezra's book in getting us to entertain this proposition, I believe that there are ways in which the book can't work and the Lucretian identification can't be made to stick. Or, the book can work only otherwise than it proclaims. By this I *don't* mean that there are many readers—not ipso facto incompetent or forever exiled from significance—for whom the book will be too densely difficult and broadly allusive; too arbitrary; too exclusively a product of "old" Eurocentric high theory and Comparative Literature; and too blindly absorbed in the U.S. major-league theory game, indifferent to defections among the spectators or changes going on outside the stadium. Many such readers there will be, but the book's liabilities, some of them due to the scale of its aspiration, will be evident even to readers most willing to play along.

Admittedly, the book bargains, though perhaps not sufficiently, for its own limiting contingencies. In theory, any possible contingency could be covered by the Lucretian thinking that renders it predictable in principle and constitutive in practice. Yet this theoretical coverage will not necessarily forestall practical criticism of some of the book's apparent contingencies. For example, two of the essays—on Freud and on *Measure for Measure*—have previously been published, while those on Descartes and Cervantes might just as easily have been: this is another set of occasional academic essays that does not quite come together as a book. Neither the three concurrent narratives nor the claimed overarching Lucretianism suffice to produce a strong, perspicuous connection to Lucretius throughout the book, nor do they produce logical transitions between discrete chapters. Although Lezra justifiably declines to produce a chronological history-of-ideas, the disrupted chronologies and contexts of the book don't help to produce coherence. Nor, in fact, does the genealogical argument. Lezra has noticed, instructively I believe, that a good deal of what seems important to us in theory and intellectual history "rhymes" with Lucretianism. His revelation that that is so never quite adds up to a genealogical argument, however, although it does make the book into a licensed poetics of sorts. No doubt Lezra has bargained for that too, but readers will vary in their tolerance for intellectual rhyming. For much of the time, the place of Lucretius in the book seems akin to the place of the gods in Lucretius's universe: removed, untroubled, superior, uninvolved.

In my view, *Unspeakable Subjects* is at once too densely abstruse, too scattered, and too dubiously all-encompassing to gain a wide readership; paradoxically, Lezra begins to seem too well qualified for his own good. Even sympathetic readers (still us?) will tend to focus on the chapters that deal with what is most familiar and professionally pertinent to them. Fortunately, they should not be disappointed. For me, the personal focus meant attention to the early modern assimilation of Lucretius in the first place. I can only wish that Lezra had said more about that, since what he does say is highly suggestive. His speedy assimilation of this material into a contemporary-theory context came as something of a disappointment. I turned next to the chapter on *Measure for Measure*: it is a fine critical meta-commentary, previously published in *ELH*, on the advent of "history" and the limits of representation (substitution) in the play. My next stop was *Don Quixote*, of which Lezra strikes me as an excellent close reader, though the relation to Lucretius becomes tenuous in the course of two differently thematized chapters. (Spanish passages are translated and key Spanish terms are glossed for the benefit of those who, like me, do not read the language.) Lezra's discussions of Shakespeare and Cervantes are firmly situated in current professional contexts, rendering them accessible and useful to readers who don't necessarily want to swallow the book whole. I leave the chapters on Freud and Descartes to those more professionally committed to interpreting them than I am, though I will add that throughout the chapter titled "Freud's Sickle" my Renaissance expectations were set for the arrival of Marvell's Mower. His failure to appear felt like a missed appointment.

So, then, are we all Lucretians in fact rather than just for the sake of argument? My review so far has suggested a less categorical answer than "yes" or "no": instead, "maybe," "to some degree," or "to varying degrees," since we don't comprise a fully homogeneous or self-identical intellectual community. There is one respect, however, in which we may be getting less rather than more Lucretian at present. The current academic turn toward religious and "spiritual" themes, not least in Renaissance studies, sometimes looks disconcertingly like another Ficinian book-burning among the humanists, another resigned embrace under pressure of what Lezra calls, in Ficino's case, "Christian-medieval forms of life." Not the least useful contribution of *Unspeakable Subjects* is its reminder of what it might mean *not* to be a Lucretian at this juncture.

Religion and Culture in Renaissance England. Edited by Claire McEachern and Debora Shuger. Cambridge and New York: Cambridge UP, 1997.

Reviewer: Elizabeth Hanson

I am sure I'm not the only scholar of Renaissance English culture who, while searching through microfilm for a projectors' pamphlet on the Virginia colony, or a marital advice book, or a treatise on usury, has found herself scrolling past pages and pages of stuff on transubstantiation, predestination, or the proper decoration of the communion table and felt a guilty recollection that, as Claire McEachern writes in her introduction to *Religion and Culture in*

Renaissance England, "religion, in fact, was culture in early modern England" (11). I say *recollection* because, like many working in this field, I recall a time when the study of Renaissance literature *was* the study of certain historically specific versions of Christianity. During my first stab at graduate studies in the late 1970s, at a fairly conservative institution, I wrote papers on topics such as "The Theology of Presumption and Despair in the Orgoglio Episode of *The Faerie Queene*," or "Anglican Ideas of Adiaphoric Ritual in the Poetry of Robert Herrick." The method of these exercises was to research extensively the writings of theologians most closely allied to the known affiliations of the poet in an effort to reconstruct all the distinctions and structures of their presumptively coherent and consciously held belief systems. Then one undertook to show how the poetry under consideration exquisitely expressed these belief systems. While this expression could be demonstrated to be wonderfully dynamic, the aim of interpretation was nevertheless to account for every last detail of a work by revealing its function in a theologically inflected design. When I returned to graduate work in the early 1980s, this time at a much more theoretically *au courant* graduate school, everything had changed. Now the court was the privileged explanatory context, although it would rapidly be joined by colonial expansion, print culture, domestic politics, emerging capitalism, and the nation. More important, though, the theoretical assumptions had radically shifted; the literary text, now understood to be continuous with the "social text," was the expression not so much of consciously held ideas as of desire and thus of the unconscious. The text was powerfully, revealingly out of control, betraying the contradictions and fissures that beset the early modern subject and his (or her, but mostly his) ideologies and social structures. For me, this transition was hugely liberating. No longer did one have to tirelessly demonstrate the beautiful coherence of repugnant or alien ideologies. Nor did one collapse (usually late at night) into despair, because, like a mechanic who discovers a large, unidentifiable bolt lying in the driveway after the engine has been reassembled, one has realized that a prominent part of the poem just won't fit into the explanatory edifice one has so painstakingly erected. This moment was simply the inevitable encounter with contradiction—what the critic now sought rather than feared. I still think that this was critical progress, permitting the development of more supple and honest, not to mention new, reading practices. The cost, however, was that Renaissance religion ceased to be an object of detailed scholarly attention. That many

Renaissance English minds were powerfully preoccupied with Christian sacrifice, and the issues about community, ontology and representation which it generated, began to slip out of critical sight.

Religion and Culture in Renaissance England undertakes to remedy this situation, to bridge the discontinuity between what can crudely be called old and new historicisms, by bringing some of the questions of recent critical practice together with a focus on religion. The essays in this volume are divided into two groups; the first six are, in McEachern's words, "concerned with how religion figured the contours of English group identity," while the remaining five "deal with the exchanges and affinities between religious and literary language." Put more simply, the first group deals with the culture broadly construed (including nonliterary texts such as Hooker's *Laws of Ecclesiastical Polity*) and the latter with literary texts. In general, the essays that make up this volume are well researched, subtle and original in their analysis, each a valuable contribution to the scholarship on their announced topic. What is striking about the volume as a whole, however, is its theoretical uncertainty. McEachern notes at the outset that "the aim of this collection is to bring the practices and insights of cultural study of the Renaissance to bear upon the dimension of Renaissance culture which is arguably most pertinent to its concerns" (2), suggesting that it will be an easy fit. Religion, she implies, is just some (hugely significant) content that cultural studies methodology has inexplicably overlooked. But the essays themselves suggest a much more resistant relationship between cultural studies and religion, and in the process raise some interesting theoretical questions.

The first three essays focus on the politics of Protestantism. Patrick Collinson demonstrates how the Bible, particularly the minor prophetic books, functioned as a source of national identity, furnishing both imaginative and rhetorical materials which served to "contort . . . and drive . . . inwards" a patriotic nationalism derived from other sources. David Scott Kastan offers an elegant, detailed account of the various Henrician attempts to produce an English Bible, focusing on the political dance between the Reformers and the monarch. He concludes that "the English Bible did help accomplish the break with Rome and encourage the idea of England's own election, but it never became an effective agent of Tudor absolutism," emerging "more in spite than because of the Crown and Church" (62). Jesse Lander examines the various editions of Foxe's *Acts and Monuments* and the interests they served, and concludes that "far from being the summation of Elizabethan Protestantism, this collection of books, produced by a wide range of individuals responding to diverse interests and pressures, provides further evidence of the discontinuity and heterogeneity that typify the English reformations" (89). These three essays share a nontotalizing, nonteleological approach, alert to contingency, fluidity of alliances, and tactical maneuvering. They also frame their analysis in terms of the emergence of the nation as an "imagined community." Benedict Anderson is frequently invoked here as is Richard Helgerson, with the implication that the process of imagining community is a collective process beset by contradiction and unintended consequences. These essays focus on religious aspects of the culture but in the service of understanding the emergence of an institution which, in the long run, would prove fundamentally secular.

Anderson also sets the agenda for Debora Shuger's essay on "the imagined community of Hooker's *Laws*," in which she charts the relationship between elite authority in popular religious experience in Hooker's writings and the traditions on which he was drawing. She concludes, in contrast to Helgerson, that while Hooker asserts that "religion supplies the moral buttresses holding up the political order," his "concept of the Church as 'visible mystical body' [is] premised on the disjunction between 'society and society supernatural'" (136). Shuger's reading of Hooker is meticulous and subtle, attentive to the tensions and complexites of his writing, as well as emphatically connected to religious experience per se, a characteristic which, I think, distinguishes it from the earlier essays in the volume. The next essay, by William J. Bouwsma, about Hooker as a "humanist-rhetoricion," is also careful and nuanced. At the same time, though, Shuger's and Bouwsma's essays are marked by their methodological conservatism, a reappearance in them of some habits of traditional intellectual history. The object of analysis in both essays is what Bouwsma calls "Hooker's thought" (144), an entity acknowledged to reveal interesting tensions but which nevertheless is asserted to be less unstable than might at first appear. The work of each essay is to painstakingly unearth the intellectual traditions within which Hooker was working and the problems he was addressing, until what might have appeared to be either pure ideology or a tissue of contradictions is instead revealed as a complex historically specific, but nonetheless individual and coherent, vision. In other words, the Author makes an unannounced comeback in these essays, apparently trailing pre-poststructuralist assumptions about the coherence of the subject, the priority of that subject to the play of language, and his apparent separateness from the material forces of his world. Although the essay writers might argue that, for them, the Author had never died (fair enough), the theoretical underpinnings of that concept do not easily align with the ways of thinking about culture implicit in Anderson's work.

The essays in the second half of the volume reveal, albeit in widely varying mixes, the critical tensions evident in Shuger's essay. Janel M. Mueller's fine essay on depictions of burning at the stake in *Acts and Monuments* shows explicit poststructuralist investments, announcing at one point "my purpose . . . is not to plot the history of an idea, but to trace the conceptual mechanisms that allowed the body to function in specific discursive patternings" (176). Mueller demonstrates that burning functions, first in the actual experience of Protestant martyrs and eventually as a poetic trope, as a way to figure the relation between the bodies of individual Christians and of Christ, an alternative to the model of ingestion and incorporation underpinning the Catholic mass. The essay is informed throughout by a sense of the subject's dialectical relation to discourse. At the same time, though, I was struck once more by the coherence Mueller seemed to attribute to the discursive phenomenon she was examining. The trope of burning is an elegant solution to a conceptual and existential problem; in Mueller's account there are no eruptions of unconscious desire in this language, no returns of the repressed. Similarly, in Michael Schoenfeldt's illuminating reading of the gendered strategies in Aemelia Lanyer's and John Donne's devotional poetry, every linguistic effect he identifies works toward the fulfillment of the poet's religious expression. "Donne and Lanyer show how the devotional subject is drawn to articulate desires which transgress the precepts of the society it inhabits" (228). Notice that, if the "devotional subject" is transgressive, nothing is acknowledged to transgress the devotional project itself. It is as though Schoenfeldt is attempting, through his convoluted syntax, to disavow the rather old-fashioned stance that pervades the essay: that the poetry he explicates is the coherent expression of the (albeit gendered) religious vision of its authors. There is no disavowal in Richard Strier's argument in "Milton Against Humility" that "Milton does throughout the corpus, have a coherent ethical position—an ethical position that is ultimately, I will argue, distinctively classical rather than Christian." Strier sifts through the various traditions—classical, Catholic, and Protestant—regarding the value of man, and demonstrates (persuasively, I think) that in his polemical writing and major poetry, Milton hews to a notion of rationally valuing oneself according to one's actual acheivements and capability. The idea-cluster of the coherent authorial vision is less in evidence in Richard McCoy's essay on Shakespeare's "The Phoenix and the Turtle," which reads this poem and the last sonnets to the young man in terms of both their courtly context and the religious resonance of ideas of sacrifice, memorialization and resurrection, although, if there is an argument in this essay, I could not figure out what it is.

The essay that presents some of the theoretical tendencies I am tracing here in their most extreme form is Robert N. Watson's account of "*Othello* as Protestant Propaganda," a reading which, I suspect, will strike most readers as simply cracked but which I found one of the more riveting essays in the collection, although I remain unpersuaded by its argument. Watson argues that *Othello* is an allegory which "transposes solifidianism—salvation by faith alone—into the realm of marriage" (234). Iago is a Jesuit, tempting Othello (the Christian soul) to ask for proof when only faith will let him rest secure in Desdemona's (that is, Jesus') love. Watson hastens to explain that "this allegorical level is secondary, recessive, and protean; it quickly becomes absurd if attached to every turn of phrase or plot" (236), although this caveat does not always save him from such absurdity. But he continues, asserting that the validity of his reading is to be measured at the points in the play where the allegory is presented, "in ways that could affect at least the subconscious minds of an audience for whom these theological questions were matters of life and death, eternal as well as temporal" (236). Watson reminds us, in other words, that religion is the thing that separates absolutely modern hearts and minds (even those of people who identify themselves as Christians) from those of people living in the Renaissance. Moreover, as any allegorical reading implies, religion manifests itself not simply as desire but also as conscious knowledge, of Scripture, of theological questions, and of strategies of representation. However alien this reading may be to my own experience of the play, it reminds me that my own receptors may be deaf to the meanings that Shakespeare may have been consciously trying to produce.

Here, I think, we come to the heart of the problem which religion poses for current Renaissance criticism and which manifests itself throughout this volume. Early modern cultural studies, whose practices and insights are supposed to be operating in these essays, evolved not only from Marxism (as the editors assert) but from the Foucauldian construction of the subject as an epiphenomenon of discourse and power and from Derridean ideas of textuality. The theoretical underpinnings of cultural studies (however attenuated now) are poststructuralist, attentive to the illusoriness of the subject's autonomy, the play of desire in language, the instability and bad faith of binary oppositions. There is, of course, also a privileged content to cultural studies; politics (power) and sexuality (desire) sometimes appear to be all that the cultural studies model recognizes as culture. But power and desire are not only privileged categories of experience in cultural studies, they also are the solvents that act on the firm categories of earlier historicisms. If religion has not been recognized by cultural studies, at least beyond the point where it can be transposed into sexuality or politics, it is not only because its practitioners have weak radar for the spiritual. Rather, it is because, as an alien system of conscious knowledge, Renaissance religion seems to force us in directions antithetical to poststructuralism, to reconstruct rather than deconstruct, to pay careful attention to individual differences of opinion, to recognize distinctions that are now epistemically meaningless. Their appearance in these essays of categories such as the author, the history of an idea, and the valuing "coherence," bespeaks the usefulness of these habits of thought for the task of respectfully piecing together the complex intellectual and emotional edifice that was Renaissance religion. But the reflexive nature of these resurrections, the failure to acknowledge the powerful critique to which these categories have been subjected, also attests to the difficulties of thinking like a poststructuralist while thinking *about* religion. One essay in the volume does attempt explicitly to do this: Lowell Gallagher's piece on the stigmata as a kind of rhetorical figure. I have left it unmentioned up to this point because it seems so different from the other contributions: here, one mysticism a "postmodernist sense of textuality" (113) seems to subsume another. The essay brings together elements which, in other parts of the volume, seem irreconcilable—such as empathy with religious experience and poststructuralist methodologies. Ultimately, however, the essay seemed too obscure to open up a new path others might go down. Thus, ultimately the volume fails to bridge that discontinuity between old and new historicisms. It leaves us like Troilus, struggling with bifold authority, trying to synthesize apparently irreconcilable ways of seeing. I could wish that the editors and contributors had confronted these problems more directly, but they have adumbrated an important theoretical problem and given us some good essays in the bargain.

Issues of Death: Mortality and Identity in English Renaissance Tragedy.
By Michael Neill.
Oxford and New York: Clarendon Press, 1997.

Reviewer: Emily C. Bartels

Michael Neill, in *Issues of Death: Mortality and Identity in English Renaissance Tragedy*, proposes that we look at tragedy as one of "the principal instruments by which the culture of early modern England reinvented death" (3). He finds Renaissance England "in the throes of a peculiar crisis in the accommodation of death—one that reflected the strain of adjusting the psychic economy of an increasingly individualistic society to the stubborn facts of mortality" (30)—to the shameful, if not also horrifying, lack of differentiation and distinction that death inevitably would bring. Tragedy, Neill argues, "provided audiences with a way of vicariously confronting the implications of their own mortality, by compelling them to rehearse and re-rehearse the encounter with death" (31). It was both "an instrument for probing the painful mystery of ending" and "a vehicle of resistance to the levelling authority of death" (31).

As the above excerpts of Neill's prose attest, the book's argument is bold, broad, and clear. Death is not merely, in Neill, a theme of early modern tragedy; it is what lies, crucially, "at its core" (1), and at the core of the culture's probing explorations of self. And tragedy, in Neill, provides mixed responses. Neill builds on competing strains of criticism that see tragedy either as denying or triumphing over death (for example, James Calderwood's *Shakespeare and the Denial of Death* [1987] or Kirby Farrell's *Play, Death, and Heroism in Shakespeare* [1989]) or as asserting anti-Christian fears of annihilation (for example, Robert Watson's *The*

Rest Is Silence: Death as Annihilation in the English Renaissance [1994]). For Neill, who sees in "all drama" "the dialectic tendency . . . to incorporate contradictory and subversive voices" (32), tragedy works both with and against the absoluteness of ending, ideologically, thematically, and structurally, to produce death as at once "the supreme occasion for exhibitions of individual distinction" (34) and the unnerving ultimate in indistinction.

The book's frames of reference are at once wide-ranging and historically specific. Choosing to limit the study to secular contexts, Neill examines the way an intriguing selection of cultural and dramatic forms are filtered through and into Renaissance tragedy. In the first part, on the "trope of apocalypse" and the project of "discovery" (42), he reassesses the defining features and historical place of macabre art and its relation to the newly "reinvigorated science of anatomy" (102). In looking at the Dance of Death, for example, he challenges the assumption that what lies behind its "morbid grotesquerie" is a "pathological loathing of the flesh and its frailties" (66). Instead, he sees in the "shocking nakedness" (66) of the Dance's figure of Death a sign of death's power to deface or strip away "the constituent forms of social"—and sexual—"identity," to embody and impose a "fearful sameness" (67). Neill then finds that figure—and its haunting insistence that death lies within the secret "'inner' self" (43)—emerging, as a "Renaissance innovation" (114), in depictions of the dissected body. For Neill, anatomy's "moralizing treatment" of the body (118) provided a crucial link between the "exploration of self-consciousness" (140) and the concurrent revision of death, tying the self to a body that inevitably betrayed its own mortality.

The leap from this "species of didactic tragedy" (118), happening in anatomy theaters, to the tragedies of the Renaissance stage, is, the book suggests, not huge. Indeed, in the book's first part, Neill links his discussion of macabre art and anatomy to a discussion of *Othello* and *The Changeling* and the ways in which the discovery of "death within" (118) structures both plays. In the second part, his focus is explicitly on the form of Renaissance, especially revenge, tragedy, and the "psychological and affective consequences" of its "fiercely end-driven narrative design" (45). For Neill, tragic drama is defined by its end, the thing "the tragic dramatist most wishes to bring about" as well as what he, like his characters, "most dreads" (204). Hence, in a sustained and provocative treatment of *Hamlet*, Neill rethinks "the whole overworked question of Hamlet's delay in terms of the play's effort . . . to imagine an end for itself"

(217)—an end that, when it comes, is lathered in "unallayed narrative anxiety" (240). He then considers the "painful transformation in relations with the dead" that occurred as the erasure of purgatory left Protestants with the "intolerable burden" (244) of remembering, and "re-membering" (251), the dead, and looks at the ways revenge tragedies, and again *Hamlet*, expose and respond to that new pressure.

The final part of the book examines the relation between tragedy and the funereal arts, whose tropes, props, and pageants Neill offers as an obvious literal and figurative backdrop to tragic drama. Any breach in the "decorum" of that pageantry—by its "displacement, stinting," or what he calls its "abruption"—had to produce "powerful dramatic meanings" (288). Although such markers as "tombs and monuments" are, Neill argues, "deeply equivocal devices," betraying "the instability of all worldly achievement" at the same time as they celebrate "fame's triumph over death" (341), it is nonetheless through them that tragedy "articulates its challenge to the undifferentiating power of death" (46). In Webster, for example, the Duchess of Malfi's tomb, like Cleopatra's monument, becomes part of a "symbolic system" that registers "the eternizing artifice of the play itself" (331), promising to "overtop and outlast all the vain architecture of courtly grandeur" (352).

As the above description should attest, this book is expert at weaving a variety of cultural forms seamlessly into a richly detailed tapestry of meanings. Renaissance tragedy, as Neill displays it, plays fluidly into and against the conventions and motifs that, in turn, testify to the inherent theatricality of those forms themselves. It is death that sets the bounds here, not some artificial divide between different kinds of representation, even though *Issues of Death* is predominantly a "drama" book. In fact, although Neill imagines the book as a set of "essays" that take on the issue of death from "a variety of perspectives" (42), to extract Neill's readings of Renaissance tragedies from the larger context he builds around them would be to forfeit the experience of what is one of the book's incredible strengths—its ability to see connections between ostensibly distinct moments and modes of cultural expression.

At the same time, however, the readings of plays here—even those, such as *Tamburlaine* or *The Spanish Tragedy*, that Neill treats only briefly—are overpowering, especially in their ability to make sense, simultaneously, of both larger structures and smaller features. For example, in order to understand Gertrude's curious description of Ophelia's suicide, Neill juxtaposes the "hollowness of [her] consolatory artifice" to the "sordor and mockery of the grave-digging sequence" (233) that follows. These moments, he argues, become "variations on the theme of 'mirth in funeral and dirge in marriage'" that runs centrally through the play, exposing the cemetery as a "place that both invites narrative and silences it" (234). Add to this the intriguing question Neill poses, of why the play does not end there, in the graveyard, where it logically might, and Gertrude's narrative becomes both a sign of the play's and the characters' unfulfillable desire "to put a form on the inchoate matter of experience" (218) and a signpost of Hamlet's dilemma—of the impossibility of "re-membering the violated past" without "repeating the violation and spreading the taint" (251). In the end, Hamlet's story, like Ophelia's (and, as Neill also suggests, like the Ghost's), is an "untellable tale" (225), whose meaning depends on "the sequence of broken and truncated funerals" (303) which Neill locates at the play's structural core.

Compellingly written and argued, complicated but clear, Michael Neill's *Issues of Death* is as engaging a study as it is perceptive. It is sure to prove a crucial resource for subsequent interrogations not only of the representation of death but also of the workings of tragedy and the inscription of self—all issues which are, as Neill demonstrates vividly, intricately tied.

The Stuart Court and Europe: Essays in Politics and Political Culture.
Edited by R. Malcolm Smuts.
Cambridge and New York: Cambridge University Press, 1996.

Reviewer: Pauline Croft

This lively and wide-ranging volume of essays originated in a conference at the University of Massachusetts (Amherst) in 1993. The editor's introduction emphasizes that in the early seventeenth century, England, Scotland, and Ireland were ruled by an aristocratic and gentry elite whose educational and social culture was broadly European, rather than narrowly British. Latin was still an international language, and most educated men knew some French. Events in Paris, Madrid, and Vienna often were considered more interesting, and more important, than the affairs of the localities or of Scotland and Ireland. The history and the culture of the seventeenth century, inside and outside Whitehall, cannot be understood without paying serious attention to European developments.

This theme is taken up by Jonathan Scott and J. A. Sommerville, arguing powerfully for a greater appreciation of the continental dimension in political ideas. Scott emphasizes that the extreme fear of popery, probably the central theme uniting the three "British crises" of 1618–48, 1678–83, and 1688–89, only makes sense when we realize that between 1590 and 1690, Protestantism had been driven back from controlling one half of the landed area of the Continent, to a mere one fifth. Across Europe, the Reformation seemed in retreat and even in danger of annihilation. It was still securely entrenched in England and Scotland, but Ireland was a perpetual reminder of the threat posed by enduring Romish beliefs. Anti-Catholic paranoia must be understood against the immediate background of European history. In a similar plea for a broader perspective, Sommerville trenchantly dismisses the much touted idea of a "common law mind," distinctly English and virtually universally accepted. Instead, he demonstrates that there is plenty of evidence that continental-style ideas of natural law, and of absolutist royal powers, were widely held. Proponents of them can be found at the English court itself. The apparent consensus in political ideas usually turns out to consist of mere platitudes and generalizations which disintegrate on any probing; there was a real difference between those arguing for a traditional, limited monarchy and those intent on extending the powers of the Crown.

Smuts also contributes a perceptive essay on art and the material culture of majesty. He points to the significance of the peace of 1604 with Philip III of Spain and the Archdukes Albert and Isabella in the southern Netherlands, which permitted the growth of a group of great Jacobean collectors who came of age in a postwar environment. The Stuart court was notably cosmopolitan, promoting "not just a fashion for collecting but a special subculture, which linked appreciation of art to foreign travel, diplomacy and new forms of knowledge." Nevertheless, the older quasi-medieval style of court display in jewels, clothes, and lavish food still consumed far more of the Crown's resources than did the purchase of

Charles I's superb picture collection. This is a valuable reminder that advances in taste must not be exaggerated, but set securely in a contemporary socioeconomic context.

Hans Werner points to the impact of the Thirty Years War, a pervasive theme in plays, entertainments, and masques after 1618. He analyzes an extraordinary forerunner, a production of London citizens in 1614, entitled "The Hector of Germanie," which set out an agenda of hostility to Catholics at home and support for Anglo-Calvinist aggression abroad. The anti-Spanish message also demanded that England accept her responsibilities as the leader of Protestant Europe. Literary evidence vividly demonstrates here that the gulf dividing Stuart foreign policy from the wishes of most of its Protestant subjects was already present several years before the outbreak of continental war in 1618. Charles Kay Smith, in a complex piece of literary investigation, points to French influence in the transmission of epicurean ideas into English poetry of the 1640s and 1650s. The court-in-exile of Henrietta Maria became familiar with the use of *libertin* thought to counter religious dogmatism, hypocrisy, and intolerance, then transferred the technique to combat Puritanism in England. Nancy Klein Maguire writes on Louise de Kerouille, Duchess of Portsmouth and mistress of Charles II. She deployed exceptional patronage and remarkable skills in political mediation between the king and his leading courtiers, channeling French influence on English politics. Maguire places a hitherto peripheral figure centrally in the structures of both court and politics.

All these contributors fill out Smuts's proclaimed theme of the constant interaction between Whitehall and Europe. However, as Geoffrey Parker indicates in a concluding piece, others, though scholarly, tend to miss their opportunity by adopting a largely Anglocentric, or perhaps Britocentric, focus. Martin Butler argues persuasively that the struggle to find a coherent imagery for the Union of England and Scotland was central to the development of the masque in the years between 1604, Samuel Daniel's *The Vision of the Twelve Goddesses*, and 1640, William Davenant's *Salmacida Spolia*. Richard McCoy begins by emphasizing the collapse of James I's peaceful foreign policy in 1618, but his elegant discussion of the emergence of the myth of Essex in the 1620s, as the epitome of principled military activism and noble opposition, makes no further continental comparisons, although they would be very fruitful. Caroline Hibberd offers illuminating insights into the character of Charles I, with his disposition to view politics in terms of personal honor, always a concept that included a degree of physical violence, as with the duel. Ronald Hutton's scrutiny of the evidence for (and against) Charles II's Catholicism is a model of rigor, but suggests only briefly at the end that Charles "saw religious questions primarily in terms of *raison d'état*," in common with the overwhelming majority of European rulers. Annabel Patterson traces the literary debate over concepts of English character during the second Dutch war of 1665–68, pointing to the ambiguities by which a reluctant admiration for the Dutch was contrasted with a perception of court-Catholic, pro-French corruption at home.

The collection produces an occasional sense of missed opportunity, as the European dimension slips too often out of focus. Nevertheless, this is a distinguished volume, ranging well beyond the usual limits of a narrowly conceived court culture. It illuminates many of the crucial interactions between the British Isles and Europe in the seventeenth century, and the cumulative effect should alert scholars to the other possibilities of creative comparison which remain to be explored.

Women and Literature in Britain, 1500–1700. Edited by Helen Wilcox. Cambridge and New York: Cambridge UP, 1996.

Reviewer: Susanne Woods

Helen Wilcox has edited yet another collaborative effort on behalf of the recovery and intelligent consideration of early modern British women writers. This one is more ambitious than her earlier work in the field, the important *Her Own Life: Autobiographical Writings by Seventeenth-Century Englishwoman* (1989, with Elspeth Graham, Hilary Hinds, and Elaine Hobby), which tried to situate women's autobiographical voices in their seventeenth-century context. In *Women and Literature in Britain, 1500–1700*, Wilcox has gathered twelve fine scholars of the early modern period to try and provide both an introduction to women's literary role and production and a provocative reconsideration of more general topics, including humanism, religion, the stage, and scientific and courtly writing. In general, the volume is a resounding success.

The book is divided into two sections, six chapters on "Constructing Women in Early Modern Britain" and six on "Writing Women in Early Modern Britain." The first section includes essays by Hilda L. Smith on humanist education and women, Suzanne Trill on religion and femininity, Valerie Wayne on advice books for women, Jacqueline Pearson on women as readers, Ann Thompson on women and the tradition of male cross dressing on the stage, and Bronwen Price on women's ways of knowing in the rising age of scientific inquiry. The second section begins with Margaret W. Ferguson on issues surrounding women and writing in the renaissance and continues with Helen Hackett on courtly writing, Elizabeth Hageman on women's poetry, Elspeth Graham with life writing and the idea of the self, Betty Travitsky on prose writing, and Ros Ballaster on "The First Female Dramatists."

Despite occasional overlap (between parts of Pearson's and Ferguson's essays, for example), the book provides a thoughtful, and largely coherent, introduction to early modern British women writers, of particular use to English majors, graduate students, and the generation of professors who received their doctorates in total ignorance of early women writers. Scholars already familiar with the topics will find little new here, although some of the essays are a pleasure to read for the style and learning of their distinguished authors.

If the essays have a common thread, it is their effort to get beyond the obvious surfaces and "binaries" of the complex textures of women's contexts and their written responses. As Wilcox notes in her introduction, "it is vitally important that we recognise . . . uncertainties and asymmetries if we are to read the early modern period accurately" (4). Many of the essays also share varying degrees of poststructuralist jargon, as they seek to "problematize" the social construction of gender and writing. In some of the essays, the result is clarity and sophistication, such as Ann Thompson's excellent summary of the recent debate on issues surrounding the use of boy actors on the stage (108). In others, the search beyond the surface may be less clear but is still provocative and illuminating. Bronwen Price's essay on "Feminine Modes of Knowing and Scientific Inquiry" ably deconstructs the beginning (and apparent inevitability) of scientific empiricism: "If the seventeenth century marks the inception of such scientific practices, they were also defined . . . precisely in reference to resistance and difference—what they excluded or suppressed, what lay outside and beyond the frontiers of knowledge they attempt to establish" (120). Her reading of Margaret Cavendish's philosophical poems as "explorations of modes of knowing that exceeded the boundaries of knowledge being founded during the sixteenth century" alters three centuries of ignorant dismissal of what Cavendish accomplishes in her "eccentric"—off-center—verse.

Less successful, unfortunately, is Suzanne Trill's essay, "Religion and the Construction of Femininity." In it, she seeks to show that religion and gender are complex and vexed social constructions, and she has some interesting things to say about Anne Askew and Anna Trapnel in particular. But it is hard to get past some of the awkward writing, not all of it the result of jargon. Someone should have edited these two sentences, which, presumably, form Trill's principal thesis: "The fact that they did not wholly conform to the expectations governing proper feminine behaviour problematises the stability of the category 'woman': it highlights the fact that the characteristics associated with that category are socially constructed rather than naturalised or universal givens. It is my contention that women's involvement with religion in this period brings the instabilities of this category to the fore" (31). Following, as it does, Hilda Smith's lucid and persuasive "Humanist Education and the Renaissance Concept of Woman," prose like this does a great disservice to the good ideas Trill is trying to convey.

Among the rest of the essays, I want to cite Hageman's introduction to women's poetry, Travitsky's to women's prose, and Ballaster's to women's drama of the period. These three are filled with useful information and sophisticated interpretation, clearly presented, and provide a fine introduction to women's work in the traditional literary genres associated with the period. Of the essays dealing with less traditional genres, I particularly like Valerie Wayne's on women's advice books, which raises interesting issues of authorship, publication, and gender construction. These, however, were personal favorites; other readers will undoubtedly want to point to other essays in this rich and useful collection.

The study of early women writers is no longer in its infancy. As the essays in this book amply declare, it is now impossible to think of the early modern period without the presence of women's voices complicating almost every aspect of the historical and literary picture, from humanism to the new science, religion to genre. Pieties about the use of boy actors, or audience, or literacy must be tested anew, as our assumptions not only about women's roles but about the entire period become subject to revision. Men, too, occupy subject positions, fashion themselves in a complex and changing gendered world, negotiate issues of class and authority, and hold varying mirrors up to an unstable nature. Resurrected from their long burial, these who are neither men nor women, but who were men and women, move past the wit of the gravedigger and back onto the stage. The essays in this volume help to re-present their culture more fully than in the intervening past.

Shakespeare and the Authority of Performance.
By W. B. Worthen.
Cambridge and New York: Cambridge University Press, 1997.

Reviewer: Cary M. Mazer

For more than a decade, W. B. Worthen has been mapping the paradigm shifts in "stage-centered" Shakespeare criticism and its intersection with performance practice. Now Worthen has drawn together several of his published articles and book reviews and knit them into a book-length polemic about the scholarly and theatrical discourses that govern both performance and scholarship. The thesis of *Shakespeare and the Authority of Performance* is compelling in its simplicity: both performance practice and performance criticism (or, more accurately, the ways theatre practitioners describe what they do, and the way scholars talk about the results of what practitioners have done) invoke the "authority" of the playwright, simultaneously deferring to and laying claim to the artistic validity and cultural status of "Shakespeare" (in inverted commas—Worthen's term for icon that the dominant culture and the Shakespeare industry have created) and to his putative authorial and directorial intentions. At precisely the historical moment that literary theory and textual scholarship have problematized authorship, intentionality, the stability of the text, and the ways the playscript is read and interpreted, stage practice and the scholarly industry that has invented itself to describe it have both clung tenaciously to the notion of a singular, knowable and comprehensible author, the transcendent genius whose intentions can be found, replicated in the theater, and analyzed in performance criticism.

Worthen offers a scathing critique of Shakespearean directing; Shakespearean acting theory, training, and practice; and the lion's share of scholarly Shakespeare performance criticism. In critiquing theatrical practice and analysis, he is not siding with the literary "text" against theatrical performance. Indeed, the "text versus performance" debate, he argues, has misstated the relationship between the script and the performance that is made from that script. Playscripts were indeed created for the theater; and theater pieces can and should still made from them. But the theater, he observes, must be seen as "a fully nonauthoritative transmitting agent"; after all, he asks rhetorically, "using texts Shakespeare never fashioned (modern editions), personnel Shakespeare never knew (the director, actresses), theatres Shakespeare never imagined (modern technology, architectural and scenic conventions), and actors and audiences informed by 440 years of history, how can *any* production claim to stage an authoritative *work* of Shakespeare?" (12, Worthen's emphases). He suggests, instead, that we "regard the stage, and stage practices like acting and directing, not as the natural venue where Shakespeare's imagined meanings become realized, but as one site among many where 'Shakespearean' meanings are produced in contemporary culture" (38).

Worthen begins by cataloguing the prevailing literary theories that offer a more fruitful explanation of the relation of the "text" to the various ways it is read, reread, performed, and reconstructed. This is no easy task, to a large extent because of vocabulary: ever since Roland Barthes, the word *text* can be taken to mean not the "work" itself but the interpretive "field of play" acted on by subsequent readers and analysts. Even the word *performance* has taken on additional meanings (not all of them useful) in recent literary theory. Surveying a wide range of theorists and critics (G. Thomas Tanselle, Peter Shillingsburg, Jerome McGann, Gary Taylor, Michael Bristol, and others), Worthen tries on for size various working definitions of *text*: the text as "work," the text as "textuality," the text as "material object," and the text as "score." He explores the relationship between *version*, *text*, and *document*; considers the performance as a *version* or an *iteration* of the initial work; and measures the *proximity* and the *congruence* of the performance to the script.

There are dangers in spending the first quarter of his book on these terms and theories. Those readers already familiar with textual studies and literary theory may be tempted to conclude that performance is just another critical exercise (and a somewhat messy one, at that), rather than a site of cultural production with its own properties and functions. Those readers who are naive performance critics—precisely the readers Worthen hopes to inspire and cajole into a more sophisticated outlook and methodology—might be overwhelmed by these theories and their vocabularies. Once they see how vigorously Worthen has been swimming with the sharks, they just might choose to stay out of the water themselves.

Worthen is on much firmer ground when, in his next two chapters, he talks about performance practice or, rather, about the discourses of performance practice. "This is not a book about performance itself," he states, "but about how a relatively narrow, professionally invested body of people talk about it." In examining how theater artists talk about their work, Worthen is doing something "rarely done in literary or theatre scholarship—taking theatre practitioners at their word." If, as Bertolt Brecht observes, "the proof is in the pudding," Worthen is "more interested in what we are asking the pudding to prove" (42).

Worthen begins with a chapter on the director, who "comes into being at the moment that 'drama' gains an independent existence as literature, a mode of being a cultural authority independent of theatrical production" (47). In the nineteenth century, when the "author" momentarily became transcendently important in literary studies, the theater had to an invent the director, for "the 'director' summons the 'author' into the discourse of modern performance" (48). But the Frankenstein's monster has refused to die. The director has prevailed, as an illusory site of authority and stability, in the face of a century-worth of anxiety and uncertainties about authorship, both in literary studies and inside of the theatre itself ("a theater in search of an author finds one in 'Shakespeare'" [54]).

Worthen identifies this self-authorizing invocation of the playwright in the theories of several contemporary Shakespearean directors: in Peter Brook's celebrated quest for the "secret play"; in Jonathan Miller's desire to liberate the play's "after life" from its original performance; and in Charles Marowitz's desire to "rape" the script in performance. And, although neither Marowitz nor Miller appears to be slavishly attached to notions of intentionality and Shakespearean authority, and though the two appear to take antithetical approaches to the script, Worthen sees both Marowitz and Miller (whom he brackets) as asserting a claim for authority in a world that discounts the theater as a merely reproductive art form. Both directors, he argues, while recognizing the director's responsibility to create new work from old scripts, nevertheless make claims to be in contact with an originary genius whose texts are there to be appropriated or re-created.

Worthen similarly critiques the discourses of contemporary acting practices, particularly the extraordinary consensus about voice-production and verse-speaking that has arisen through the books, workshops, and television programs of John Barton, Cicely Berry, Kirstin Linklater, and Patsy Rodenburg. Taking his cue from the pioneering analyses of Richard Paul Knowles and others, Worthen sees in such voice training theories the construction of an elaborate discourse, not only about the authentic Shakespeare (or, as Linklater has come to believe, the authentic Earl of Oxford), but about what constitutes an authentic voice, an authentic emotion, and the actor and the character's authentic "self," even though such definitions of character and self have been contested by recent scholarship. He goes further, situating verse and voice in an essentializing view of the naturalized physical body (what Worthen calls "authorized embodiment"), even though the stability of the body has similarly been contested. He demolishes Neil Freeman's fetishizing of First Folio punctuation as actor cues ("M, O, A, I, doth sway his life," as Granville-Barker once remarked about W. W. Greg). And he sees the assumptions about character (and the character's "journey"), documented in the essays by Royal Shakespeare Company actors in the *Players of Shakespeare* series, as a natural extension of these assumptions about body, verse, voice, and text. The actor's individuality, he argues, ought to be "the final point of resistance" (144–45) to authority; instead, it becomes the ultimate means of authenticating the author's transcendent, trans-historical creation.

In his final chapter, Worthen surveys several decades of scholarly performance criticism and analysis, much of which, he claims, depends on the vocabulary and critical categories derived from literary criticism (an accusation that could be leveled against Worthen himself, in his first chapter), in particular from the (now old) New Criticism. In much of this writing, he observes, "The modern stage becomes a site of interpretation, rather than a place of production, a place where meanings are found, not made" (159). And he rightly criticizes criticism that offers to "read" contemporary performance, including some of the more sophisticated scholarship that offers to "textualize" performance: "Textualizing the performance is finally a way merely to reread the text" (173). Worthen saves his most earnest and sophisticated analysis for a detailed survey of performance criticism that tries to do more. He examines scholarship that tries and, he feels, often fails to put performance criticism on a new theoretical footing, or that appropriates the vocabulary of performance to other ends (Harry Berger, Jr. takes his knocks here, as does much speech-act theory, which, Worthen observes, "oddly removes speaking from ... theatrical practices" [178]). He also takes a long, detailed look at scholars who, he argues, succeed, such as Anthony P. Dawson, Barbara Hodgdon, and Susan Bennett, who anchor performance analysis in a recognition of the material conditions of theater production, and in the relation of theatrical performance to competing sites of cultural production and appropriation. Finally, Worthen calls for a new paradigm of performance criticism, one that eschews the simplistic "skirmishes" between text and performance whereby performance "remain[s] captive to the disciplines of the past, the disciplines of the text" (189), and which, instead, views the material conditions of the theater as a site of cultural production.

He is appropriately less confident (and somewhat more modest) in his calls for a new aesthetic of performance, one that will not be tied to fallacies of authority, intentionality, and meaning. If only, he seems to be saying, actors and directors could learn from what we might teach them; if only actors could create characters that are based on early modern or postmodern definitions of character and subjectivity, definitions that New Historicist scholarship and postmodern theory have taught us; if only actors could create characters without a "journey," for, as he argues about Deborah Findlay's account of playing Portia in 1987, "to play the character's journey from the character's perspective, freighted with the weight of Shakespeare's transcendent morality, is to reproduce the ways the play naturalizes the character's behavior to its larger suasive purposes, its attempt to achieve the effect of the real" (139).

He is unpersuasive, however, when he cautiously offers models of what might be a new "postmodern" paradigm of character. That Brian Cox's Titus, in 1987, should whistle "Hi-ho, Hi-ho" when setting the table for Tamora's feast may invoke a postmodern ironic self-referentiality; but does it present a new aesthetic of characterization or of embodiment? And does Anthony Sher's use of a monkey as the model for his Fool, in 1982, necessarily represent a postmodern breakthrough in approaching character? According to a much quoted anecdote, Michael Williams, preparing to play the Fool in 1968, visited the monkey house of the Regent's Park Zoo and bumped into Alec Clunes, who pointed out the monkey he had used as the model for his fool in 1962. Actors, it seems, have been monkeying around with the Fool for decades without benefit of postmodernism.

Even more problematic are Worthen's proposals about directing, using Peter Sellars's 1994 *The Merchant of Venice* as his test case. (For one thing, his analysis of this production—which I did not see—is ill situated in the book. His discussion hinges on how character is constructed and how actors represent character; yet his discussion precedes the chapter on acting in which he discusses this.) Worthen wisely hedges his bets about the production, and about the performance piece to which he usefully compares it, Anna Deavere Smith's *Twilight: Los Angeles, 1992*, which was similarly inspired by the Los Angeles riots and which similarly modifies the relation of the actor's emotions, body, and identity to the character she is representing. The pieces, he seems to argue, are postmodern, or perhaps they aren't; characters are depicted without having emotional journeys, or perhaps with them. Smith's aesthetic of representation of the "Other" defies Stanislavskian paradigms of identification—or perhaps it doesn't.

I do not object to Worthen's caution in making claims for Sellars's *Merchant*, but his faith in there being a way performance can replicate what theory has discovered about indeterminacy and multivalence and transgressive ideology, and his belief that a postmodern performance aesthetic potentially might hold the answer, smacks of the same solepcistic interventionism of the naive authorial-intention-besotted performance-critics he criticizes in chapter 4: now that *we* have identified how it all really works, things would be better if theater artists would only learn from *us*. In both cases, this leads to self-conscious art: On the one hand, productions that fetishize illustrative moments (for example, Isabella's response to the Duke's proposal at the end of *Measure for Measure*) now that scholars have identified such moments as interpretive cruxes; and, on the other hand, self-consciously postmodern productions (and postmodernism is self-conscious, if it is anything), like Sellars's *Merchant*, which sometimes feel as though they had been staged for the exclusive benefit of postmodern scholars capable of analyzing them.

Now, I confess that I take perverse delight in what might be called un-self-conscious theater: Beerbohm Tree and Augustin Daly, Donald Wolfit, the neo-Victorian Cedric Messina seasons of the BBC Shakespeare, and Kenneth Branagh's childish picture-book Shakespeare films. There's something to be said for un-self-conscious—or perhaps I should call it *falsely* self-conscious—theater: theater that wallows in naive authorial-intentionality in the worst way, that never questions its own claims to be doing it *right*, that replicates prevailing ideologies (both of Shakespeare's time and of its own), that blindly accepts the high-brow (or middle-high-brow) cultural claims for Shakespeare's timeless transcendency, and that willingly participates in the tourism and "Heritage" industries. So long as there are scholars such as Dawson, Hodgdon, Bristol, Bennett, and others to analyze these productions, to remind the world of the fallacies they practice and of the hegemonic uses to which they are being put, what harm are these productions doing? Such un-self-conscious productions are more revealing of their own times (and of ours): the artists' hands are dirtier, so they leave more fingerprints. And the productions are, I find, more fun to write about, much more so than postmodern productions that blind-side you with their self-consciousness.

Perhaps the same case can be made about the naive, un-self-conscious performance criticism. Sure, I'd much rather read Hodgdon's analysis of a production's intertextual dialogue with pop-cultural representations of the play's iconography than yet another performance critic's "reading" of a production's "success" or "failure" in "realizing" the playwright's "intentions." But, so long as there are scholars like Worthen to situate such scholarship in larger critical practices and in the larger culture—as he does with such clarity and virtuosity in *Shakespeare and the Authority of Performance*—then this scholarship will, in the long run, have so much more to teach us about ourselves, our professions, and our theatres.

Index

Abel, Lionel, 41
Adelman, Janet, 69
Albanese, Denise, 230–32
Alleyn, Edward, 77
Alter, Jean, 113
Anderson, Benedict, 269
Ariosto, Lodovico, 51
Aristotle, 243
Ashley, Katherine, 165
Askew, Anne, 281
Auden, W. H., 51
Austin, J. L., 28, 30
Avery, Bruce, 233–35

Bacon, Anne, 165, 166
Bacon, Anthony, 167
Bacon, Francis, 123, 249
Bacon, Nathaniel, 166
Bacon, Robert, 167
Baker, David J., 213–19
Baker, J. H., 78
Bakhtin, M. M., 219
Ballaster, Ros, 280, 281
Barber, C. L., 237
Barnes, Barnabe, 187–210
Bartels, Emily, 273–75
Barthes, Roland, 244, 283
Barton, John, 46, 285
Baudrillard, Jean, 103
Benjamin, Walter, 125, 237
Bennett, Susan, 286, 288
Benveniste, Emile, 20, 31
Berger, Harry, 19–73, 286
Berry, Cicely, 285
Bersani, Leo, 252
Bertie, Richard, 165
Bevington, David, 229
Bingham, Richard, 219
Blank, Paula, 234
Blayney, Peter, 228
Bloom, Harold, 242–243
Blount, Charles, 180

Bodley, Thomas, 228
Boose, Lynda, 92
Booth, Stephen, 50
Bourne, Elizabeth, 175–176
Bouwsma, William, 269
Boyarin, Daniel, 251
Boyarin, Jonathan, 251
Bradley, A. C., 66
Branagh, Kenneth, 254, 256, 288
Braunmuller, A. R., 124, 129
Brecht, B., 284
Bristol, Michael, 219–22, 229, 283, 288
Brook, Peter, 284
Brooks, Cleanth, 237
Bryson, W. H., 78
Bulwer, John, 200
Burt, Richard, 89–90
Butler, Martin, 278
Byrne, Muriel St. Clare, 171

Calderwood, James, 273
Callaghan, Dympna, 213–19
Castiglione, B., 233
Cavanagh, Dermot, 134–160
Cave, William, 200
Cavell, Stanley, 19, 20, 23, 24, 37, 54–55, 59, 65–73, 243, 252
Cavendish, Margaret, 281
Cavendish, William, 165
Cecil, Robert, 149–150, 155–56, 167, 173
Cecil, William, 165, 172, 176
Cerasano, S. P., 77–93
Cervantes, M., 261, 263, 265–66
Champion, Larry S., 129
Chaw, Richard, 97
Clare, Janet, 88–89
Classen, Albrecht, 171
Clegg, Cyndia Susan, 92, 135
Clifford, Margaret, 166
Clinton, Elizabeth, 174
Clunes, Alec, 287

Cohen, Walter, 125
Coke, Edward, 193
Comensoli, Viviana, 223–24
Conway, John, 175–76
Conway, Lady, 166
Cox, Brian, 286
Cox, John D., 225–29
Cressy, David, 94–105
Crewe, Jonathan, 260–65
Crooke, Helkiah, 249
Cromwell, Thomas, 176
Croft, Pauline, 80, 276–78
Cunningham, Karen, 148
Cusack, Sinead, 47

Daiton, Thomas, 200
Daly, Augustin, 287
Daniel, Samuel, 278
Darlington, Ida, 80
Daubeney, Catherine, 176
Davenant, William, 103, 278
Dawson, Anthony, 286, 288
Day, Angel, 175, 176
Daybell, James, 161–86
de Gratzia, Margreta, 225
Dekker, Thomas, 102
della Porta, Giambattista, 190
Derrida, Jacques, 20, 261
Descartes, R., 261, 263, 266
Dessen, Alan, 113
Devereux, Robert, 168–69, 178–79
DiGangi, Mario, 230–32
Donne, John, 41, 103, 270
Douglas, Archibald, 217
Downame, John, 193, 194
Drury, John, 175
Dryden, John, 103
Dudley, Lettice, 178–80
Dunsworth, Felicity, 227
Dutton, Richard, 89–90

Earle, John, 200
Edelman, Lee, 252
Elam, Keir, 245
Elias, Norbert, 249
Eliot, T. S., 237, 239
Elliott, John R., 227
Elton, G. R., 78
Elyot, Thomas, 233
Emck, Katy, 244
Emerson, Ralph Waldo, 24, 69, 70, 73
Enterline, Lynn, 19, 21, 22, 25–36, 257–59

Epicurus, 260, 262
Epp, Garrett, 227
Erasmus, 125
Erickson, Amy, 79
Erickson, Peter, 20–21, 24, 26, 41, 48, 49
Evans, Blakemore, 113, 242
Evans, Maurice, 46

Farrell, Kirby, 273
Ferguson, Margaret, 280
Fermor, Nicholas, 174
Ficino, M., 262–66
Findlay, Deborah, 286
Fletcher, Angus, 19, 22–24, 47–41
Foucault, Michel, 20, 261
Fowler, Elizabeth, 233–235, 241–247
Foxe, John, 268, 270
Freccero, Carla, 246
Freeman, Neil, 285
Freud, Sigmund, 27, 31, 61, 71, 261, 265, 266
Frye, Northrup, 237
Frye, Susan, 253–56

Galen, 196
Gallegher, Lowell, 272
Garber, Marjorie, 248–49
Gaskill, Malcolm, 87
Gawdy, Bassingbourne, 174
Giese, Loreen L., 77–93
Gillet, Charles Ripley, 92
Girard, René, 237, 238
Goldberg, Jonathan, 230, 250, 252
Goldman, Michael, 130
Gosson, Stephen, 201–2
Gowing, Laura, 77–93
Grafton, Anthony, 247
Graham, Elsbeth, 279, 280
Granville-Barker, H., 285
Greenblatt, Stephen, 237, 239, 250–252
Greene, John, 200, 202
Greene, Robert, 102
Greene, Roland, 233–235, 246
Greene, Thomas, 96, 246
Greenfield, Peter H., 227
Greg, W. W., 228, 285
Greimas, A. J., 20
Grey, Katherine, 167
Grossman, Marshall, 19, 21–24, 51–64
Guicciardini, Francesco, 188
Guilpin, Edward, 91

Index

Guy, J. A., 78

Habermas, J., 238
Hackel, Heidi Brayman, 228
Hackett, Helen, 280
Hacquenghem, Guy, 252
Hageman, Elizabeth, 280, 281
Halpern, Richard, 236–40
Hammer, Paul, 156
Hammill, Graham, 248–52
Hanson, Elizabeth, 266–72
Hart, Jonathan, 241–47
Hatton, Christopher, 149
Hayward, John, 155
Hegel, G., 261
Heidegger, M., 261
Helgerson, Richard, 269
Helmholz, Richard, 80
Henderson, Diana, 229
Herrick, Robert, 103, 267
Heywood, Thomas, 199, 223
Hibberd, Caroline, 278
Higgins, Anne, 226
Highley, Christopher, 213–19
Hillman, David, 248–52
Hinds, Hilary, 279
Hitler, Adolph, 216
Hobby, Elaine, 279
Hodgdon, Barbara, 286, 288
Holdsworth, William, 77
Holinshed, R., 136–38, 148
Honigmann, E. A. J., 124, 128
Hooker, Richard, 268, 269
Houlbrooke, Ralph, 177
Howard, Jean E., 253–56
Hutson, Lorna, 91
Hutton, Ronald, 279

Inglis, Esther, 164
Ingram, Martin, 79, 80, 88

Jacoby, Derek, 47
James, Henry, 24, 65–66, 71–73
James, Mervyn, 139, 155
Jardine, Lisa, 247
Jed, Stephanie, 234
Jones, Ann Rosalind, 234
Jones, Emrys, 126, 130
Jones, W. R., 78
Jonson, Ben, 45, 89, 90, 91, 102, 103, 113
Jordan, Constance, 94–108

Joyce, James, 238

Kafka, Franz, 41
Kahn, Coppélia, 257–59
Kant, I., 261
Kaplan, M. Lindsay, 77–93
Kastan, David Scott, 225–29, 268
Kermode, Jenny, 77–93
King, Henry, 48
King, Rodney, 213
Kipling, Gordon, 226
Knight, G.Wilson, 237
Knowles, Richard Paul, 285
Knutson, Roslyn, 228
Koestenbaum, Wayne, 247
Kott, Jan, 237
Kyd, Thomas, 197–98, 275

Lacan, Jacques, 20, 21, 27–30, 52–55, 58, 261
Lander, Jesse, 268
Lanyer, Aemelia, 270
Leavis, F. R., 237
Lee, Sidney, 65
L'Estrange, C. Ewan, 79
Levin, Harry, 245
Levin, Richard, 41
Lewis, Wyndham, 239
Lezra, Jacques, 260–65
Linklater, Kirstin, 285
Lisle, Honor Lady, 172
Lobanov-Rostovsky, Sergei, 252
Lodge, Thomas, 245
Lomazzo, Paolo, 187, 191–92, 196
Lowe, Lisa, 28
Lucretius, 260–66

Macchiavelli, N., 136, 233
McCoy, Richard, 270, 278
McEachern, Claire, 266–72
McGann, Jerome, 283
Machin, Lewes, 230
MacIntyre, Jean, 227
McLuskie, Kathleen, 227
Maguire, Nancy, 278
Manley, Lawrence, 94–105
Marlowe, Christopher, 109–11, 120, 130, 230, 243, 275
Marowitz, Charles, 284–85
Marston, John, 103
Marvell, Andrew, 216–19
Marx, Karl, 238, 261

Massinger, Philip, 196–97
Masten, Jeffrey, 228, 247, 252
Masters, Betty R., 80
Mauss, Marcel, 221
Maxwell-Lyte, H. C., 78
Mazer, Cary M., 282–88
Mazzio, Carla, 248–52
Middleton, Thomas, 274
Miller, Jonathan, 284–85
Milowicki, Edward, 246
Milton, John, 51, 104, 270–71
Mitchell, Juliet, 69
Montaigne, M. 233, 247
Montrose, Louis, 94–95
Moore, Margaret, 87
More, Thomas, 44, 100
Morrison, Paul, 242–44
Mowat, Barbara, 228
Mueller, Janel, 270
Mundy, Anthony, 199

Nashe, Thomas, 102
Navarre, Marguerite de, 245
Neal, Lisa, 247
Neill, Michael, 273–75
Nevill, Anne, 167
Newdigate, Anne, 166
Nietzsche, Friedrich, 73, 260
Nixon, Richard, 53
Norbrook, David, 155
Norris, Bridget, 172–73

Olivier, Laurence, 254
Orlin, Lena Cowen, 19–24
Orrell, John, 226
Overbury, Thomas, 193

Paré, Ambrose, 190
Park, Katherine, 252
Parker, Geoffrey, 278
Parker, Patricia, 252
Parson, Robert, 156
Paster, Gail Kern, 249
Patterson, Annabel, 89, 90, 129, 136, 279
Pearson, Jacqueline, 280
Percy, Dorothy, 168–69
Perrot, John, 148–50
Pollard, Tanya, 187–210
Potter, H., 78
Potter, Lois, 19, 22, 23, 42–50
Price, Bronwen, 280

Prynne, William, 200
Puttenham, George, 235

Rabelais, F., 125
Racine, Jean, 242–44
Rackin, Phyllis, 225–29, 253–56
Ralegh, Elizabeth, 173
Rasmussen, Eric, 228
Rendell, Steven, 245–46
Rodenberg, Patsy, 285
Rowe, Katherine, 249–50
Rowley, William, 224
Russell, Elizabeth, 163, 166, 167
Ryan, Kiernan, 236–40

Sawday, Jonathan, 250
Schelling, F. W. J., 249
Schoenfeldt, Michael, 252, 270
Scott, Joan, 259
Scott, Jonathan, 277
Schwarz, Kathryn, 251, 252
Scudamore, Mary, 174
Sellars, Peter, 287
Serres, Michel, 262
Seymour, Edward, 167
Shakespeare, William, 19
—Plays: *All's Well That Ends Well*, 19, 39, 45; *Antony and Cleopatra*, 48, 257–59, 275; *As You Like It*, 61, 230, 244–45; *Coriolanus*, 28–29, 257, 259; *Cymbeline*, 257; *Hamlet*, 38, 40, 47, 52, 111, 122, 126, 238, 242–44, 249, 274–76; *1 Henry IV*, 30, 38, 44, 51, 52–64; *2 Henry IV*, 51, 57; *Henry V*, 21–22, 58, 110, 216–19, 254–56; *2 Henry VI*, 112, 256; *3 Henry VI*, 126, 127, 256; *Henry VIII*, 22, 254; *Julius Caesar*, 238, 257–59; *King John*, 109–33; *King Lear*, 19, 31, 32, 37, 41, 43, 48–49, 52, 54, 56, 59, 68–71, 117, 264; *Macbeth*, 19, 42, 43, 44, 47, 50; *Measure for Measure*, 21, 30, 32, 35–36, 38, 39, 41, 42, 45, 47, 89, 119, 263, 265, 286, 287; *Merchant of Venice*, 42, 43, 45, 113, 238, 239, 259, 287; *Merry Wives of Windsor*, 40; *Midsummer Night's Dream*, 59; *Much Ado About Nothing*, 19, 42, 43, 47; *Othello*, 29, 38, 40, 48, 115, 271, 274; *Pericles*, 238; *Richard II*, 44, 46, 52, 134–160, 231, 255–56; *Richard III*, 40, 51, 111, 112, 245, 255; *The Tem-*

pest, 52, 61, 73; *Titus Andronicus*, 32–35, 115, 257, 259, 286; *Troilus and Cressida*, 39, 128, 251, 272; *Twelfth Night*, 50, 245; *Two Gentlemen of Verona*, 113; *The Winter's Tale*, 33, 47, 52, 219, 251
—Poems: *Phoenix and the Turtle*, 271; *Rape of Lucrece*, 32, 34–35, 257
Sharpe, J. A., 79
Shaw, Fiona, 46, 256
Sher, Anthony, 286
Sherman, William, 247
Shershow, Scott Cutler, 219–22
Shillingsburg, Peter, 283
Shipley, Elizabeth, 97
Shuger, Debora, 266–72, 269
Sidney, Philip, 125, 235
Smith, Anna Deavere, 287
Smith, Charles Kay, 278
Smith, Hilda, 280, 281
Smuts, R. Malcolm, 276–78
Sommerville, J. A., 277
Spenser, Edmund, 19, 50, 51, 89, 90, 92, 100–102, 215–19, 267
Stafford, Dorothy, 174
Stallybrass, Peter, 253
Stevens, Scott Manning, 252
Stokes, Adrian, 167
Strier, Richard, 270
Stuart, Arbella, 163–64, 177
Stuart, James, 226, 231, 278
Stubbes, Philip, 192–94, 200
Swetnam, Joseph, 234

Talbot, Elizabeth, 166, 176–77
Tanselle, G. Thomas, 283
Tasso, Torquato, 51
Taylor, Gary, 41, 283
Thompson, Ann, 280
Thomson, Peter, 229
Thoreau, Henry, 66, 73
Threfall, David, 46
Throckmorton, Mary, 165

Throckmorton, Thomas, 165
Tourneur, Cyril, 45
Trapnel, Anna, 281
Traub, Valerie, 230
Travitsky, Betty, 280, 281
Tree, Herbert Beerbohm, 287
Tresham, Muriel, 165
Trill, Suzanne, 280, 281
Tudor, Elizabeth, 165, 227
Tuke, Thomas, 187, 192, 193–94
Turner, Victor, 101
Twain, Mark, 221

Vickers, Nancy, 251
Virgil, 51
Vives, Juan, 191–92

Walker, Garthine, 77–93
Warner, Deborah, 256
Wasson, John M., 227
Watson, Robert, 271, 273
Watterson, Bill, 221
Wayne, Valerie, 280, 281
Webster, John, 275
Weever, John, 91
Weimann, Robert, 109–33
Welles, Orson, 239
Werner, Hans, 278
Westfall, Suzanne, 226
Wilcox, Helen, 279–81
Williams, Michael, 287
Willoughby, Elizabeth, 169–70
Wilson, Robert Rawdon, 246
Windebank, Thomas, 167
Wittgenstein, Ludwig, 24, 28, 70–71, 261
Woods, Susanne, 279–81
Worthen, W. B., 282–88
Wynne-Davies, Marion, 223–24

Young, Richard A., 245

Žižek, Slavoj, 27, 30, 31, 249